NORMA FARNES was b[...]media introduction as a Resear[...]castle, working for Jack Clark[...]on to become an agent and m[...]of the theatre inevitably led t[...]ng in such shows as *Hair, O[...], Jesus Christ Superstar* and *Evita* among others. She lives with Jack Clarke, her partner for twenty-five-years, in London, Yorkshire, Sheekeys and The Ivy.

From the reviews of *Spike, an Intimate Memoir*:

'Fascinating . . . a devastatingly candid account of an extraordinary Jekyll-and-Hyde personality.'   *Daily Mail*

'Compelling . . . Part showbiz memoir, part personal exorcism, it is one of those books you wish you had never started but . . . cannot stop reading, so revealing is it of the tortured individual that lurked behind the public façade.'   *Observer*

'It is probably the most significant book that will ever be written about Spike. The insights into Spike's character are endless and both fascinating and harrowing to read, and we would never really understand Spike without them. That he achieved so much in the last 36 years of his long life, despite his huge problems, speaks volumes for Norma. For this, we owe her a large debt of gratitude. Her book is essential reading.'

MIKE BROWN, The Goon Show Preservation Society

'No-one is better placed to write the definitive biography of Spike Milligan, Britain's most mercurial comic genius, than Norma Farnes – his agent and personal assistant for 35 years. Spike was both a man of contradictions and a brilliant comic writer and this comes through on every page of this well-written, insightful biography.'   *East Anglian Daily Times*

Spike
an intimate memoir

Norma Farnes

TED SMART

This edition produced for The Book People Ltd,
Hall Wood Avenue, Haydock, St Helens WA11 9UL

Harper Perennial
An imprint of HarperCollins*Publishers*
77–85 Fulham Palace Road
Hammersmith
London W6 8JB

www.harpercollins.co.uk/harperperennial

This edition published by Harper Perennial 2004

1

First published in Great Britain by Fourth Estate in 2003

A catalogue record for this book
is available from the British Library

ISBN 0 00 773643 6

Set in Minion by Rowland Phototypesetting Limited,
Bury St Edmunds, Suffolk

Printed and bound in Great Britain by Clays Ltd, St Ives plc

For Spike
  for changing my life

and

for Jack
  for making it better

Foreword by Eric Sykes

Many people have written varied descriptions of the life and times of Spike Milligan but nobody is more qualified to give us an accurate version than Norma Farnes, his manager, mentor and troubleshooter for thirty or more years. Spike had three wives who knew the outside view, but Norma knew what went on inside the lad. When the spotlight was on him and the applause prolonged Norma would be in the shadows happy for the lad, but in the many instances of trouble she would be foursquare in front of him deflecting the flak and the bullets, pouring oil over troubled waters until the next time.

Because of the shocking state of my eyesight I am unable to read the book so all I can say is, it feels right. I can assure everyone who reads the book that it is a truthful version of the man himself, although knowing Norma as I do, it has been written with sympathy and a warm heart and heaven help anyone who speaks badly of Spike. Norma is still protective of him and her memory will always remind her of the good times.

But being a Yorkshire girl straight, stubborn and honest this is not a book about the virtues or the vices of Spike but a true version of the man she looked after for years, protecting, encouraging and on occasions gently chastizing. She and Spike made a good team and, sticking my neck out, I believe without the steadying influence of Norma, Spike may well have gone before his time.

September 2003

Foreword by Spike Milligan

I first met Norma Farnes at the same time she was meeting me. I did not know then that it would be a relationship which would last what appears to me to be 300 years, during which I aged prematurely due to the terrible inroads she was making into my private life – like lending me money when I was skint. This was heroic on her behalf because she was skint.

It was due to her that I spent the money very slowly, not exceeding more than £3 on a dinner I gave for the Prince of Wales; and he, suspecting a very small outlay, brought sandwiches. I got him to autograph one for me which I proceeded to eat on the anniversary of the Battle of Trafalgar; for the simple reason one of my ancestors was mortally wounded on the fore deck of H.M.S. *Victory* and never forgave Nelson and, in fact, on his death bed was heard to say 'F . . . Nelson' but he never did and nobody was to blame.

This foreword is written for my Damager/Saviour's book – God help me.

In the dark days at the beginning of the 300 years we spent

together I told her I wasn't making any more decisions. She said she'd make them if I stuck by them – she's been doing it ever since – so everything is her fault, and I'm still working for her.

December 1998

Acknowledgements

I want to thank Louise Haines, my editor, for all her encouragement; my friend Diana Noble-Jones for always being there; Beryl Vertue for her support in those mad early days; Janet Spearman for running my life; Alan Clare and Jack Hobbs for enriching it, and Grandma and Desmond Milligan for all the laughs.

My special thanks to Eric Sykes for all the years he supported me against the 'Raging Mad Milligan' – Spike's own phrase – and for his enduring friendship. I can't do better than quote Spike: 'a piece of gold in showbusiness'.

Chapter One

'What's he really like?'

Whenever and wherever I was introduced as Spike Milligan's manager and agent I waited for the inevitable question. In not far short of thirty-six years it never altered. It was not one that could be answered in a few words so I generally made do with 'Interesting' or 'Don't ask', the latter reserved for the days when either Spike or I had slammed the phone down on the other, or in his case perhaps flung it through the window. Then came the second question.

'How on earth do you put up with him?'

Sometimes I wondered myself, though not for very long. My answer was invariably 'He's very stimulating.' The truth went much deeper. He could be lovable, hateful, endearing, despicable, loyal, traitorous, challenging, sometimes all of these things in a single day, but always original and never boring. I remember days of laughter and tears, exuberance and despair, and not a single one that was monotonous.

While I was with Spike he went through depressions,

marriages, numerous affairs, and very many tantrums. And at the same time there were always those flashes of inspiration, occasionally genius, that made him comedy's most influential innovator in the last fifty years, and a fascinating human being. People either adored or detested him. Nobody ever dismissed him with 'Oh, he's okay.' His disciples – and I use the word advisedly – worship him to this day. To them he could do no wrong, a view not shared by everyone, including me.

When I walked into Nine Orme Court, Bayswater, on a stormy winter's morning in January 1966 I never imagined I would spend the better part of four decades with the truly extraordinary man who was about to interview me. Perhaps the weather was trying to tell me something.

I had been looking for a job in television production but then I spotted an intriguing advertisement in the *Evening Standard*:

> Showbusiness personality requires personal assistant. Must be bright and efficient. Good shorthand and typing speeds. Bayswater area. Ring Alfred Marks Bureau, Notting Hill Gate.

That would do for the three months I reckoned it would take to get into television, and Bayswater was only a fourpenny fare and two tube stops from my flat in Kensington. I rang up and the salary was attractive too. I did not have any money so that was in the job's favour. The girl at the agency wanted to know my shorthand and typing speeds, where I had worked previously and whether I had references. I satisfied her on all those counts. Then she seemed to hesitate.

'Yes?' I said.

'Just one thing,' she said. 'You'd be working for Spike Milligan.'

In her dreams.

'No thanks. I've heard all about him. Not for me.'

'He really is a very nice man. Do go and see him.'

Spike was a notoriously turbulent character, but it would pay the bills and provide an introduction to the world I was interested in. And after almost three years as secretary and researcher to a driven newspaper and television journalist, being Spike Milligan's assistant should not be too daunting. I had had all the temperament bit, curses, tantrums and books being thrown across the office. Surely it could not be much worse than that. Was I in for a surprise.

Even after Spike's death I still have my office at a strangely quiet Number Nine, where I manage his affairs for his children. His presence lingers and it will for as long as I remain his surrogate. Every time I arrange for a new edition of his books or scripts I recall the circumstances, the rows, the highs and lows that gave birth to them. If I am asked to do something that I know would not be right for him I hear his whisper. 'That's right, Norm. You tell 'em!' Other great talents, household names, worked at Number Nine, but it was Spike's moods that coloured the days and set the tone.

Strangers often wonder, even suggest with a knowing look, that there must have been something going on between me and Spike for the association to have lasted. But there never was and that is perhaps one of the reasons we stayed together. He was my greatest friend and I was his, though I told him when I thought he was wrong and that did not always go down too well. As well as his manager and agent I was his peacemaker and confidante, and what confidences there were.

Spike had his own explanation for why we stuck together so long.

'I've always fought against being dominated by strong women. You're one but with you there's one important difference. You're in my corner.'

And I always was.

*

A long stay was the last thing on my mind when I entered the stately Edwardian house for the first time. I walked into a bright reception area with a red carpet which continued on up the stairs and landings. The receptionist was friendly and we chatted until the switchboard buzzed. 'You can go up now,' she said, 'it's the first door on your left.'

As I walked upstairs I wondered whether Spike Milligan would be as extraordinary as his public persona. He had converted the post-war radio audience to his crazy, anarchic sense of humour with *The Goon Show*. As a performer he was guaranteed to fill West End theatres: his unrehearsed antics convulsed spectators and unnerved the actors appearing alongside him. By the time I met him he was famous in South Africa, New Zealand, Australia, Canada and the United States, where he had gathered a following among students and – something that baffled him – intellectuals. Yes, it was rumoured that he was unpredictable and eccentric. Well, I had had a dose of that already and decided in advance that my stay with him would be for three months only.

I stepped into a small cold room. French windows were open to a balcony and let in an icy draught. He was apparently oblivious to the temperature, no doubt because he was sitting there in a thick grey ribbed sweater, black corduroy trousers and a black woolly hat topped with a pompom. He looked up but did not greet me.

'It's freezing in here,' I said.

'Yes,' he said. 'I hate the Americans.'

Well, naturally. That explained everything. I later discovered that this reply summed up Spike's convoluted logic, and its speed was typical of him. He would always fly to the conversational winning-post while others laboured over the hurdles of qualification and explanation, and he expected you to fly with him. If you could not, then bad luck. Should I tell him that the Romans invented central heating and not the Americans? I decided to leave it.

I looked around the office. On top of a filing cabinet to his right were some packets of Swoop bird seed. Reminders of his family crowded every available surface. Drawings by his children; a very old toy dog; a much-cuddled teddy bear; two pairs of baby boots; a wool bonnet; and a large brown rosary which lay beside a smaller green one underneath a picture of a benevolent Jesus Christ. I wondered what His views were about all that went on in that room. Although there was electric light numerous oil lamps were dotted about, two on top of an upright piano before which stood a rickety chair. Shelves packed with files lined three walls and the fourth was covered with photographs of his children. A large Victorian bureau, double doors open wide, revealed numerous compartments, all open and filled. Every file, cassette and tape it contained looked to be neatly labelled. Under another window was a divan bed. What initially seemed chaotic had a streak of unorthodox order about it, not unlike the workings of his mind, as I would find out. Even a glance told me that this room was a refuge to him, and somewhere to kip when he felt like it.

He opened the conversation with a few desultory questions, none of which amounted to much. I waited for him to get down to business. And waited.

The Bureau had said he was forty-nine but at first glance he looked older, with what is now called designer stubble and was then considered the sign of a man too lazy to shave. There was an air of vulnerability about him and, despite my first impression, something childlike in his manner which made him seem younger than his years. We talked about this and that. Then, without any warning, looking me straight in the eye, he said, 'You won't mind if I shout at you from time to time, will you?'

I had had experience of that sort of thing before. 'No. Not if you don't mind if I shout back.'

He appeared crestfallen. 'You must never do that. It would break me up.' I could tell from his expression that it would.

Suddenly he got up, took one of the packets of Swoop and sprinkled some seed over the balcony floor and the empty window boxes. 'Morning, lads,' he said, looking into the sky. Within a minute or so there were half a dozen pigeons tucking in.

He turned to me, pointing at the birds. 'That's Hoppity. He's a bugger, first every time. I reckon he's an argumentative sod, always in fights. I bet that's why he's lame.' He sat down behind a table and gazed at me, nothing rude about it, more of a dispassionate survey, I felt. 'You've got legs just like Olive Oyl,' he said. 'Who'd want to make love to an elastic band?'

'Another elastic band.'

He grinned. 'You'll do for me.'

I wondered whether he would do for me.

He told me that at the end of February he was going to Australia to see his parents and do some work. When he came back at the end of June he would be in touch. I had not bargained for that but decided to stick with my job at the Independent Television Companies' Association (ITCA) in the meantime, keeping an eye open for a vacancy in television production. I quite fancied working for Spike so if nothing spectacular came up I would wait for his call.

June came and went and he had not rung. Then the Alfred Marks Bureau called. They wanted my permission to give Spike my telephone number, which he had lost. A few minutes later the phone rang.

'Spike here. I'm back from Oz. Do you want to come and see if you still want to work in this madhouse?'

I had had long enough to consider whether it was the right move but there would be no harm in seeing him again. So off to Number Nine for the second time. And I met a completely different Spike: bright, alert and brimming with energy. Yes, I thought, I'll give it a whirl, if only for a few months. It might be fun.

I told him I would have to give a month's notice to the ITCA so could start at the end of August. That was fine by him because he was taking his family on holiday to Tunisia so would see me again on 29 August. He took me downstairs to a room immediately behind reception and left me with his agent, David Conyers, to sort out the details. David suggested I start early and have a week to settle in before Spike's return. It was all very informal. Yes, I thought to myself, it could be very pleasant working here.

Chapter Two

I could have been born in a different galaxy from the frenetic world of Number Nine. In fact it was at 45 Barnard Street, Thornaby On Tees, on New Year's Eve 1934. The town, tucked between Middlesbrough and Stockton, was still suffering from the deprivations of the Depression. My father was lucky with a construction job at ICI Billingham, a dangerous occupation but comparatively well paid. My mother was a rarity in those pre-war years because she was a working mum and served behind the counter of Robinson's, an upmarket department store.

At that time sons and daughters generally lived in the same neighbourhood as their parents and family ties were strong, if somewhat binding for those with an instinct to break the mould. After school, when my friends had tea with their mums, I went to my maternal grandmother's house, two doors away from our own. When Mum finished work she often came for tea with us, not a dainty Ritz-like affair with cucumber sandwiches but a knife and fork meal with ham and salad or a Newbould's pork pie.

My parents were judged to be somewhat unusual. They were among the very few people on our street to cast their votes for the Conservative Party and did not mind who knew it. And although my straight-as-a-die Dad conformed to the archetype of the working man in that he was a sports fanatic, there the resemblance ended. He went to his barber every Saturday morning, not just for a haircut but a manicure. He must have been the only manual worker on Teesside to do so. He was also a non-smoker and almost teetotal, but could be persuaded to have a whisky at Christmas. And he was potty about variety theatre.

As soon as he decided I was old enough Dad took me with him to the Middlesbrough Empire on Wednesday evenings, Saturdays too if there had been a change of act during the week. The ritual never altered. At the interval he would say, 'Come on. We'll go and see Ally at work in the Circle Bar.' In fifteen minutes Ally could serve more pints than it is possible to imagine. Although a big woman she would swoop gracefully from customers to the pumps, arrange six pint glasses in a hand as big as a navvy's and fill them with just the right amount of froth on top. Then in one fluid movement she would bang the pints down, take the money, scatter change on the counter and somehow pull another six.

Visitors from out of town were told not to miss Ally. Even the artistes came to witness her performance. 'She's a class act,' my father claimed he heard one customer tell a comedian who had died before the interval. 'Better than owt on stage. So far, that is.'

Dad's favourite acts were peerless comic Jimmy James; Wilson, Kepel and Betty, the sand dancers; comedians Rob Wilton and Billy Bennett, and the incomparable G. H. Elliott, who, blacked-up, sang 'Lily of Laguna' hauntingly as he glided across the stage. Above all Dad idolized a great ballad singer, fiery Dorothy Squires. After meeting in the Empire bar they became friends and he looked out for her, not that she needed any help because she could be as tough as a bar-room brawler. Whenever she was within travelling distance of Thornaby Dad would be in the audience, and through all her tempestuous affairs he was the one who listened quietly to talk of her latest love and the inevitable parting which had given her so much pain – temporarily at least, for there was always a new man in her life. (This was before she married Roger Moore.)

Dad knew that Dorothy could be a demanding monster with the hide of a politician, and, like many of that breed, she was often ruthless and unforgiving. But because of her talent he excused her frailties. She was the very opposite of my mother. Mum never threw tantrums, was content with her lot and, in the jargon of today, she gave Dad space to enjoy his interests. It was not all one-way traffic, though. Mum took the view that what was good for him was good for her so she went to the local dance halls with her girlfriends. Strange as it may seem, I am sure neither of them strayed.

My parents often went backstage to see Dorothy after the curtain came down and one evening, when I was about twelve years old, they took me along with them. I was utterly bewitched by this glamorous singer.

As well as inheriting my parents' love of entertainment I also picked up their pecuniary habits. In those depressing times half the men in our street were unemployed and dependent on the dole and often the pawnshop. If they could wangle something new for the house it would be on hire purchase. My parents considered this a device of the devil. If they could not pay cash they did without.

Religion played a large part in my mother's life. She said her prayers every night until she died so it was not surprising that I was sent to Sunday School from an early age. It was never a chore to me and at fourteen I was asked to teach the younger children there. I did it for three years until I fell out with the new vicar.

Everyone in my extended family seemed content with their way of life, as they remain to this day, and yet in my teens I had an urge to get away, to broaden my horizons and to travel. There had to be something more interesting than a future in Thornaby.

Many people reminisce about golden school days but they could not end soon enough for me. I was good at shorthand and typing, becoming sufficiently proficient to teach both for a time at night school, but did not shine at anything else apart from sport. After I left at sixteen my first job was at Head Wrightson, a local steelworks, as receptionist, typist, telephonist and general dogsbody. The manager, a Mr Cussons, treated everyone with charm and courtesy and inspired a family atmosphere. But as with most families, there was an awkward one, the pinstriped junior manager of our small office. Bombastic and opinionated were his better traits. One day some money was found to be missing and he as good as accused me of stealing it. When I went home that evening I told my father. He was furious.

'Right, I'll come to the office with you and have it out.'

'No,' I insisted. 'I'll do it myself.' I did not want anyone to think I was a wimp.

Dad advised me to confront him and demand that he should call the police. When I did he spluttered like a pricked sausage and I knew I had come across my first bully. He flushed and scuttled out of the office, but did not have the grace to apologize, although the missing money was not mentioned again. In my remaining time there he kept out of my way, which was fine by me. But after eighteen months I got itchy feet and successfully applied for a job as shorthand typist at ICI, then the largest employer on Teesside, at Kiora House, a mansion two miles north of Stockton.

I was there for three years, at first in the typists' pool under the strict eye of Winnie Gatenby. She was not the Miss Brodie type, more Mother Hen, because her girls were definitely not *crème de la crème*. Rather we were young, boy crazy, and spent our days discussing the shortcomings or otherwise of the young men who worked in the building and what had happened at the Saturday dance at Saltburn Spa. Winnie often had to crack the whip, which she always did rather apologetically.

It was a very happy office. There was the usual flirting but cupboards were used for their intended purpose and it was all fairly innocent. I have no memories of winters at Kiora. It always seemed to be summer, with sandwich lunches on the lawn, where we would bask and gossip until it was time to return to work. It was then that I developed a crush on a BBC television news-reader, Kenneth Kendall. I cut his photograph out of the *Radio Times* and stuck it on the wall to the left of my desk so I could gaze at it every time I flicked back the typewriter carriage. My dream was to meet him but as he was out of reach I was left with the local talent. I was quite devoted, however, and when we were moved to another ICI country house, down came Kenneth and up he went on another wall in our new home.

But I felt restless, and soon afterwards I realized a long-held ambition to go to modelling school. I had always been interested in fashion and grooming. ICI gave me a leave of absence and Dad the necessary wherewithal, and off I went to the Lucy Clayton School in Grosvenor Place, London, which was then considered to be the very best. There I joined twenty girls for a month-long course. Although at five feet five I was an inch too small to qualify for the Mannequin Certificate, the all-important diploma for those who wanted to follow in the footsteps of Barbara Goalen and my idol, Fiona Campbell-Walters, I graduated in every other respect.

It was an exciting month. The girls were different from my friends at home. All were extremely clothes-conscious and some very blah, but others brought a mixture of accents from all over the country. This was at a time when anything but an educated southern accent was a problem for the ambitious, so those of us from the Midlands and North Country were encouraged to lose them. I was an eager learner. We were shown how to use cutlery, how to make introductions and, most importantly, how to look after clothes and shoes. Of an evening we met in coffee bars – the new rage to hit London and later to spread to the provinces – and talked excitedly about how the course would change our lives. When we parted, sometimes close to midnight, I travelled safely to South London where I was staying with a cousin.

The experience opened the door to a glamorous new world and gave me poise and confidence. It had never been my intention to make a career of modelling, but when I returned to Thornaby I was offered evening and weekend jobs by Robinson's and a hairdresser who had made a name for himself on local television. So typing was interspersed with fashion shows but my feet became even itchier than before. Local girls and boys seemed drab in comparison with their metropolitan counterparts. Nonetheless recruiting nights continued with my best friend, Pat Howden, at the dear old Saltburn Spa. We never missed a Saturday night of flirting. And we started planning for our summer holidays.

After a taste of London sophistication I was thirsty to travel further afield than Blackpool, where my parents used to take me every year. Package holidays were then in their infancy and flights expensive. Only the moderately wealthy took a ferry across the Channel and drove down Route Nationale 7 to magical places such as Juan-les-Pins, St Tropez (then still a fishing port), Cannes and Nice. But our imagination was fired by news stories of young people who had hitch-hiked their way to the sun and we were desperate to do the same. The trouble was that our parents were equally desperate to save us from the white slave trade, which they were convinced flourished twenty-two miles the other side of Dover. Throughout the winter of 1953 we pleaded our cause.

France! The home of the Folies Bergère, teeny-weeny bikinis, chic, garlic and Gauloise cigarettes. Mum was fearful, Dad apprehensive, but eventually they gave their permission, with one big proviso: I must not do anything that might bring shame to the family. Not the shame that dare not speak its name – coming back pregnant – but even losing you know what. Mum had heard that girls purposely dressed skimpily to catch the eye of drivers as they raced to the sinful south and she was adamant that my clothes should be modest. The same condition was placed on Pat so we left Thornaby dressed demurely in passion-killing long shorts. As soon as we were out of sight we changed into pairs that were short and tight enough to make sitting down an artful manoeuvre, packing the long ones at the bottom of our rucksacks to be retrieved on our return.

Those cheek-popping shorts served us well and they certainly made drivers take their eyes off the road, so much so that we were able to disdain offers of lifts from lorries and small cars; luxury sedans and saloons became our favoured mode of transport. We were careful to stay on the main road to the south, never hitched after five o'clock and as travelling was free we stayed at decent hotels, not only because they were cleaner but because they might contain eligible young men.

Over the next few years I went back to France and visited Italy and Spain with Pat and then another friend, Aideen Thornton. On the second trip I met someone who made a lasting impression, though we knew each other for only a few days.

It happened on the Champs Elysées. Aideen was taking my photograph with the boulevard's nameplate in the background so I could show off back home. Then as it was her turn a tall man in his late twenties asked, 'Would you like me to take both of you?' Talk about hearts stopping. He was a young English Gary Cooper, slim, smart and outrageously handsome. Unbelievably, he said he was hitch-hiking. Hitch-hiking! He looked as though his everyday conveyance should be a Rolls.

'Where to?' I asked.

'Juan-les-Pins. And you?'

There was no hesitation. 'Juan-les-Pins.'

He smiled captivatingly. Would we care to join him for coffee? Would we. Over coffee he proved to be a fabulous raconteur. He knew Paris like a native and the afternoon whizzed by. How about dinner at this tiny bistro? How could we refuse? With him I would have shared a baguette on the beach. John, as he was called, told us he was staying in Paris for three or four days and between us we soon persuaded Aideen that we should do the same, to see the sights, of course.

He was the most charming man I had ever met, always immaculate in a spotless white shirt and one of those famous public school ties. He showed us Paris as expertly as, and a lot more charmingly than, a tourist guide but every evening at nine o'clock he turned Cinderella. He would look at his watch, apologize and leave. I wondered who she was.

On the morning we were to say goodbye he arrived with two brown carrier bags. His luggage. I could not believe it. True, he said. Inside the first, very neatly folded, was his underwear, plus three or four white shirts, a toilet bag and a jar of Frank Cooper's coarse-cut marmalade. In the second was a pair of shoes by John Lobb, complete with trees. They weighed a ton. Definitely an eccentric, I thought. Why did he not carry everything in a rucksack like other hitch-hikers?

If I had asked him to wear brown boots in London he could not have been more horrified. 'Oh dear me no. Most definitely not.' There was a suggestion of a shudder. In his world rucksacks were definitely not *de rigueur*. I was glad he had not seen us on the road.

'We must meet in Juan-les-Pins,' he said. Not only a charmer but a mind reader. 'Let's split up now, go our separate ways and meet in three days. At the Hotel ———.' I have forgotten the name of the hotel but not him.

We made Juan in two days. The next afternoon we met, as arranged, at his hotel, naturally the one with the most stars of any in the resort. He was draped languidly but elegantly in a chair at the best table with a glass of wine. He seemed as delighted to see us as we were to see him and we arranged to travel to Cannes, the queen of the Riviera. The next morning we met outside his hotel at the arranged time, but he had forgotten something in his room. Great. I would go with him. I wanted to see inside this famous hotel.

'Come along,' he said. But instead of going into the hotel he walked away from it.

'Where are you going?' I said.

'To my hotel.'

'Isn't this it?'

He laughed. 'I couldn't afford their prices.'

I was disappointed although I should have realized that if he chose to hitch-hike he too must be on a budget. Aideen and I followed him along side streets well away from the promenade, through a quiet courtyard, and stopped at a brightly painted house which looked like a private home.

He invited us up and ushered us into his barely furnished room. He had his back to us as he sorted through a drawer and I caught a glimpse of a passport on the wash stand. I thumbed through it quickly and the shock rocked me on my heels. 'John Huggins, Clerk in Holy Orders.'

'You're a clergyman!' I gasped.

He nodded. 'A vicar.'

'How come you're hitch-hiking?'

'It's a bit complicated.'

'Uncomplicate it for me.'

It was the only time I saw him slightly embarrassed. 'You see –' he started, almost in a whisper, then hesitated.

'Go on.'

'I was caught kissing a girl in the vestry.'

'Well, I suppose the vestry isn't the place for that, but it's not criminal.'

Again a hesitation, then a cough. 'It was a shock to my wife.'

Not as big a shock as the 'wife' was to me. I could excuse a kiss. But a married man . . .

After it happened, he explained, everyone thought it better that he should leave the district. I suppose it had shocked the strait-laced among his parishioners but even in those days the offence did not seem to merit the punishment. That was why he was in France. He had no private means but was bilingual and worked as an interpreter. He explained his disappearance every evening: he was being hired by wealthy tourists who might lose thousands at the casino if they said 'Oui' at the wrong time.

'I've let everybody down,' he said, looking so crestfallen I could have hugged him. 'The church, my wife, the family, they're all very critical, except my brother, Jeremy. But he's different. He's an actor.'

I had never heard of an actor called Jeremy Huggins.

'His professional name is Jeremy Brett,' said John.

The name meant nothing until I saw Brett many years later as an unforgettable Sherlock Holmes. He was good-looking all right, and female viewers swooned over him, but John was the more handsome brother.

After this discovery a black cloud seemed to have settled over Cannes, but being only twenty, I found my spirits revived in the days that followed, and I was dazzled once more by his charm. The two of us went out together on our last night in Juan before leaving for Cap Ferrat. As we left the bistro he repeated what he had done in the vestry. It was our first and last kiss. A street photographer spotted us and took our picture. His resulting panic was out of all proportion. 'My wife's put a detective on me! It'll be a divorce if she sees the picture.' Paranoid no doubt, but the next morning as he said a more formal goodbye he gave me a gardenia. I knew he could not afford it, which made it all the more touching.

'Meet me in Juan when you decide to go home,' he said. 'I'll show you how to travel back in style.' He explained his method. Before leaving he visited the best hotel to find out from the concierge whether he was expecting any English visitors who would be driven to the Riviera by their chauffeurs. Their employers considered it cheaper to send them back to England for the month or so of their holidays and then ring for them when they decided to make the return trip. He travelled back with the chauffeurs, who 'appreciated the company.' He was unashamedly elitist about it. 'I get the chauffeurs' names and registration numbers and choose the best Bentley or Rolls available.'

Trust John Huggins to have worked that one out. We said we would meet when we returned to Juan, but that never happened as Cap Ferrat had its own unattached attractions. We have never met since, but as you can see, I have never forgotten him.

All holidays come to an end and once more it was Saturday nights at Saltburn Spa. There I met Michael Williams and we fell in love. He was an officer in the Merchant Navy, good-looking and reliable but fun, in fact every working-class mother's dream of a suitable son-in-law. We had wonderful times when he was on leave and became unofficially engaged. Everyone, including me, expected us to walk down the aisle. But a new man, not yet in my life, put paid to that.

After five years at ICI I was ready for a change. I stopped going to Saltburn Spa because Pat had moved to London and I was more or less engaged. Kenneth Kendall still looked benignly at me but one day I had a few words with him. 'It's time we moved on.' What I needed was a more demanding job. I was lucky because that same evening I spotted just what I was looking for in the local newspaper:

National newspaper journalist needs hard working secretary
with good shorthand typing speeds. Clock watchers need not
apply. This is a challenging post and merits a commensurately
higher than usual salary. Telephone 4500.

That was more like it. I made an appointment, dressed with
care and set off with all the aplomb of a Lucy Clayton graduate.
I sat in the waiting room and was about to leave after fifteen
minutes when a girl walked out of his office, looked at me and
mouthed one word: 'Bastard'.

Although based in the north-east Jack Clarke was probably at
that time the U.K.'s highest-paid journalist. Savile Row suits and
the latest sports cars were his badges of success. He had worked
in Fleet Street and become a news editor, but decided he could
make more money as a freelance investigative journalist. Jack
would travel anywhere, any time to get an exclusive where others
had been rebuffed, so he prospered. When I met him he
employed six reporters, two photographers and a cine man, and
supplied national newspapers and television stations with stories
from the region. At the time, however, I did not know much
about him.

When the 'bastard' opened his office door, I saw a man in his
mid-thirties, five feet nine or so, with a receding hairline but very
well groomed and wearing a bow tie. Not dapper but smart. I liked
that. He had twinkling blue eyes and, though no Hollywood
heartthrob, had something about him. He smiled after the
departing girl. 'Come in, if she hasn't put you off.' How could he
know? I soon found out that he read people very well, and quickly.

It was unlike any interview I had had. Questions about all
sorts of things; current affairs, gossip, all discussed at a whirlwind
rate as if time was money. He asked me courteously enough if
I would mind taking some dictation, handed me a pad and
pencil, then rattled off a letter at about one hundred and thirty
words a minute, which I only just managed to get down.

'Now type it.' He must have noticed my expression. 'If you don't mind, and you want the job.'

I typed the letter quickly and confidently handed it to him. He read it and reeled back in his chair, as if in shock. 'Christ! Didn't anyone teach you punctuation?'

The bosses were not rude like that at ICI. Who did he think he was?

'When people dictate they normally indicate commas and full stops. You didn't. I'm a secretary. Not a graduate in grammar and punctuation.'

He grinned. I got three months' trial at fifteen pounds a week, about fifty per cent above the going rate, plus a wonderful if tough initiation into the world of newspapers and television. I did not know it then but it was the beginning of the road to Number Nine, Orme Court.

In addition to being his secretary I was the office's general dogsbody, tea lady and wages clerk. I typed reporters' copy when they phoned in their stories, read them over to Jack on the telephone if he was out of the office, altered them according to the Clarke gospel and then dictated them to the nationals. The work never seemed to stop. I wondered if Jack ever spared the time to see his wife and children.

The reporters' room was thick with smoke, the desks dotted with a dozen mugs or so containing milky dregs of tea leaves and stubbed-out cigarettes. I could not believe the bad language they used and Jack was probably worse. The Sunday school teacher came out in me and I imposed a penalty of sixpence for a curse, which enhanced the contribution he made to nuns who called every month for donations to their missionary order.

Jack's television work was fascinating to me. When ITN came on air he soon became their man in the north and when the region's broadcaster, Tyne Tees, was launched he had a weekly political programme and appeared in a nightly current affairs magazine. About six months after starting work for him I became his researcher and consequently he thought it would be a good idea if I met some of the producers. I got to know one very well, Malcolm Morris, a crinkly-haired, bespectacled young man who was bubbling with ideas. When Malcolm was appointed Programme Controller he gave Jack his own shows, which he wrote and produced.

Increasingly, I made the round trip of eighty miles to the studio at breakneck speeds in one of Jack's sports cars (this was before the days of speed limits). One evening, when his show finished after ten, we were both hungry, having existed since early morning on canteen sandwiches, and he suggested dinner. That was a surprise because until then it had been very much a boss and employee relationship but I was famished and agreed.

In those days in the provinces most dining rooms and restaurants closed their doors around 8.30 p.m., but an Italian restaurant on the outskirts of Gateshead was daring enough to stay open as long as there were customers to serve. That evening I saw Jack in a new light. This often abrupt dynamo of a man changed into an attentive host. I found it difficult to believe I was with the same person who was so focused in his work that anyone who got in his way had to look out. Even the waiters seemed to find him charming. I found him attractive and fascinating. Whether, like an angler, he had been casting his line for a catch I do not know but by the end of the evening, I was hooked and ready to be hauled in.

In the meantime Michael Williams had gone back to sea and I simply stopped writing to him. My parents were sad about Michael, but they never knew the real reason we drifted apart. This is not to say that Jack changed overnight, only when we were out together, after hours. Whenever something went wrong in the office he flared up at the incompetents who had caused it, me included. Then of an evening that dazzling charm would return.

As I became more researcher than secretary I also began to help Jack cover some stories and I was there when he met his match. He had unrivalled sources at the Army's Catterick Camp, then the biggest in the country, and discovered that a certain eligible lieutenant in the Greys, who happened to be the Duke of Kent, was about to announce his engagement to Katherine Worsley, who was not royal or even titled but the daughter of Sir William Worsley, the Lord Lieutenant of the North Riding. Jack's photographer got a picture of the Duke's arrival at the Worsley home, Hovingham Hall. This was an exclusive and within hours of its publication reporters and photographers were sent to the sleepy village, which was still very feudal in its outlook. Journalists slaked the thirsts of locals in the Hovingham Arms but they were a tight-lipped lot. News editors were screaming for something new. Even Jack could not make any headway. Then he had an idea.

At that time he owned one of the very first E-type Jaguars. I had often wanted to drive it on quiet country roads, but his answer was always 'No'. Fair enough, I suppose, since I had not got a driving licence. Now he smiled at me.

'There's time to kill so why don't we give you a lesson in the Jag? The lanes round here are very quiet so it should be all right.'

I was so excited at the prospect that I was taken in. Silly me. Then I became nervous. What if I smashed it up?

'Nonsense!' he said. 'You've always been keen enough before. All cars are the same. Four wheels and an engine. Get in and I'll show you how.' So for ten minutes I was given a lesson by an unusually quiet, patient Jack Clarke. Until the car hiccoughed.

'For Christ's sake, woman!' He turned puce but somehow stifled his anger. 'It happens to us all.' Then he smiled once more. 'Excellent. Do you feel more confident now?'

I nodded.

'Good, because I've got an idea. You've always wanted to be a reporter. Now's your big chance. Katherine's girlfriends are driving past the gatekeeper with flowers and stuff. To congratulate her, I suppose. I want you to do the same.'

'You're out of your mind.'

'No I'm not. You'll see. It'll work. The reporters and photographers are all in the pub so nobody will recognize you.'

'How about the gatekeeper? He'll stop me.'

'He won't if you drive at him as if you don't intend to stop. Just give him a casual wave.'

I do not know why I fell for it but I did. Off we went to Helmsley for a giant bouquet and then half a mile from Hovingham he stepped out of the car and I was on my own, with firm instructions to get into the Hall if I could. If Katherine was not there I was to hand the flowers to the butler or footman and remember everything I saw, furniture, pictures on the wall, and ask if the Duke was there with her. If she came to the door then I was to remember what the engagement ring looked like and wish her all the best from Jack's agency.

I drove off – quite well, actually – at a steady twenty-five miles an hour, never faltering, and waving to the gatekeeper who saluted and opened the gates. I skidded to a halt at the huge door, got out of the car with trembling legs, rang the bell and waited. The door swung open to reveal a liveried manservant, a young, very good-looking one. I opened my mouth but the words would not come. How dare Jack put me in this position. I thrust the flowers into his hands. He looked at me expectantly and then the words tumbled out.

'I'm not a friend of Katherine Worsley. My boss is a journalist and made me come to ask if the Duke is here with Katherine and if not where are they?'

He looked at me impassively. More blurting.

'Is Katherine at home? Is the Duke here? I didn't want to do this. He made me. I'd have lost my job if I'd refused.'

He took pity. 'The Duke isn't here. He's with Miss Katherine at Nawton Hall.' Which, I knew, was where the Countess of Feversham lived.

I jumped in the car. It was such a relief to drive off. Did I say drive? More accurately, hiccough past the gates where Jack was waiting, along with thirty or forty reporters and photographers who had heard that an E-type had been admitted to the Hall. I pulled up and stalled the engine as I had forgotten to take it out of gear.

I made straight for Jack, absolutely furious. 'Don't ever put me through that sort of thing again!' I yelled. He put me back into the car and got behind the wheel.

'Tell us what happened, love,' one of the reporters shouted.

Jack put the car into gear. 'You can read all about it tomorrow,' he told them. And we roared off.

From such flimsy details he wrote a story that made several page leads and one of our photographers got an exclusive picture of the Duke and Katherine leaving Nawton Hall, the first of them both together.

'I'll never do that again,' I said. But I did, and I got better at it. The best was when I was sent to a local Lady who had held a charity sale of fashion clothes but instead, it was rumoured, had put most of the proceeds into her handbag. After Jack had broken the story hinting at her misdeeds her ladyship was very wary of the Press when she held a second sale. When I was dispatched to the manor, in the E-type again, she was delighted to show a 'model from London' around. After chatting for a quarter of an hour we were bosom pals. 'I do hope we come across one another again,' she said as I made to leave. 'It's so nice to meet a working gal.'

And then KERPOW. A camera bulb flashed in my face. Somehow the reporters had got to the front door again and one of them shouted at her ladyship, 'I thought you said reporters weren't allowed in the house. What about her?'

'I'm certainly not a reporter,' I said, quite truthfully. 'He's obviously mistaken me for someone else – dreadful man!'

'Riff raff,' agreed her ladyship.

Head held high, I walked disdainfully through the throng of

pressmen, some of whom I recognized, and got into the car quickly. And this time, thank God, I drove away smoothly.

Jack was delighted with my description of the house, Lady ——, and the clothes on offer. He wrote his piece, with carefully guarded hints about the proceeds of the previous sale having shrunk by the time they reached the charity, and sure enough, the nationals splashed with it.

'I should get a bonus for this. I got the story and you've made money out of it,' I told him.

'But you couldn't have written it.'

'Without me you wouldn't have had anything to write about.'

'But you're on a salary.'

'Yes, as a secretary and researcher. Not an undercover reporter.'

He sighed. 'You win.' He gave me a generous bonus and I now realize that this was my first stab at negotiating.

Life in Jack's office could be tough. I still remember going home after a particularly bad day. The reporters had ragged me, Jack was in an impossible mood because one of them had lost a story to someone else – 'You'll be lucky to hold down a job on a sleepy country weekly' – and in his fury he started to throw things around the office.

The sheer pressure of the day made me burst into tears when I got home. My dear mother was mortified. I can still hear her now. 'Dear oh dear. For goodness' sake don't go back there any more. All this upset. It's only a job. I'll have a word with Dick Colclough at the Town Hall. He'll get you a respectable job in his department. There'll be none of this upset there.'

The tears dried up immediately. 'What do you mean – a job at the Town Hall? I couldn't stand it. Boring, boring, boring! If you think I'm going to let Jack Clarke browbeat me you're wrong. When I go in tomorrow I'll give him a piece of my mind.'

Mum could not understand my reasoning then and to the end of her days wished I had gone to the Town Hall or stayed at ICI, married a local boy, settled down and provided her with grandchildren. But I was not interested. The same determination not to give in to Jack's forceful personality would serve me well as I refused to wilt when times were bad with Spike.

When I arrived at the office the next morning Jack behaved as if nothing had happened. That was yesterday's news and therefore history as far as he was concerned.

Jack and I had a vibrant, loving relationship for almost three years. He would leave his family: this week, next week, after Christmas, sometime, never. Eventually I realized I took second place to them, though I knew he adored me. It had been the most wonderful and exciting time of my life and he would always be in my heart, but the time had come to part. I was desperately sad and I think I decided then that this journalism lark was not for me. Jack had opened the door into the world of television and I was fascinated by it.

Back in the office I looked at Kenneth Kendall. 'It's time to move on again,' I told him. I was ambitious and determined to find a production job in television. There was only one place for that – London. I made a vow. I would never have another affair with a colleague or a married man. I had learned my lesson. I never did.

Pat Howden, my friend from hitch-hiking days, had gone to work in London a year or so earlier. She had asked me to join her but I did not want to leave Jack. 'Idiot!' she said. 'There's no future in that.'

Since then I had spent the odd weekend in London, staying in the flat she shared with four other girls. I got on well with all of them, particularly Diana Holloway, a lovely Welsh girl. When Pat moved to Paris to join her future husband I telephoned Diana to see if I could bum a bed for three or four weeks until I found a flat. 'You can have the spare room and it'll help us with the rent,' said the ever practical Diana. So off I set for my new home, a flat with two double bedrooms, both with two single beds, and a box room – the one I was to use – in a Victorian house on the Fulham Road.

I have no trouble remembering the date I moved in because as I walked through the front door a television newsreader announced, 'Marilyn Monroe has been found dead.' 4 August 1962. Marilyn was, and still is, someone I idolize. Instead of an evening of celebration for the start of a new period in my life it was one of mourning. 'Welcome to London and all its glitter,' I thought glumly.

I unpacked my case in the box room, squeezed six outfits into the built-in wardrobe, turned a small table under the window into a dressing table, shoved my suitcase under the bed, and Norma Farnes of 32 Langley Avenue, Thornaby sank onto it to mourn Norma Jean of Tinsel Town. What a depressing start to my new life.

The next morning my eyes opened to sunshine. No time to waste. Up bright and early to find some temp work to pay for my share of the expenses.

Household duties were on a roster basis. The one who did the shopping also did the cooking, and it soon emerged that only Diana and I were prepared to splurge on extravagances to relieve the interminable diet of chops and mince. Diana worked in the Burlington Arcade and told me there was an employment agency round the corner, Nu Type. I put on my glad rags and was interviewed by a Mrs Long, who tested my shorthand and typing speeds. Satisfied, she eyed me. 'You're very well groomed, very smart. You'll be easy to place.' She made me feel like the final piece of a jigsaw. I said I needed temporary work until I found something permanent.

'No trouble,' she said. 'Felicity Green – she's Woman's page editor on the *Daily Mirror* – wants someone for a week.'

I was familiar with newspaper work, loved the job, worked hard and Felicity gave a glowing report. Mrs Long was delighted.

'You'll be a wonderful advertisement for the agency,' she said. I did not give a damn as long as I got the plum jobs.

My second assignment was with Granada Television in Golden Square, another familiar medium; the third with a peer in sumptuous offices in Half Moon Street, which was easy-peasy, just answering the phone, typing a few letters, plus walks in Green Park. Within weeks I was earning more than I had dreamed possible, and happy to work evenings and weekends.

Two weeks after I arrived in London, when we were relaxing in the flat on a Saturday morning, the front bell rang. It was my father. Mum had sent him to make certain I had not been debauched by the big city, that I was not living in a hovel or suspect neighbourhood, that my flat-mates would have met with her approval and that my employers were not gangsters or white-slave traders. His anxious face soon relaxed into a smile. Then I noticed a large carrier bag. Food for the needy: lamb chops, pork chops complete with succulent kidneys, fillet steaks, sirloin steaks and pork sausages, just to make sure I did not die from malnutrition. These visits went on for five months until I told him it would have to stop. Instead I agreed to travel home once a month, which I did for many years. He was always there, waiting for me on the platform at Thornaby station.

After a year or so I started wondering whether I should get a 'proper job', that is, a permanent one. I still wanted to become a television producer so was happy when Mrs Long found me a job as assistant to the information officer at the Independent Television Companies' Association (ITCA), Television House, not far from Covent Garden. But as I found out the ITCA's rôle was mostly administrative, serving as the industry's watchdog.

My boss liked to use his wartime title of major. On my first day he went to lunch at 12.30 p.m. precisely. At five o'clock he telephoned. 'Are you coping, my dear? Good. I knew you would be. No point in coming back to the office now.' A cough. 'I'm afraid I fell among thieves.' As he did most days. Although he was almost a caricature of the retired Army officer he was very kind and I liked him. However, after a couple of years covering up for him he was abruptly fired and I took over his responsibilities.

Every month since I started there had been obituary meetings to update the planned coverage for the funeral of Sir Winston Churchill, and like him they went on for ever. Three days after we had said goodbye to the major Sir Winston died and I was thrown in at the deep end, having to liaise with each television station to let them know what their rôle would be. Up to that time the longest outside broadcast had been two hours but this would last five. We all worked night and day but it was worth it when newspapers acclaimed our coverage, which they reckoned was superior to the BBC's.

I saw the cortège as it passed our offices and remember wondering how such a small coffin could contain this giant of a man. All those who worked on the funeral were given a specially printed brochure, *The Valiant Man*, which is still one of my treasured possessions.

Then I was offered the major's post. All very well, I said, but what was in it for me? I could have a secretary and my name on the door. How about increasing my salary? Two pounds a week was the offer, far less than they had paid the major. It was decision time. I could not even consult Kenneth because he had been lost in the various moves. But I did not need to. This had been a man's job and I wanted a man's rate of pay for it. Oh dear no! That would never do. Equal pay simply was not on as far as they were concerned. But it was for me. So after two years it was time for a change. The ITCA was too much like the Civil Service for my liking. I would seek temporary work until I could find a job in television production. Something to tide me over for a few months would be ideal.

Chapter Three

Well, I thought, as I walked into Number Nine on 22 August 1966, it may be for no more than a few months but it will be very convenient. Only fifteen minutes from the flat, famous writers and performers working in the building and television producers and directors coming to see them all the time. It would not harm my c.v. when I applied for the television job. And I had a whole week to get to know my way round the office before Spike returned.

David Conyers introduced me to the head agent Beryl Vertue, and showed me to my office. It was in the basement, which had originally housed the kitchens and butler's sitting room and was now occupied by me and three delightful, friendly girls, Pam Gillis, Tessa Batson and Barbara Alloway. Pam and Tessa would go on to become successful agents, but that was some years distant. That first day I went out for lunch with Pam, beginning a tradition we maintain to this day, and she gave me a rundown of who occupied Number Nine and what they did.

The office buzzed with talent. Spike had founded a writers' co-operative, Associated London Scripts or ALS, and looking back now, it seems most of the best British comedy of the Fifties, Sixties and Seventies emerged from this small group of people. I knew all about the famous Eric Sykes, Spike's closest friend and co-founder, who was on television every week with Hattie Jacques in *Sykes and A . . .*, which for many years held the record for longest-running series. Then there were Ray Galton and Alan Simpson, who wrote Tony Hancock's best material, then moved on with *Steptoe & Son*; Johnny Speight, a prolific comic writer and creator of *Till Death Us Do Part*, and Terry Nation, who had battled endlessly to get the BBC to screen his invention, the daleks, in the *Dr Who* series he had written. Spike was unusual among the writers, in that he wrote solely for himself and starred in his own programmes. That was not the only characteristic which set him apart. There was always a host of limousines parked outside Number Nine, with one exception. While the others purred to a halt in their Rolls and Bentleys Spike would squeeze impudently and incongruously into a space between them in his Mini, which he drove so furiously and with such a complete disregard for speed limits that nobody would travel with him. David and Beryl also represented other writers and artists who worked from home but frequently called in at Number Nine. Pam reeled off a list of names so starry I nearly choked on my lunch. It seemed a dream place to be.

Unlike the stuffy ITCA the building was never quiet. It hummed with an incessant babble of voices; ringing phones; voices raised in frustration or enthusiasm; gags being tried out; people running up and down stairs, and a non-stop trail of show business personalities popping in to see their friends. As the days passed I got to know David and Beryl a lot better. He was easy-going but quietly efficient and she was an absolute star, giving me so much help and advice. At the end of the week she told me, 'Remember, when you have a bad time with Spike I'm here with a shoulder to lean on.'

I arrived early on Monday, 29 August to make sure I was there before Spike. I need not have bothered. He did not show up. Not that day, not the next, not Wednesday, in fact not any day that week. I went to see David.

'What's happening? Where is he?'

David's smile was benign, the sort you get from a kindly and sympathetic grandparent, perhaps with a hint of relief in his expression. 'Don't worry. He'll turn up.' A sigh. 'He always does.' That was it. Nobody had heard from him, knew where he was or seemed all that concerned about his absence.

By the middle of the second week there was still no Spike. I had had enough and went back to David.

'I can't wait any longer, doing nothing except twiddle my thumbs. It's not on, so I'm off.'

David seemed at first amazed, then amused and finally his face creased into a careworn smile. 'He'll be here soon enough, I assure you.' He peered at me, as if weighing me up. 'Somehow I have an idea you're just what he's looking for. You might hit it off.' He smiled again. 'Give it another week. Please.'

Much later I discovered he had decided I had the mettle to cope with Spike, and he had also kept to himself the fact that Spike had got through five typing pool secretaries in the previous eighteen months. He was not to know that I had served my apprenticeship with another volatile character.

At the close of the second week a private line telephone arrived on my desk. 'You'll need it,' David explained. 'He's never off the phone. It's better this way. He won't be able to block the switchboard.'

I used the time to get to know everyone in the office and was feeling quite settled, but when I went to Number Nine at the beginning of the third week I had resolved to call it a day on the Friday unless things changed. On the Tuesday they did. My phone rang and the receptionist, Ann Thomas, announced, 'It's him. On the line.' Click. There was a pause, then came a voice in a low, flat monotone.

'Are you the girl I chose?'

'Yes,' I said, nothing else; I sensed there was more to come.

'Are you sure you're the girl I chose? I can't trust that lot in the office. It would be just like those buggers to take on someone else while I was away. Someone suitable for them and not for me. Bastards.' All this was said in a voice empty of drama or emotion. He had not finished. 'When you first came to see me you were wearing a hat, a sort of black and white fake fur, weren't you?'

'That's right.' I found it strange he should remember that.

The voice continued in its detached way.

'Well, I'm ill. I'm in a mental home in Friern Barnet. I was on holiday with the family at the Skanes Palace Hotel in Tunisia. I had a terrible row with my wife. It all got too much for me. So I left them, came home and put myself in here. The only thing to do.' A pause. 'Will you wait at the office for me?'

Before I could reply he had replaced the receiver.

Another two weeks passed without a word from him. Then one morning Josie Mills, Beryl's assistant and Frankie Howerd's manager, skipped down the steps to the cellar.

'Spike's just walked in.'

Simultaneously the phone rang. It was Ann. 'He's arrived.'

David clattered downstairs.

'He's back,' he said, in a voice that was both relieved and tinged with the unspoken suggestion that a peaceful interlude was about to be shattered.

Pam and I looked at one another and giggled.

Seconds later the phone rang. It was Ann again. 'He wants you to go up.'

Up the stairs I went to room six on the first floor, my note-book in my hand ready to take dictation. Now I would get an explanation. I opened the door and he glanced at me quickly. No niceties, no formalities, just the glance.

'Yes. You're the one I chose.' He paused and opened his diary. 'It's Norma Farnes, isn't it?'

'I hope so.'

He looked at me quickly. I sat down on the chair opposite him.

'Okay. Let's get down to it.' He slid several pieces of paper across the table. 'This is what I'm working on. A children's poetry book. All the poems are about animals. What do you think?'

I read quickly.

> Said a tiny Ant
> To the Elephant
> 'Mind how you tread in this clearing.'
>
> But alas! Cruel fate!
> She was crushed by the weight
> Of an Elephant, hard of hearing.

Then another.

> A very rash young lady pig
> (They say she was a smasher)
> Suddenly ran
> Under a van –
> Now she's a gammon rasher.

And another.

> A baby Sardine
> Saw her first submarine:
> She was scared and watched through a peephole.
> 'Oh come, come, come,'
> Said the Sardine's mum,
> 'It's only a tin full of people.'

There were several more. I had never read any of his work before and wondered why on earth he wanted my opinion.

'Well?' he prompted.

'They're enchanting,' I said, meaning it.

He smiled. 'Good.'

As I was to find out, disagreement could have led to 'What do you know about comedy?' or 'Since when did you become a judge of what's funny and what isn't?' But we were in our honeymoon period.

He took the pieces of paper from me.

'Enough! The poems can wait. There are more important matters to deal with. *The Amazonian rain-forest for one.*'

'What about the poems?'

He looked at me, incredulous. 'Get a sense of proportion. Forget the rain-forests and we're all in trouble.' He picked up the phone. 'Get me Ted Allbeury.' Then an aside to me. 'He has lots of radio contacts.' Ted had run a pirate radio station and was now a successful author. Spike waited on the line then looked at me as if he had forgotten I was there. 'Come to think of it, as you're here you can help.'

So much for my passport to the entertainment industry. Instead I found myself plunged into a campaign to save the Amazonian rain-forest and got given a nature lesson.

'Always remember, the earth's resources are finite. The stupid bastards who run the world need a lesson in that. But they don't bloody care.'

Welcome to Spike. Long before the importance of the world's rain-forests became accepted wisdom he had been alerted, how I do not know, to the need to preserve them. Later others joined in but it took Spike, with his wide following, to start the crusade in the U.K., as he would also do with campaigns to save the seal, the whale, the elephant, the rhinoceros and the lion.

That first day initiated me to the foibles of that exhilarating man. Okay, I reflected, when it was time to leave, I have given myself three months, but if it turns out to be as interesting and challenging as it promises then that could stretch to six. Because this was more of a commitment than I'd anticipated the next day I took my bits and pieces to the office, including my pin-up photograph. By then poor Kenneth had been given the old heave-ho. Anthony Hopkins had taken Kenneth's place after I had seen him in *A Lion in Winter*, and once he was pinned to the wall I was ready to face the world. But could I be as confident about coping with Spike?

Day Two was an introduction to the single-minded dedication Spike was always prepared to devote to what he considered to be an injustice, an affront or a con. On this occasion Lord Fraser, owner of Harrods, was the enemy, as apparently he had been for more than a year. The reason for this was that Spike had bought a ladder from the store (it had to be Harrods, not a hardware store or builders' merchant where most people would buy a ladder). Spike was adamant that the bolts were insecure and therefore the ladder unsafe. The department head was dubious, however, and would not exchange it. So Spike, as was his way, aimed for the top man. Nothing else mattered on the second day I worked for him: Harrods and Lord Fraser were in the wrong and justice had to be done, honour salvaged and punishment meted out.

Victory did not come immediately but later Lord Fraser wilted under the torrent of letters, raised the white flag and sent a new ladder. Spike was relentless and won almost every battle of this nature. 'Don't let the bastards get away with it,' he often said, and he never did. Over the years he had many run-ins with Harrods, over chairs, lace tablecloths, white envelopes he did not consider sufficiently white. Despite it all he would never shop anywhere else. Indeed, the following day, when we ran out of toilet paper, I said we could get some from the shop round the corner. Not a bit of it: Harrods was his corner shop. He rang and had them delivered by taxi, the fare being three or four times their cost. That was typical.

In my early days at Number Nine I had the feeling that the girls in my flat thought life there was one long cabaret but it was anything but that. Popularly it may have been known as 'The Fun Factory', where incredibly talented people were a laugh a minute, yet although I had a lot of laughs, the reality was very different. Eric Sykes summed it up. 'Every business has its products. Show business is no exception. One of them is humour. And that is a very serious business.' They certainly set about it seriously, which is not to say that they were not funny as well. Whereas work for Spike could start at two or three in the afternoon if he had been working on a script until the early hours, the rest of them started any time between ten and eleven. They all had their own idiosyncratic way of writing their material. But one thing they had in common was that all of them, bar Johnny, were six feet or more tall. When Eric introduced me to his old RAF mate, Denis Norden, and his writing partner Frank Muir, both six feet four, I wondered whether it was height that made them all able to see the funny side of life.

In the office opposite Spike were Ray Galton and Alan Simpson – the lads, or the boys as far as he was concerned. I walked in one day and did a double take. Both their long frames were stretched out on the floor, facing each other like bookends and throwing out lines and suggestions. This was how they got their inspiration and flat out on the floor was how they liked to work. It sounds relaxed but actually they were intensely disciplined and set a target each day of how much they needed to write between the hours of ten and six. Then office hours were over. Immaculate, charming Ray, with his handmade silk shirts by Turnbull and Asser, was an inveterate clubber, and smart, football-loving Alan more of a gourmet and an expert on vintage wines, which they could both, and still do, consume in amazing quantities without any apparent effect.

Eric worked on the next floor up. He was and still is the consummate professional, and according to Spike the greatest droll comic and writer of the last fifty years. I soon found out that he could spend days, sometimes weeks, mulling over an idea, and then when it was clear in his mind write it up at great speed. He was terribly busy writing and performing in *Sykes and A. . .*, but liked a round of golf whenever he had the chance. He dressed the most conservatively, generally coming to work in an immaculately tailored suit or blazer. Eric has survived them all and now, clinically blind and deaf, he is still writing and busy as an actor on stage, television and film, always giving the same thought and preparation to his performances as he does to his writing. Having known Spike longer than anyone, Eric and he had a remarkable bond.

By the time I arrived at Number Nine Terry Nation had already left. Johnny Speight still arrived there most days. The first series *of Till Death Us Do Part* had been broadcast earlier that year, and he was basking in the success. He was very busy, a stewpot of ideas, writing *Till Death* and mulling over plots for plays, but also happy to indulge his taste for the finer things in life. Dressed casually in the latest fashion by Blades or Mr Fish, he would appear in the late morning, chat to Eric and then pop in to see Spike. This amazing self-educated East Ender was a truly original thinker, unfettered by received opinions on any subject, and so wise. And a great observational writer. He thought Spike was at his best when his humour was at its blackest and, no matter what trouble he was in, Johnny always excused him. 'What do you expect?' he would ask. 'He's not like the rest of us. He's a true genius.'

The co-operative lived up to its ideal, and everybody was on first-name terms, always popping out together for lunch or supper at the end of the day. Johnny in particular was generous to a fault. Very early on he took me to lunch at a famous restaurant, the White Elephant at 28 Curzon Street. I've forgotten what my first course was but he was drinking whisky with his.

'You need a white wine with yours,' he said, and ordered

it, the most expensive half-bottle on the menu. Johnny then explained to the waiter what he wanted for his main course. A baked potato filled with caviar.

'Go on,' he told me. 'Try one.'

'Not caviar on a baked potato! It's outrageous.'

'Don't be silly,' said Johnny. 'It's a Soviet peasant's lunch.'

Just as Pam had promised, I was soon brushing shoulders with many household names, who always had a joke for the girl from Thornaby. Tommy Cooper, a naturally funny man who was unsure of his talent and could never understand why people laughed at him, often called to see Eric and they would have a whisky or three while they discussed 'the business'.

The Goon Show was no longer running but the Goons were still friendly. Peter Sellers often called from Hollywood to chat things over with Spike. Pete and Spike had an extraordinary and lasting relationship, even though Pete was often disloyal. Over the years similar acts of treachery – and with Pete, it really was treachery – from others meant they were damned to oblivion but Spike always forgave Pete with a shrug, saying 'That's how he is.' Anyone else would have 'died yesterday', as Spike put it.

The most cheerful and refreshingly normal of the three was Harry Secombe, who popped in now and again. Fame had not gone to his head and his diminutive Welsh wife Myra made sure it never did. He once told me that after a rapturous reception at a Royal Command Variety Show at the London Palladium he returned to his wife on a high. Then he described in great detail, several times in fact, his performance as the star of the show and the applause he won, reinforcing the tale with a bit of business. 'Right, Harry,' said Myra drily, 'now you're finished go and bring the coal in.' He loved her for bringing him back to earth.

Harry was a caring man and always placatory when there was trouble between Spike and Pete. While the other two were not made of the stuff of faithful husbands, Harry always went home to Myra as quickly as possible after a performance. In his day he could drink whisky with the best of them, Eric, Tommy and the incorrigible toper Jimmy Edwards, but later swore off it for the sake of his health and Myra. As a result he was blessed with the sort of happy family life denied to Spike and Pete; on the other hand, without being unkind, he did not carry the burden of their unique gifts.

Frankie Howerd often dropped in to see Eric. I can still see his hunched figure, in suits that never seemed to fit. He was a man in doubt of his talent, insecure and lonely, always wondering how long it would be before the phone stopped ringing once more. It had happened before in the early Sixties when comics like him were thought to be as outdated as the old eight-reel films, but he was born again when he appeared with Peter Cook at The Establishment Club and demonstrated that, as an old trouper, he was a master of satire; next to Frankie the Footlights crowd could look like amateurs.

Sometimes Frankie seemed desperate to be reassured of his popularity. One evening, long after we first met, I was dining with a friend at Spike's favourite restaurant, the Trattoo, off High Street Kensington, and noticed Frankie shuffle in. He looked around to see if he could recognize anyone, then spotted me and, with that wonderful wide-mouthed smile, sidled over. Leaning forwards so nobody else could hear, he whispered, 'Can I join you?'

If Spike had been with me Frank would have darted out of sight as quickly as possible because he was always on tenterhooks about what Spike might say and in awe of his inspirational wit. Frankie's humour was crafted, rehearsed, and his apparent spontaneity honed to perfection. That evening – and there was nothing unusual about this – he thought he was once again washed-up. In that hoarse whisper of his, with genuine bafflement, he said, 'The worrying thing is, you see, I don't know why people find me funny. I have nightmares about it.'

My companion, a fan, was quite astonished and his enthusiasm reassured Frank, who became expansive and happy. By the time we were about to part he was a different man. 'Do you know,' he said quietly, looking over his shoulder like the music-hall comic he was, 'you've made me feel so much better.' He felt in his inside pocket. For a moment I thought he was going to offer to settle the bill but I did not hold my breath. I knew his reputation. 'Next time,' he beamed, 'you must let me pay.'

This was, of course, years later, but quite early on I would find myself leaving the office only to rejoin the gang at the Trattoo of an evening, chatting and listening to Spike's friend Alan Clare, the talented jazz player, on the piano. Though I did not know it at the time, these days marked the beginning of some of the most important friendships of my life. After Jack Clarke I had sworn never to get romantically involved with anyone I worked with and perhaps this is what made things last.

Meanwhile, Diana and I had become close friends and carried on living together while other girls came and went. One of them was New Yorker Camille Marchetta, who was a lot of laughs, tough and hugely ambitious. She worked for an agent whose clients included film stars and famous writers. She also had an idea she could write, 'Better than some of the clients.' We all have our dreams, I thought. Well, she was brave enough to pack in a good job and return to New York to do it. And write she did. Her television series ran and ran and made her famous. *Dallas* was its name.

As the months passed the Number Nine blend of business and play came to seem more and more natural to me. Spike had recently been a sensation on the stage in his improvised play, *Son of Oblomov*, and was now being courted by impresarios to take it to Broadway; Barbra Streisand was just one of the people who pleaded with him. I believe he would have been a huge success and become a world-wide star if he had agreed, but he did not like Americans so that was the end of that.

In the autumn he presented me with a list of five hundred

names for his Christmas cards. 'I'm going to draw my own for about two hundred of them,' he said. Ridiculous, I thought. He cannot possibly mean it.

'Get on to the Times Drawing Office in Maddox Street and tell them to put two hundred sheets of their best quality white cardboard paper in a taxi. I need it in the next hour. Then ring Sandfords and tell them to send me a dozen black calligraphy pens in another taxi.'

'How are we going to pay for them?' Silly me. I did not realize that the Times Drawing Office knew him of old.

'Just do it. Pay the taxi when they are delivered and get David to send me the bill. I've got to get on with them before somebody interrupts me. Some bastard is bound to spoil it.'

The cardboard was delivered later that morning. By the time I left the office he had drawn two hundred cards.

Spike could also be mean and nasty, particularly to the people he loved most. Spike's wife Paddy was nearly twenty years younger than him, and scatty and undisciplined in contrast to his fanatical sense of organization about everyday things. While we had already spoken many times on the phone my first clear memory of meeting her brought about perhaps the worst moment I had yet experienced with Spike.

Paddy was doing her Christmas shopping in the West End and ran out of money, so she came to the office to get some from Spike. She was tall, nearly six foot in high heels, and very elegant. Spike was at the Mermaid Theatre. I told her not to worry, she could have whatever was in the petty cash box. Forty-five pounds would do, she said. When Spike returned a few hours later I said Paddy had called in and mentioned the money I had given her. He went berserk.

'What on earth possessed you to give away *my* money?'

'She's your wife and needed it to get home.'

He went into a tirade. 'That's no reason to give away *my* money. Would you give *my* money to a tramp in the street?'

'No. I leave that to you.'

That infuriated him because it was true. We had a resident tramp in Bayswater and when Spike went out for doughnuts and cakes (another Milligan obsession) he would always give him a few quid.

'You gave away *my* money,' he raged. 'I can do what I like with *my* money. You can't. And that includes giving it to Paddy. It was *my* money so you must pay it back.'

'All right,' I said. 'If that's how you feel I'll pay it back at three pounds a week.'

'Right. Done. Accepted.'

Fuck him, I thought.

Half an hour later, on his way out, he appeared in my office. I waited for him to speak.

'You've learned your lesson about not giving my money away,' he said. 'Forget the forty-five pounds. I don't want it.' He went out before I could say anything. In less than an hour he was back, with a magnificent pot plant. He placed it on my desk.

'You have a dress this colour. I thought you'd like it.' Before I could thank him he had gone. Later that afternoon he gave me a copy of the 1955 *Picturegoer*. On the front cover it said 'Goons are Inside.' It also contained a write-up of his split-screen film, *The Case of the Mukkinese Battle Horn*. 'It's in Schizophrenoscope,' he quipped. 'I want you to have it.'

And so I learned the lengths he would go to avoid saying 'sorry'. It was soon after this that he fell out with his manager and I was given the job and started taking care of his business affairs. Not long afterwards I received the Christmas card he had drawn for me. Clipped to the card was a tiny envelope addressed in the smallest of writing, which I discovered was the style he used when sending his children messages from the fairies. Screwed up inside was a twenty pound note and the message, 'To save you counting it's twenty pounds.'

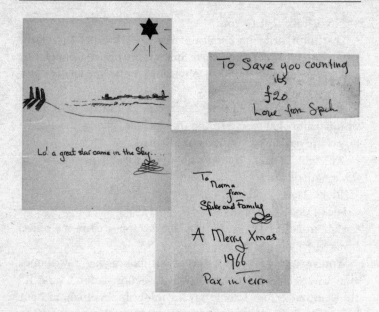

Lo! a great star came in the Sky....

To Save you counting
it
£20
Love from Spike

To
Norma
from
Spike and Family
A Merry Xmas
1966
Pax in Terra

The year was coming to an end and it was decision time. Did I want to stay at Number Nine? Eric, who remained Spike's greatest friend, warned me that his every mood permeated the building: when Spike was buoyant so was everyone, when he was down voices were hushed and people moved warily. Should I give it another few months? I consulted Anthony Hopkins. He seemed very much at home at Number Nine. He agreed we should give it a whirl.

Chapter Four

In all the time I knew him Spike was never boring. When you consider his parents' characters this becomes understandable. Leo Milligan grew up in County Sligo, Ireland, and followed family tradition by joining the Army at the age of fourteen. Unusually he took dance classes and was soon appearing both on military and civilian stages – sometimes blacked up for a song-and-dance act, at others dressed up as a cowboy to demonstrate his skill with a lariat. He was also a mean trumpeter. This last skill served him well and he ascended the ranks, going to India as Lance Bombardier, trumpeter. He did not neglect his Catholicism and it was at St Ignatius Church, Kirkee, in 1912, that his eye was caught by the beautiful organist. Like her future husband, Florence Kettleband came from an Army background, emigrating with her family from their Leicestershire home to India at the age of eight. She was a trained contralto and when Leo heard her sing he was smitten. They married two years later and it was not long before they started performing at regimental theatres as a double act. In Ahmednagar, on 16 April 1918,

Florence gave birth to their first son, Terence Alan Milligan, a troublesome baby. As Leo often told Spike, 'You never stopped bloody screaming.'

The next year the family travelled on leave to England, having to be rescued when their ship struck a reef. When they finally made it back Florence got measles, which turned into pneumonia, and temporarily she went blind. To the end of her days she maintained that her sight was restored by a faith healer, and certainly her own faith never wavered, however much her older son liked to tease her about it. After she recovered the family returned to India where Leo, with Florence at his side, seemed to spend more time touring on stage, entertaining the troops, than he did on the barrack square. One of their greatest successes was putting on rodeos, with Leo trick-riding like a cowboy. These skills were entirely self-taught, another Milligan family trait. Spike joked that Leo liked the rodeos because his stetson covered a problem: he was completely bald. The rest of the time he wore a black wig which looked like 'a dead cat nailed to his head'. One day a kite hawk snatched it from his pate and until another one arrived from England Leo wore his topee, even indoors. Spike enjoyed his parents' shows, but he was an unwilling spectator to their passion for hunting. They would fire at 'anything that had feathers or fur on it'. He went on to devote a large part of his life to trying to protect wildlife.

The Milligans moved on to Burma, and their second son, Desmond Patrick, was born in Rangoon on 5 December 1925, soon after Leo had been promoted Acting Regimental Sergeant Major. They continued their comfortable colonial existence until 1933, when the post of RSM was abolished in Leo's regiment and they were sent back to England and a two-room flat in Catford. The country was still in the grip of the Depression, but it was not long before, at the age of sixteen, Spike was at work by day and earning another ten shillings a night to sing with a band at a dance hall in South London, doubling on guitar and double bass, both of which he had taught himself to play. Leo was less successful. He set out for interviews in a Homburg and grey kid gloves, with a silver-topped ebony cane, ready to consider offers from deserving employers. They did not realize what a bargain they were getting in an ex-sergeant major who could throw a lariat, ride bucking broncos and do a soft shoe shuffle. It took twelve months but finally he got a job with Associated Press. He and Spike always said he was a journalist but as those were the days of closed shops this might have been stretching the truth, which was never a problem for Leo. Spike always remembered how Leo reacted when he was sceptical about his claim to have shot a tiger. 'Let me ask you something, son. Would you rather have an exciting lie or the boring truth?' There was a lot of his father in Spike.

When he was nineteen Spike met the one true love that remained constant throughout his life, in the window of a shop in Lewisham High Street: a gold-plated Besson trumpet, price totally beyond him. No problem. He had enough for a deposit and bought it, figuring the rest could come from his employer. His bosses disagreed. Spike was still playing the clubs but his day job was with a wholesale tobacconist where he would wrap parcels of cigarettes and tobacco. It was conveniently cold in the warehouse so he wore his overcoat and some of the cigarettes found their way into its pockets. Spike sold them on at a cut price, but was caught by the foreman and arrested.

Leo had missed the drama of the theatre and wasted no time in offering his services as advocate. After several rehearsals at home to hone his act he was ready to take centre stage at the police court. As ever, the boring truth was disregarded. Theft? Nonsense. Entrepreneurial flair in a time of hardship. 'Look at him,' he declared to the magistrates, pointing a finger at Spike. 'His crime was a love of music. He needed the money to buy a violin and study classical music, but he was so poor he could never – you hear – never afford one. His only way was to pilfer stockroom goods and sell them. This has afforded him a second-hand violin which, even now, he is learning to play. Have pity on this boy. As a result of his action he could become a virtuoso.'

It was a triumphant performance. As Leo correctly reckoned, burgeoning classical violinists got far more sympathy from magistrates than trumpeters. Spike was discharged and played his gold-plated trumpet in the Harlem Club Band, all because of an exciting lie.

Although Spike's family was Army on both sides he was not keen to join up when Britain declared war on Germany in 1939. He was conscripted the following year, on his twenty-first birthday, and took this trumpet with him to the 56th Heavy Regiment, Royal Artillery. Every morning he would sound the reveille, and aspects of the life must have recalled the pleasures of his childhood. It was at this time that he acquired a new name. In the services there were three common nicknames: Clarkes were called Nobby, Joneses Taffy, and tall and skinny ones often became Spike. He decided this was preferable to Terence and so, to everyone apart from his mother, Spike he was from now on.

Spike saw a lot of action in North Africa then moved to Italy, escaping injury until he was caught in heavy fighting outside Naples in 1944 and blown up by mortar fire. Although his wounds were slight the stress of battle and the sight of his friends perishing had caused him intense suffering. He was diagnosed with combat fatigue, the Second World War term for shell-shock. This episode was, though he did not know it at the time, the first manifestation of the illness which would dog him for the rest of his life.

After he recovered Gunner Milligan joined an Army dance band and reached the rank of sergeant. As soon as peace was declared in May 1945 he was posted to the Central Pool of Artists, whose rôle was to entertain the troops waiting for de-mobilization. One day he was practising guitar in a rehearsal room, when tall ex-Gunner Bill Hall, a brilliant violinist, invited him to form a trio with a double-bass player, Johnny Mugrew. Spike accepted, reckoning they sounded like Le Hot Club de France, a famous Parisian jazz combo. It was when they were playing at the Officers' Club in Naples that he was struck by one of the cabaret acts, 'someone from Mars, Gunner Secombe H., singer and lunatic, who had been pronounced loony after a direct hit from an 88mm gun in North Africa. He rushed on chattering, screaming, farting, sweat pouring from him like a monsoon.' Spike could not understand a word Harry said and thought he was 'a Polish comedian', although they had met in North Africa.

The Bill Hall Trio was a great success and on demob they were offered officer status if they would continue to play for the troops for six months. They accepted and Florence was able to tell the neighbours that her son was a 'banjo-playing officer'. It was then that Spike developed his first manic act, which would eventually lead to *The Goon Show*. A natural front man, Spike would do the links between songs, and these quickly mutated into riffs with funny voices, then sketches, with Bill and Jimmy playing a part. He did not tell jokes as such. But then Spike is famous for being the first comic who didn't need punch lines to make people laugh. They toured through Italy and when they reached Naples the Italian Corps de Ballet joined the show. They were thrilled to have women on board, and Spike was particularly keen on the prima ballerina, Maria Antoinetta Pontani. For months Spike and Toni were inseparable and I believe she was the love of his life. They spent an idyllic weekend in Capri and planned to marry. Spike wrote home with the good news. But his mother would have none of it. 'We don't want a foreigner in this family,' she told him. Apparently Spike accepted, which I have never understood. There is no doubt he was in love with Toni and she with him and it would have been in character for him to ignore his mother's opposition. By the time I knew Spike he was someone who always did what he thought was right, regardless of anybody else's opinion. Toni married an Italian diplomat who was sympathetic to their friendship, and Spike flew to Rome to take her out. When her daughter moved to Paris it became much easier for them to see each other. This continued until a couple of years before his death.

In 1946 the Bill Hall Trio arrived back in Britain and toured the halls, earning seventy-five pounds between them a week – affluence indeed when the average wage was about five pounds – but Spike was not satisfied. After a few months he decided to go solo with his wild act. The parting was acrimonious. Bill said, 'I hope you never get another fucking job.'

Sure enough, the act flopped and Spike joined another trio which travelled around Italy, but he still wanted to succeed in his own right and returned to England in 1948. He was doing his best – 'it wasn't good enough', he said later – to break into radio. It was then he heard that the 'Polish comedian' was appearing at the Windmill in Soho. This theatre was the place for post-war talent. Alumni of the Central Pool of Artists would try out their acts there between the more risqué performances, including the famous female 'statues', nudes who were not deemed obscene so long as they did not move. Spike went along to see Harry and when they caught up after the show he was introduced to another comic performer, Michael Bentine, who was also on the bill. The three became friends and, while Spike struggled to eke out a living, of an evening they started to hang out at the Grafton Arms in Sutton Ground, Westminster.

The landlord Jimmy Grafton, formerly a major, was very handsome and a tireless entrepreneur. He had taken over the pub, was struggling to write scripts, and always had an eye for talent, becoming Harry Secombe's agent. One night in the bar, after Spike had played piano while Harry sang, they had a few drinks and told stories. Jimmy heard some of Spike's and immediately asked if he would like to write with him for Derek Roy. Roy had sung with the band leader Geraldo and now had his own comedy guest spot on BBC radio. Spike was always very dismissive of Derek Roy, the 'unfunniest man in the business', and reckoned he 'killed ninety-nine per cent of all known jokes.' But this was the break he had been waiting for.

In 1949 Spike was invited to appear in one of Roy's shows to do 'an idiot voice', which he told me developed into Eccles for *The Goon Show*. Ever hopeful of making it alone, Spike developed an act based on the voice for the music halls but quickly died a death and it was back to the Grafton Arms. He had no money and nowhere to stay but Jimmy had three attics free above the pub and offered one to Spike. He took his typewriter up there and continued to hammer out jokes for Derek Roy. Occasionally he was disturbed by a noise in the next room so he looked through the keyhole and a monkey looked back at him. Jimmy had bought it as a present for his wife. A friendship developed between Spike and the monkey but this came to an abrupt end when it bit him and the monkey was consigned to the garage.

Meanwhile Harry was prospering and had got a spot at the Hackney Empire. In the bar after the show Harry introduced him to a man Spike said 'wanted to look like a male model – posh suit, posh collar and tie, Crombie overcoat, gloves carried in his left hand and a trilby hat.' This suave fellow was Peter Sellers, who came from a stage family and made quite an impression on Spike, although he never forgot that Pete 'didn't buy a bloody drink all night': he was 'dignified but skint'.

Pete started to join them of an evening at the Grafton Arms and he and Spike became close, the attraction for Spike being that he had 'such a mad, abstract mind'. Spike and Pete had many traits in common. Both could be loyal, yet occasionally betray people without a smidgen of guilt, both liars when it suited them, both adulterers, both sometimes generous and other times incredibly mean, and both adored their mothers but could occasionally spit bile about them. They blurred the margins of fantasy and reality, loved pranks, and shared an amazing amount of talent. I experienced the good and the bad aspects of both men. Peter Medak, who directed them in the disastrous film *Ghost in the Noonday Sun*, assessed them like this: 'They were identical but with one important exception. Milligan had a heart.' That summed them up for me.

When they first met Pete was already working for the BBC. It had happened because his mother Peg, a woman as redoubtable as Florence, had a brilliant idea. In 1946 Pete rang the BBC and impersonated Kenneth Horne, the star of *Round the Horne*. He recommended an outstanding new talent, one Peter Sellers. 'Just listen to him', he said, 'and you'll recognize that he's a star in the making.'

With the proceeds of his radio performances Pete had bought a tape recorder and he and Spike started to record funny voices on it. They discovered that if they did them at the slowest possible speed when played back quickly the voices became hilarious. Spurred on by this Spike experimented with writing scripts for more mad voices. Pete and Harry, who was also doing the odd job for the BBC, showed them to an innovative producer, Pat Dixon. Pat commissioned a trial script from Spike and his co-writer, Larry Stephens, and Pete suggested some voices. Spike later described it as 'the crappiest script ever' and the BBC planners rejected the pilot programme they recorded. But Pat was persistent and the first show, starring Michael, Harry, Pete and Spike, was broadcast on 28 May 1951 as *Crazy People*. It was a hilarious, anarchic comedy sketch show. After an incredible response the planners did not hesitate to commission a second series, starting in January 1952, and increased the number of episodes from seventeen to twenty-five. And this time the BBC caved in and let them call it *The Goon Show*.

Spike's parents had tired of the cold and damp and grey of London living and decided to emigrate with Desmond to Australia. Spike was still more or less homeless so Pete took him home to meet his parents. Bill Sellers had been a church organist in Bradford before being hired by Peg's mother as pianist and driver for her touring company. Peg and he fell in love, married and became a performing team. When Spike was first taken to the Sellers flat in Finchley Bill was still doing the rounds with a ukulele act but Peg was overseeing her son's career. They hit it off and Peg agreed that Spike could move from the attic to the flat where he slept on the floor on an airbed.

One night Pete took Spike along to meet his girlfriend, Anne Howe. On the way they picked up Anne's friend, June Marlow, and Spike fell in love. The best friends married the best friends, Spike and June a few months after Anne and Pete, in January 1952. *The Goon Show* became a cult hit but the strain of producing such innovative humour led to a breakdown later that year and Spike was treated at a psychiatric hospital for two months. Over the years his depression became increasingly uncontrollable, and by his own admission he behaved abominably towards June. They had three children together, Laura, Sean and Silé, the last born in 1956, but things became so bad that in 1959 June left with the children and moved in with a porter from Covent Garden market. When they divorced in 1961 Spike was given custody. At least he could remain in the family home at 127 Holden Road in Finchley, one of the few constants in his life. It was a spacious Edwardian house in a quiet tree-lined street and he became a driving force in the Finchley Society, which he co-founded in 1971 with the aim of preserving the dignity and tranquillity of the district.

The year Spike met June was one which marked the beginning of a more lasting relationship. In 1951, while Eric Sykes was in hospital being treated for the first signs of ear trouble, he heard *Crazy People* on the radio. The writers were unknown to him. 'I thought their material was the funniest I'd heard for some time and wrote them a letter saying so, with a few pointers to how I thought it could be made even better,' he recalled. By that time Eric was already a hugely successful writer and performer. As well as writing for Frankie Howerd and with Sid

Colin for Peter Brough as Archie Andrews, then later for Tony Hancock, he wrote for American comics appearing at the London Palladium and topped the bill there in his own right. The young writers were thrilled to hear from him.

A couple of days later Eric was propped up in bed in his private room. 'Two faces peered at me through a window in the corridor, Spike and Larry. They were so grateful I'd written and thanked me.' Later that year Spike visited Eric in his one-room office at Longridge Road, Earls Court. 'He was bursting with ideas. Couldn't keep still. He said his mind was so busy inventing them he hardly had time to sleep,' said Eric. 'We hit it off and decided to share an office.'

Eric found rooms to rent five flights above a greengrocer's shop at 137 Uxbridge Road, Shepherd's Bush and they moved in. The collaboration was fun from the start, although there were a few obstacles, particularly because rationing was not over. 'At that time,' said Eric, 'oranges were still in short supply and when a shipment came in there was always a queue outside the shop. We had to wait with them until they were all sold before we could go to work.'

Eric and Spike got on extremely well because they were both idealists. An idea they had for a co-operative, with writers working alongside performers or producing scripts for their own use, at last came to fruition in the early Fifties. I suppose Spike was more of the dreamer, attracted by the vision of artists working in collective harmony. Eric told me that Spike helped to get the project off the ground and he made sure it worked in practice. They formed ALS and word soon got round among budding writers that it was worth sending them material to get advice and maybe more, if they were good enough.

ALS worked very simply. 'We would all do our own thing,' said Eric, 'but subscribe to a fund that would be there when one of us hit a fallow period. There were several rooms so we invited two young chaps who were just beginning to get the odd success,

Ray Galton and Alan Simpson, to take one of them. I had more work than I could handle so passed Tony Hancock over to them.'

They needed an office secretary and Alan knew an ambitious young girl, Beryl Vertue. She was a brilliant organizer, and her rôle developed with the business, eventually becoming agent. Then David Conyers joined them to work alongside Beryl and the co-operative multiplied into an awesome collection of talent. Spike invited along a struggling television writer, Terry Nation. Then a script came in from a young fellow called Johnny Speight. 'I thought it revealed enormous talent and sent for him,' said Eric. 'He was working as an insurance agent at the time and came to the meeting with his wife. I told him to give up his job and move in with us. He did and became one of our very best writers.'

As they became more successful ALS found better offices at Cumberland House on Kensington High Street. Then Eric and Spike discovered Number Nine. Each bought a quarter, with Alan and Ray, and ALS moved in at the beginning of 1962.

Spike's marriage was not the only thing to come to an end with the close of the Fifties. There had been ten series of *The Goon Show*, but the pressure of organizing nannies, writing the scripts, recording, then shuttling home to read the children a bedtime story, towards the end must have become unbearable to someone so mentally fragile. In January 1960 the last run began. The remaining Goons (temperamental Michael Bentine left after the second series) were being offered film and stage rôles. Spike had already written and performed in three television series, and written dialogue for and performed in some comedy films, including, of course, *The Case of the Mukkinese Battle Horn*, and his future seemed bright.

In 1961 Spike was cast in a Second World War film, *Invasion Quartet*, and fell for one of the extras, Patricia Ridgeway, who everyone knew as Paddy. She was statuesque, very good-looking, but with a weight problem she battled all her life. Spike recounted how he sighed when he first saw her on set: 'Oh, look at those legs.' He asked her out to dinner and the attraction was immediate. When she went on to appear as a nun in *The Sound of Music* Spike was bewitched by her lovely voice and proposed.

She was from a very middle-class Yorkshire family, her father a director of Monsanto. They married in Yorkshire in June the following year with the Beatles' producer, George Martin, as best man and Spike's three children in attendance. But the dignity of the proceedings was destroyed when, as he stood at the altar with his bride, Spike put on a big black moustache and turned round. The congregation tittered, but Paddy's father was appalled.

Although Spike and Paddy loved each other their temperaments clashed. Perhaps their first disagreement occurred shortly after they married, when she insisted that his children should go to private school, which he considered very Victorian. But she won and Laura went to a convent as a weekly boarder and Sean to a local private school. Soon more rifts occurred. Spike told me there were moments of great happiness but terrible rows. They were like two pieces of sandpaper rubbing against each other. Both had tempers and Paddy could be very forceful and stubborn, and with Spike's volatility, the combination was lethal. Result: rows, passionate reconciliations, and philandering by Spike.

He had a bust-up with the British Government when passport regulations changed in 1962 and his Indian birth and Irish father denied him an automatic transfer to a British passport. Instead, he became technically stateless. As an ex-soldier he obstinately, but by his lights logically, refused to swear the oath of allegiance necessary to gain a new British passport on the grounds that he had shown enough loyalty to the Crown by fighting for the country. Instead he obtained an Irish passport, and began a love-hate relationship with the English. Later Prince Charles tried to persuade Spike to take the oath, pointing out that he had had to swear his allegiance to the Queen. And Spike said, 'Yes, but she's your mother.'

On a professional level, things became quieter for Spike. This marked the start of his obsession with the BBC. Like Harrods, it became a target for his campaigns of letter writing: I think this was a warped compliment from Spike, because he believed they were both great institutions which should maintain their standards. Then he was cast by impresario Michael White in *Oblomov*, based on Ivan Goncharov's humorous novel about a Russian aristocrat too indecisive to leave his room. The run at the new Lyric Theatre in Hammersmith was a disaster, but somehow Spike persuaded Michael to let him re-write the play and call it *Son of Oblomov*.

After the first night at the Comedy Theatre in December 1964 Michael was certain they had a hit, and Spike's performance was hailed by critics and actors, who fought to get seats. He had hit a brilliant streak of inspired humour and it all came pouring out during the run. He often stood the script on its head and improvised, which brought the best out of some of the cast, shattered the nerves of the remainder and provided much hilarity for the audience, some of whom saw it again and again because each night was guaranteed to be different. It ran until April 1966 when Spike was so tired he had to call a halt.

The money poured into ALS and Spike became convinced that, rather than sharing a secretary from the pool, he should have a dedicated personal assistant. The others did not agree. Nobody else had one so why should he? He did not argue. He just moved out, taking his furniture with him. Eventually Eric and Johnny brokered a compromise. If Spike would pay half the PA's salary then ALS would match the rest. With honour salvaged on both sides, Spike moved back in and employed me. It was love, light and peace again. But for how long?

Chapter Five

Many managers rightly have nightmares about their clients' fondness for booze. Certainly, a day without wine was like a day without sunshine as far as Spike was concerned, but his normal consumption at dinner would be less than a bottle. Occasionally he had a few too many with friends and could be happily tight, but for all his numerous tantrums, traumas and depressions there were only two occasions when I saw him really the worse for drink. He was doing a one-man show at the Wimbledon theatre, but it seemed safe enough to accept an invitation to a morning tasting of Australian wines. He was fond of them and one of the first to extol their qualities. He had left for the tasting in what he considered to be quite a smart turn-out – that is, a striped shirt and wide red braces, no jacket – and said he would return to the office after the tasting, do some writing and leave in time for the show that evening.

It said 11 a.m. to 12.30 p.m. on the invitation. When he had not returned by three o'clock I rang New Zealand House – an unlikely venue for an Australian wine tasting but there we are

– to see if he had left. No, but he was leaving very soon. At four o'clock I rang again. Yes, he was on his way. It was ten to six before he staggered into the office, gave me an inane and happy smile and stumbled upstairs.

Josie Mills was still in the office. I asked her to bring me some black coffee and steeled myself while she fetched it. With a steaming cup in my hand I marched into Spike's office and lifted his head off the desk so that he could drink. He did not want it, 'horrible stuff,' and giggled. God, what was I to do with him? He staggered from the chair, laughing, and stretched out on the floor. I tried to pour coffee down his throat, but he refused. More stupid laughter. I could have kicked him. But he had a show to do at 7.30 p.m., so I tried to pull him up. He flopped down again, too heavy for me.

I shouted for Josie and while I took him by the shoulders she grabbed the only thing available at the front: his braces. They stretched and he stayed exactly where he was, like something in a Laurel and Hardy sketch. Spike had hysterics. What a hoot.

Between us we managed to get some coffee down him and by 6.30 p.m. it had started to have its effect and we got him as far as the steps outside Number Nine. I hid the keys of his Mini in case he decided to drive to Wimbledon. While Josie stayed with him I ran to the Bayswater Road and hailed a taxi. I got in the cab and directed him to Number Nine.

We pulled up outside and he said, 'It's Spike Milligan then.'

I nodded. Most taxi drivers seemed to know where he worked.

'Wait here and I'll get him. Then you can take him to Wimbledon.'

'No, I can't. Too far and I'm going home for my tea.'

It was just our luck to get an awkward one.

'I'll give you an extra ten pounds.'

His beady eyes never blinked.

'I said I was going home for my tea.'

'All right. I'll double what's on the clock and give you an extra tenner.'

Spike appeared at the top of the steps outside the front door, propped up by Josie, and beamed at the taxi driver.

The taxi driver took one look at him. 'I'm going home for my tea.'

I could have screamed. Spike had heard everything but I tried to calm the situation by explaining that the driver had not had anything to eat all day and needed his tea, hoping to appeal to Spike's sympathies for the working class. Fat chance. In ringing tones he addressed the whole of Orme Court. 'The fucking English taxi driver won't take me, so the fucking English audience won't see me.' With a whirl and the suggestion of a stagger, he turned and marched back into the building.

Johnny Speight was upstairs nattering with Eric. Neither man was averse to a drink so when I barged in on them they understood the situation immediately.

'Take my driver,' said Johnny, gazing hopefully at Eric's collection of malt whiskies. 'I'll wait here.'

Johnny's driver had spent hours on end waiting for his boss all over London so he was not fazed by the situation. He would be delighted to take Spike to Wimbledon. There was one condition. I had to go too. Spike started to play me up as soon as we were in the car. 'By the way,' he said, 'there's another condition. You must stay in the theatre with me.'

I got Spike into the car and we made it to Wimbledon at 8 p.m.

The theatre manager was outside the theatre, jumping from one foot to the other, a nervous wreck. He turned to me and said, 'It's not as though I could put an understudy on.'

Spike went on stage, by now on a high, and gave one of his best performances while I stood watching on. At the end there was a standing ovation and he turned to me in the wings, arm outstretched, and announced, 'My manager, Norma Farnes.'

The old sod! I had had a fraught day, felt like death and probably looked like it. I knew from experience that he would have to win the round so, despite my appearance, I went on to take a bow. As we walked to the dressing room he said, 'You're a winner. We're off to the Trattoo for dinner and you can have the best champagne they've got.'

As I took the first sip, or more likely a gulp, I said, 'I've put up with an awful lot of shit today for this.'

He grinned. 'You'd better enjoy it then.'

And so the day ended with laughter.

After the first few months I was used to the long days that shifted into evenings with the inmates of Number Nine. But although I had been shocked at the curses in Jack Clarke's office nothing had prepared me for the language that was common parlance with Spike and Johnny. It was as if they were still in the barrack room. Spike was at his worst when something annoyed him; then he could rant and rave about anything and everything. Johnny walked in one day after one of his explosions and sensed I was about to walk out. He drew me aside.

'Remember, he's not shouting at you. He's shouting at the world.' I would often have cause to remember this rationale when the going got tough with Spike.

It was Spike versus the universe when he was in a fighting mood. That was how he liked it, indeed he revelled in it. And with single-minded purpose he was prepared to devote all his frenetic energy to defeating the enemy. If there had been a meeting of ALS and he had put forward an idea the others rejected, he would go to his room, retired hurt, hang a notice on the door saying 'Go away' or something similar, and perhaps not surface for three or four days. Over time I became used to these periodic withdrawals and would tell those who queried this behaviour that for Spike it was 'normally abnormal'.

Things were not all bad. Having tried out his poems on me on my first day, Spike had devoted most of my time to fighting his various campaigns and organizing his diary. But now we had settled into a routine together he started testing new work on me. He would phone down and say, 'I'm finished. Do you want to come up?' If I did not react as he thought I should he would say, 'What do you know about being funny?' End of try-out. Or the smile on his face would fade as he read it aloud and realized it was not what it should be. 'I didn't know I could be so unfunny,' he would say and into the wastepaper basket it went.

Just as he could be incredibly mean, as he was over Paddy's Christmas money, so Spike could also be extraordinarily generous. One day in April 1967 he asked me, quite out of the blue, how I got to the office. I explained that one of the deciding factors in taking the job was that it was only a fourpenny tube fare from home and I was saving for a car.

'How much have you got?' he asked.

It was none of his business and I told him so. He laughed.

'I'm making it my business because I'm selling the Mini. If you want to buy it I need to know how much you have, don't I? I love that car and I want to find a good home for her.'

As much as he loved it, it was one of the earliest basic Minis with a bundle of faults. When it rained the interior of the car was awash because the door vents had been put in the wrong way, so the rain ran inside and onto the floor. Controls were minimal. It also had a sneck to slide half the front window open, a temperamental windscreen wiper and heater, and hard seats; with virtually no insulation, it was a loud and bumpy ride. All this I discovered later. Spike adored her.

'So tell me. How much have you saved?'

The man had a cheek. '£125,' I said. 'By next summer I'll have enough to buy a car.'

'Okay. You've got enough now for my Mini.'

I could not do it. 'It's worth much more.'

'I said £125.'

I shook my head. 'It would be like taking charity.' All my working-class instincts came to the surface: accepting an over-generous offer might put me under an obligation. But Spike was insistent.

'I want you to have it.'

'All right. I'll take it to your garage to get it valued.'

I drove it round the corner to Queen's Mews and asked Mike, the owner, for a valuation. With Spike's name on the log book, he told me, it was worth nearly three times what I had to offer.

Downcast, I returned to the office and explained.

Spike smiled, such a warm smile. 'You are looking after me, aren't you? Let me look after you.' He would not take no for an answer.

I was knocked out. The Mini, 3490 PK, became my own treasured first car. It was my first experience of his largesse, which continued throughout our relationship, though it did not prevent him from accusing me, from time to time, of giving his money away.

Back in my own office I looked at Anthony Hopkins. 'How about that, then?' Later I discovered that Anthony liked comedians, which was just as well.

Soon after this Beryl arranged a tour of *The Bed Sitting Room*, in which Spike had wowed packed audiences in the West End and received ecstatic reviews. The play was based on an original idea by John Antrobus. It was about the survivors of World War III struggling to create order while radiation caused havoc, turning them into animals and items of furniture. Spike regarded Antrobus, an ALS writer, as a wayward son, but claimed that John did not have the discipline to anchor himself behind a desk to write the play. Spike did, though, and the result was brilliant.

He was in good spirits when he returned, high on success. This meant more work for me of course. One day I had been at it non-stop until well after seven o'clock. Spike breezed into the office, relaxed and happy from an afternoon at Alan Clare's house in Holland Park. Theirs was a musical friendship: Alan had played with Oscar Peterson and at private parties for Frank Sinatra, and Spike liked to accompany him on his trumpet and chat about jazz. When he saw me Spike said, 'You look knackered.' Just what a girl needed to hear. 'You need a glass of panacea. Why don't you meet me at the Trattoo about eight-thirty?'

He was on. Off to the flat, then a bath, a quick change and a twenty-minute drive back to the restaurant for that first glass of champagne. I went up to the bar to say hello to Alan and there, sitting next to Spike, was Peter Sellers. I was completely taken aback. I would have dressed up had I known. Spike rose and gestured to me to sit between them, and being Spike he made no introduction.

'Hello,' I said to Pete. 'I'm Norma.'

'No need for that,' said Spike. 'He knows you're Norma.'

Then he pondered. 'I didn't realize you hadn't met before.'

So there was I sitting next to this Hollywood legend, a man who was perhaps the greatest mimic in the world, and the star of countless films. Charm oozed from him. No wonder his conquests ranged from Princess Margaret to Liza Minnelli, not to mention his soon to be wife, the Swedish beauty, Britt Ekland. He put me entirely at ease, as if I were an old family friend. I tried not to show how star struck I felt. I had thought I was immune to being impressed by celebrities, but the evening that followed was truly memorable. There were laughs about old times and anecdotes about his movies. I told him that his portrayal of General Fitzjohn in *Waltz of the Toreadors* was his best, and he warmly agreed with me. I learned later that, just like Spike, whatever Pete said had to be taken with a pinch of salt. If they were in a mood to please they would listen to your opinions as if suddenly you were an oracle. Everything you said, darling, was absolutely right. In a different mood your views would be met with a curl of the lip, or 'What the fuck do you know about it?'

There was no swearing that night. Pete mentioned Eric, how he missed him since he was spending so much time in the States, and how much he would like to have dinner, just the three of them. Spike recalled how, one summer's day in Orme Court, he had been driven mad by the clickety-click of Eric's typewriter pumping out yet another episode of *Sykes and A . . .*, probably because he was having trouble with his own work. He undressed and, stark naked, walked across the landing to Eric's office. 'I'm stuck on these last two lines of the sketch,' he said, handing him his script. 'Tell me what you think, will you?'

Eric had a read and looked at Spike.

'They're very good,' he said and resumed tapping.

'You bastard,' said Spike.

Without raising his eyes, Eric said, 'Well, it is rather warm in the office today.'

'Typical of Eric's deadpan delivery,' he remembered. I assumed Spike was embroidering, as was his wont, but many years later Eric recounted the same story, detail for detail.

Then it was Pete's turn. He, Eric and Spike had decided to hold a Christmas party for their children at Holden Road. It had a large garden which they decided was ideal for a firework display. A magician was hired and, excess being the order of the day, they went out and bought hundreds of fireworks. That was what children liked, yes, and they would get a magnificent view from the large window in the living room where they would hold the party.

The men devoted much thought and a lengthy lunch to planning the display. When they arrived back it was after three and they started setting them out: rockets, Catherine wheels, sparklers, thunder flashes, jumping crackers, waterfalls, rockets, plenty of rockets, and even bigger thunder flashes. It all took rather longer than expected and, being winter, it was dark before they finished, so much so that they could not see where they had put the fireworks.

'We'll have to get a torch to find them,' Pete suggested.

'Can't do that,' said Eric, 'it'll spoil the effect.'

So they crept round the garden, each with a box of matches, and because, being stars, each wanted to outdo the other, they set them off immediately. The thunder flashes were deafening, rockets whizzed dangerously close, jumping crackers pursued them. They nearly had an accident but it was a laugh and they went back to the house proudly to see how their audience had enjoyed it. As they trudged up the garden they were dismayed to see that the window had steamed up, which must have spoilt the view. When they got into the house they found the children, backs to the window, mesmerized by the magician.

Fireworks? They had not noticed.

Pete played the roles of all three of them, brilliantly, and the wine flowed with the anecdotes into the night. It was one of the happiest evenings I had spent with Spike.

But trouble was on the horizon. Beryl Vertue is as ambitious as she is gifted and she had been in negotiation with the Robert Stigwood Organization, which was interested in acquiring ALS. At a meeting in early 1968 she announced that if they made the move there would be large cash payments for all members. David and everyone else seemed in favour of the move, but of course Spike could not see any advantage in joining a large organization. Stigwood, he said, wanted to buy the talent to gain respectability. Getting into his stride, Spike reminded everyone that ALS had been started to nurture all concerned. Now the rats were deserting a very happy and successful ship. Let them go; they could sell their souls for gold if they wanted, the traitors. He was staying put. 'On my own, if need be.'

Nobody took kindly to this outburst. When I heard what had happened I looked at Anthony. Would we be on the move again or should I stay with Spike, whose demands could alter not every day but every minute? Could I leave him alone in the building? For all his tantrums Spike was the most vulnerable person I knew, and he had been so kind to me. No, I decided to stay.

The negotiations took quite some time, as they always do, but eventually the time came for them to move. Ray and Alan sold back their share of the building to Spike and Eric and, as Ray was packing up to leave, he decided his antique desk was too big and heavy for his new office and I bought it from him. When I handed over the cash he had a receipt ready.

'Don't be silly. I don't need a receipt from you,' I said.

'You need it for Spike.'

'What do you mean?'

'If he fancies the desk he'll convince himself, and try to convince you, that because it's in the office it belongs to him. That's the way it is with him. So keep the receipt,' he said. His advice proved useful in the future.

Eric was on tour with Jimmy Edwards in *Big Bad Mouse*, which they took all over the world, so come 30 April 1968 it was just me and Spike and Anthony alone in that big house. And so we remained for months on end. The others moved to grand offices in Brook Street and it was a while before we sublet the many spare rooms in Number Nine. It was nice to have my own office but when Spike was out, and then abroad in Australia, it was a strange experience to work in a building that had once rung with laughter and was now eerily quiet. I took on a receptionist, a lovely if slightly wacky Welsh girl, Tanis Davies. She was hopeless with money and always had at least two jobs. Over the years she left about five times because she was tempted by a bigger job elsewhere, only to telephone a few months later saying she missed us too much. She was incredibly loyal and, if anything, she became more protective of Spike than I was.

It was around this time that Spike Milligan Productions was set up, at the suggestion of Spike's accountant. Spike was not a director of the company, rather the company had exclusive rights to his services, and I became a director along with his accountant and his solicitor.

Beryl Vertue had asked me to join ALS when they first left Orme Court and about two months after they decamped she invited me out to lunch. We talked about the future and she told me I would waste my career if I stayed with Spike; she had been there before me and knew that he was very difficult and needed a lot of looking after. I knew she was right in everything she said, but I could not leave Spike on his own. I realized I would have to stay put, for the time being.

My flat mates thought I was mad to stick it out. But because I did an agent was born.

It happened as a result of a telephone call I took from an advertising agency. They were interested in Spike heading a big television campaign for BP. When I passed on the message Spike was blasé.

'You'd better go along and talk to them.'

'I don't know anything about negotiating a fee,' I said.

He shrugged. 'You'll have to, Norm. There's nobody else.'

I shook my head.

'If you don't go it will be your fault if I lose out on making a lot of money.'

Blackmail as well. He won, as usual.

Off I went to Service Advertising in Knightsbridge. They wanted Spike to dress as Batman for the commercial and needed a year's exclusivity.

'How much?' I asked.

'£10,000.'

If they had said £500 I would have been impressed. £10,000. I was shattered but determined not to show it.

'Oh dear,' I managed. 'I was expecting much more than that.'

'How much did you have in mind?'

That was the trouble. I did not have anything in mind. So I doubled their number.

'£20,000.'

They looked aghast, but there was no going back. I could not lower the figure.

'That's out of the question.'

I remained as composed as I could, wished them good day and went back to the office to tell Spike. He went into orbit and I was at the receiving end of another tirade.

'What do you mean? You've lost *me* £10,000. Have you any idea how much £10,000 is?'

'Don't take it out on me. I didn't want to go in the first place. I told you I didn't have any experience of that sort of thing.'

He glared and paced up and down, then cocked his head.

'Wait a minute. What did they say? How did they look? Did they drop down dead –'

'Let's wait and see. If we've lost it, we've lost it.'

He was furious. 'What kind of a fucking attitude is that? It's a lot of money,' he said and slammed out.

I did not see him for the rest of the day. Mentally he had consigned me to a hellish Siberia populated by failed agents.

Two days later the agency rang to see if I was prepared to have another meeting. I would have dropped anything to go, except perhaps a date with Anthony.

'Just let me look at my diary.' It was blank but they could not see it. 'I can't make it tomorrow but I've got a slot at eleven the next morning.'

That would be fine, they said, and I went back and settled for £18,000 with perks.

Back to Spike. I had kept him in ignorance about the second meeting. The expression on his face made the trauma of the last few days worthwhile.

'£18,000. Are you sure?'

I nodded and told him I did not want to be put through that sort of experience again.

'What do you mean? I reckon you're a born agent. The bloody nerve of it!'

He smiled. Suddenly I was his wonder girl.

'Do you want to be my agent as well as manager?'

For some reason I said 'Yes'.

Spike donned his Batman outfit, did the job and soon after the cheque arrived. Later he ran downstairs with a cheque made out to me for £1,800.

'That's your ten per cent,' he said.

I normally needed to work nearly a year for that. I could swear Anthony winked at me. Perhaps we had done the right thing after all. We would stay a little longer to get some money together before moving on. Besides, 'manager and agent to Spike Milligan' would not look too bad on my c.v. when the television job came up.

Obviously my new rôle meant I had to watch the money side of things, and that was not always easy. When he ran out of wicks for his numerous oil lamps (he dreaded power cuts) they had to be replaced immediately; no delay was brooked. So off he sent Tanis in a taxi to make the expensive round trip to Christopher Wray at World's End. I learnt to laugh off this sort of indulgence.

Most actors have an agent as well as a manager and there is a distinct difference between the two rôles. Tony Boyd, co-agent with Jimmy Grafton to Harry Secombe, who worked in the next office to me, was fond of telling me, 'You'll regret showing him you can do both jobs.'

Our professional relationship merged into friendship fairly early on, but I have never been able to answer those who ask when the change took place. It was soon after I had started to negotiate for him, however, that he made an announcement at one of our meetings (which were so informal as to make the word meaningless).

'I've made a decision. As from today I'm not making any decisions.'

I was happy to agree. 'But there's one condition. When I make a decision you'll have to stand by it.'

'Right on, baby.'

We shook hands. And that was that.

Chapter Six

Peter Sellers may have been an international star but, far from feeling left behind, Spike often felt sorry for his friend. One evening he invited Spike to dinner at his luxurious new flat at 30 Clarges Street in Mayfair. Britt greeted Spike dressed stunningly from top to toe in silver – and then went out for the evening. Spike thought that was peculiar but Pete did not seem at all surprised and showed him round the flat with its three bedrooms, one for Britt, one for their daughter, Victoria, and the other for the chef.

'Where's yours?'

'I haven't got one. I walk to the Dorchester every night, go in the back way so nobody sees me, stay the night and come back here in the morning.'

Spike was sceptical; he knew that Pete valued the truth about as much as he did monogamy.

'What has the chef got for us?' he asked.

Pete turned those mournful eyes on him. 'Britt has given him the night off. But we could do ourselves egg and bacon.'

The Hollywood star frying an egg! So that was their dinner and afterwards Spike walked him to his hotel.

The next morning he told me the story.

'Do you know, he hasn't got a fireplace in his life.' He shook his head and sighed, 'Poor Pete.'

Spike placed enormous importance on the ideal of a happy domestic life, but for him it was more often an idea than a reality. Nobody found his ideals more difficult to live up to than his wife, Paddy. He often claimed that she made him ill. This was an exaggeration but occasionally it was true. She lived in chaos, while he was obsessively tidy and orderly. Having been brought up in a military regime, punctuality had been drummed into him; for Paddy, time was something the clock kept but not her. For all his whims, Spike was paranoid about falling into debt and never spent more than he could afford, whereas Paddy was reckless with money.

When I took over as Spike's manager his accountant suggested all Spike's financial affairs should be looked after by me. Paddy had an allowance for clothes but everything else went on accounts which came to the office and were settled each month by me – greengrocer, grocer, fishmonger, butcher, chemist, garage for petrol, taxis, electricity and gas bills, rates, coal, clothes for the children and their school fees. She would go out for a day's shopping in the West End and take a minicab for the whole day while she disappeared into Oxford Street department stores. Friends thought I spent a fortune on make-up but I was a Scrooge compared with Paddy. The bills from the chemist where she bought hers were mind-blowing. After she had exhausted her monthly clothes allowance she ran up huge overdrafts, which Spike had to settle.

When I told him the bills were in his reaction varied. Sometimes he would say 'Just tell me how much and by when' or 'Give me the bottom line', or even 'Don't put me in a bad mood. I don't want to know.' On other occasions it was rocket time. His temper could be searing and their rows would be momentous. 'Are you trying to bankrupt me?' he would shout down the phone. Or he would race home to have it out with her. Their rows were cataclysmic and after some of them he returned to the office looking shattered. In calm moments Spike believed Paddy could not help herself. 'She lives life in a rush,' he once said to me. 'Sometimes the ink is still wet on the birthday cards she gives me.'

Spike was wonderful with all children, particularly his own. He had the gift of being able to understand the workings of a child's mind. That ability produced poems that have bewitched several generations of children.

Eric still recalls a Christmas, after June had left Spike, when his wife Edith invited him and his children to share Christmas with them. 'It was simply magical, and it was all down to Spike. I'll never forget it.'

On Christmas Eve Spike dressed as Father Christmas and, out of sight in the garden, put a tube through the sitting-room window and announced: 'Father Christmas is coming tomorrow. Ho, ho, ho. And you must light candles in the garden so the reindeer will be able to see their way.'

That is what they did, with lots of laughter and screams from delighted children.

Spike then reappeared as himself and gave everyone a torch. They ran through the woods backing onto Eric's house, Spike leading the way with a red light that everyone had to follow.

Come Christmas morning, which according to Eric was the best time of all, with the children screaming excitedly over their presents, Spike was nowhere to be seen. Eric did not think he had done a bunk because he would not leave his children. Edith and he searched the house and grounds, but he was nowhere to be found, and she was upset that he had missed them opening their presents. Spike did not appear until eleven. Instead of his bedroom he had slept in the attic because he did not want to be disturbed by the noise of the children.

'I need my sleep,' he explained. Eric and Edith knew Spike well enough to take this in their stride.

Although Spike and Paddy had their problems I soon realized that his difficulties came from his personality as much as his marriage. In the little details of life his eccentricities and obsessions were beyond anything I had previously encountered.

He worked at a frenetic pace, always several ideas at once, with numerous television appearances sandwiched between long sessions of writing his books, and kept up vigorous physical activity, playing squash twice a week and cycling seven miles daily on his exercise bike. Even so, he rarely ate more than one meal a day, generally spaghetti if it was a Trattoo night, surviving on doughnuts and his beloved Battenberg cake the rest of the time. Yet his energy was extraordinary. But it could all stop at any minute.

Soon after becoming Spike's agent I arranged for him to play J.B. Morton in a television programme. Morton wrote the famous 'Beachcomber' column on the *Daily Express*, which poked fun at the upper classes, and for Spike, he was 'a light in the darkness'. Because he was due on location I took the opportunity to go out for lunch. When I returned there was a desperate message from the television crew. Spike had not turned up. I raced upstairs to find out whether he had taken a nap or forgotten about it. Pinned to the door was a note: 'Fuck off and leave me alone – and that means you.'

There was only one thing for it. I told the crew to stand down. They were not very pleased because without Spike they did not have a programme. I would find scores of such notes over the years, all with different wording but expressing the same sentiment. And you could never argue with him about it.

If he was on location or on tour there would be a litany of conditions. Most important was that he had to have a quiet room. Indeed, he would inspect every one in the hotel to make sure they had given him the quietest before he could settle for the night. Once he left a comfortable bed and tried to sleep in a wardrobe because there was less noise. He was obsessed with sleep, not being able to sleep for worry about insomnia, it seemed to me at first. It never changed. He told me that if he possessed the world's top secrets and enemies kept him awake for three nights he would tell all. Once, much later, when Prince Charles invited him to spend the weekend at Highgrove, the bedroom was not quiet enough for him. So he took the blankets off the bed and slept in the bath where there was less noise to disturb him. Years later he sent Charles a blue plaque inscribed 'Spike Milligan Slept Here' to be fixed in the bathroom. And that, I am told, is what happened to it.

He could switch from euphoria to deep dismay in a second. After touring with *The Bed Sitting Room* he was heaped with praise from every quarter. In an interview director Peter Brook pronounced him 'a free genius'. 'Spike Milligan is the greatest of all theatre artists of our time.'

Spike returned to the office in buoyant mood. One day he said he wanted to show me his handiwork in Kensington Gardens. 'We'll look at the Elfin Oak, walk through the park and have lunch at Fu Tong in Kensington High Street.' He was very proud of the Elfin Oak, for without his efforts it would have disintegrated. It was a 600-year-old tree in Richmond Park which had been carved by a sculptor, Ivor Innes, in 1911, before being uprooted and moved to Kensington Garden nineteen years later, when his wife, Elsie, published a children's book, *The Elfin Oak of Kensington Gardens*. Innes maintained the Elfin Oak until he died in the Fifties.

Spike was fascinated by elves, goblins and fairies and had been held in thrall by the book as a child. In 1964 he took his daughter, Laura, to see the tree and found it very neglected, the delicate carved figures all chipped and peeling. Laura was disappointed.

'Daddy,' she said, 'what a pity someone can't mend it.'

That was all Spike needed to spur him into action. He recruited a team of helpers, persuaded Rentokil to preserve the tree and British Paints to provide the waterproof paint. The restoration was a labour of love and now he wanted to be the one to give me my first glimpse of his beloved tree.

It was one of those spring days when the sun had the warmth of an early summer morning. He bounded, and I walked, over freshly cut grass. Then yards from the unprotected Elfin Oak he stopped abruptly. His face moved from horror to ineffable sadness. I asked what was wrong. It was the tree. Part of one fairy's wing had been snapped off.

'We must go back to the office. Now.'

We walked in silence. At Number Nine he went upstairs to his room and locked the door. I had never seen anything like it and found it difficult to believe that this upset could plunge him into such despair. Over the years little things could and did tip him into depression. He possessed a vein of sensitivity that reacted all too often, sometimes unpredictably, and produced hurt unimaginable to most of us. On that occasion he stayed in his office for three days and nights, never once eating, perhaps not even drinking. His silence unnerved me. I had yet to learn to slip notes under his door when it happened. When at last he emerged and came into my office his face was grey, his body stooped. It was amazing to me that the 'vital' man Peter Brook had described in such adulatory terms was the one standing before me – all because of an act of vandalism. A week later I asked what had made him so ill.

'I'm not ill,' he said. 'I'm suffering from contemporary society. The sickness of it. Think of all the care that went into restoring those little people and animals living in that tree – and some sick yobbo snaps off a wing. They are the ones that are ill. Me? I just want to write scripts and books, poetry and music, to make the world a better place. I'm not the one that's ill. They are.'

In the late Sixties and Seventies Spike's mental state was

extremely fragile. It was not only the damaged fairy on the Elfin Oak that could trigger a depression. A picture on the wall hanging out of true could do it. As time passed it came to seem almost normal for him to lock himself in his room for days.

Inevitably this meant I spent a lot of time on the telephone to Paddy and came to know her well. She warned me that he was a self-medicator. As the tablets were on prescription he should not have been able to get them without one, but he had a supplier. He consumed Tryptozole, a damaging anti-depressant drug, with as little concern as children pop Smarties, up to six tablets a day. Paddy advised me to put placebos in his tablet bottles, so I did when I could. He did not seem to notice the difference.

How Paddy lived through the start of a depression and his brooding, raging moods I shall never know. She loved the man and to her it must have been torture. One refuge was spending, and then there were her uncontrollable splurges of gorging. 'I might as well be living in the fridge,' she told me more than once. Spike found this difficult to cope with and when he had had enough he moved into the office, which caused her to eat even more. Once he was locked in his office she would ring to talk to him, but he would not take her calls, so she either rang me or came to Number Nine to find out how he was. Although he would not talk to her he always wanted to know whether she had called. This was small comfort to Paddy. When her weight ballooned it was her turn to pop pills – diet pills. Never a week passed without her trying some new slimming aid. When those failed she found doctors who could be persuaded to give injections to curb her appetite.

During one episode she came to the office and her appearance was shocking. I told her things were bad with Spike. She sat down quickly, dived into her handbag and broke off a piece of chocolate.

'Please have some. It's Lindt and very nice.'

When I shook my head she burst into tears. 'I can't help myself when he gets a depression.'

The stress of being married to Spike must have been horrendous. The longer I worked with him the more fascinated I became by this complex character. One day he was totally incapacitated, the next a man brimming with ideas and energy enough to charge round a squash court. Why was he so driven, so talented, often impossible but so vulnerable? In a way his outrageousness was compelling; you never knew what he would do next, and so often he seemed to get away with it. For example, he suddenly announced, 'I have had this bloody black and white television on rental from Granada for nine years. Write to Sydney Bernstein [Granada's top man] and tell him I have paid for it twenty times over and he should give it to me.' I did and Sydney obliged. And when once I explained I would have to leave the office for an hour to do the household shopping, he told me not to be so ridiculous. He picked up the phone, dialled and handed it to me. 'Harrods. Give your order and they'll deliver it.'

'Don't be silly. I don't have that sort of money.'

'But I do and I need you here.'

So Harrods delivered our groceries.

There was also the challenge of such remarks as 'I'm always being overwhelmed by time wasting and you're the biggest waster of my time.'

'Get on with it' became my response.

It was probably a combination of all these factors that made me stay with him. At times he made me furious, but my heart ached for him at the first signs of depression. I learnt to recognize them. Sometimes it would be caused by something in particular, like the Elfin Oak episode, at others it just came upon him. The first indication I would get was a slowing down of his normally lightning mental responses and bouts of exercise. Then the lethargy became total. The normally open office windows were closed, his blinds drawn, the electric fires put on, food ignored.

I would sit with him when I sensed he needed the presence of another human being. Neither of us would speak. On other occasions he preferred to be alone. I once asked him to explain how he felt at such times and he gave me this poem, 'Manic Depression', published years later in *Small Dreams of a Scorpion*.

> The pain is too much
> A thousand grim winters
>   grow in my head
> In my ears
>   the sound of the
>   coming dead
> All seasons
> All sane
> All living
> All pain
> No opiate to lock still
>   my senses
> Only left
>   the body locked tenses.

He told me he had written it in the psychiatric wing of St. Luke's Hospital from 1953–4, and I realized that the poor devil had suffered like this for decades with little hope of a cure. At such times he could not bear any form of noise. His definition of noise was different from other people's: the ring of a door bell, the shutting of a door seemed to him as bad as the sound of a pneumatic drill. Unless one had experienced it, he said, it was impossible to imagine the feeling of utter desolation that followed.

It was devastating to see him in this state, huddled in a chair, his shoulders rounded, his legs up against his chest. No matter how desperate he felt I never feared he would commit suicide because he loved his four children too much to put them through such an ordeal. But his habit of self-medicating worried me. He could so easily forget how many he had taken. Even worse than Tryptozole was a dreadful drug, Tuinol, which had the advantage of bringing him out of the trough more quickly than other medication, but after recovery would plunge him into even deeper misery than he was suffering before. I was told that eight Tuinol was a lethal dose so I started to sneak into his office when he was in the bathroom to see how many he had used. But he had his secret supplier so I could never be sure how many he had taken. Those were nightmare days.

As soon as Spike sensed that the black dog was about to take over he moved into his office, which must have seemed like a womb to him. There he was self-sufficient and I made sure the outside world could not intrude. He felt he was better alone, and above all was determined that the children should not see him. His system closed down to such an extent that he neither ate, drank nor went to the loo.

When I came to know him better I used to push notes under the door so he was aware that I was still in the office. I felt it was a comfort for him to know there was somebody else in the building. Often I stayed until nine-thirty or ten and would then write another note to let him know I would be home in twenty minutes if he wanted someone to talk to. On reflection I wonder whether this was more for my peace of mind than his.

Sometimes the phone would ring at two or three in the morning.

'Are you awake?'

'No.'

'Well, you are now.'

On those occasions he never discussed himself or his depression. He just wanted to talk to somebody.

'Tell me about yourself,' he would say. 'Are you all right, Norm?' And then we would chat inconsequentially, sometimes for an hour or two.

I knew he was emerging from a depression as soon as a note appeared on his door. It meant he was preparing to come back into the world. It would say, 'Leave me alone,' or something else, less polite.

Then he would come out of his office, his whole appearance changed, with large purple bags hanging over his cheek bones, his body hunched and his gait unsure. The next stage would be a curt, nasty, 'Why do you keep me unemployed?' But I always shrugged it off.

Chapter Seven

On 7 November 1968 Spike wrote in his diary, 'I should shoot her.' I got married the following day. To me he said, 'Keep your own flat and let him keep his. You've been very happy for nearly a year together. Don't cock it up.'

John Hyman was everything I considered I was not: educated, professional, liberal and only too ready to agree that there were grey areas which needed to be discussed on most topics. He was quite different from Spike, who shared a number of liberal ideas with him, but did so vehemently leaving little room for argument. John seemed well-balanced and reliable. He was an extremely successful solicitor, with offices in Harrow and Regent Street, and did not expect me to give up the job I enjoyed.

I was so busy that sometimes I wonder how I fitted a private life around it. We met on New Year's Eve. I was dating a BBC director but he was in Scotland and snowed in. A friend dragged me out to a party in Pinner and I was immediately charmed by him.

We did not follow Spike's advice and moved in together.

Spike's version of married life was not an example I wanted to follow. There was no doubting Spike and Paddy's tremendous mutual attraction. Within minutes of meeting he told her, 'I'm going to marry you.' But their relationship oscillated between tender love and furious rows. They would argue, she would not give in, he would accuse her of being an iceberg and then move into Number Nine. As well as his office he had a large sitting room on the next floor up. It was furnished in the style beloved of Edwardian gentlemen, with a fireplace, deep armchairs, oil lamps and walls lined with bookshelves. Once he had taken up residence he would greet me in the morning and still be there when I left at night.

During these periods he always asked if Paddy had phoned, just as he would when he was in a depression. She would not sit in at home, however, as Spike thought she should, but went out with friends. I am certain she never had an affair. Which is more than could be said of him, although he loved her very much. She did not only have to deal with Spike's depressions; when he was living at Number Nine Spike would also spend time with what I came to call the Bayswater Harem. He did not try to hide it from me, indeed he claimed he had slept with three leading ladies during one theatre run. He was not the first man who thought there was one rule for him and another for his wife, but if you had asked him he would have professed a complete belief in a faithful marriage. Once I asked him, straight out, what he was up to. He gazed at me sadly out of his blue Irish eyes. 'Oh, Norma. I'm sleeping with some of them. One day I'll pay for my sins.' He had not entirely forgotten his Catholic upbringing.

There seemed to be anything between half a dozen and a dozen women in the harem at any given time. While he embraced the sexual emancipation of the Sixties and Seventies and enjoyed cocking a snook at authority, Spike still lived part of his life according to Victorian values. He always stood when a woman entered a room, helped her into a chair, arranged corsages when they were his guests at dinner and insisted on paying their taxi fares home. Nearly all his intimate girlfriends were friendly with one another and few seemed jealous about taking their turn in his bed. He seemed to have the knack of persuading them that there was nothing unusual about such an arrangement.

Spike's love life was his business and I was determined not to sit in judgement. To paraphrase Johnny Speight, he did not trouble me and I did not trouble him. I soon got to know Liz Cowley, his long-standing girlfriend, a diminutive, bubbly and highly intelligent Canadian journalist who became Deputy Producer of the BBC current affairs flagship programme, *Tonight*. She was at least his intellectual equal and great fun. Sometimes he found it difficult to cope with her independence. Because she did the same as him and slept with other partners he also considered her amoral. It takes a man to work that one out. She never showed the slightest jealousy and I think that irked him more than he liked to admit. I always thought she was ideally suited to him. They continued to meet until two years before his death. Spike would say to me, 'Ssh. I'm in town because you need to see me.' Then came a grin and a wink.

He and Liz first met when she was working for *Reveille*, an armed forces orientated newspaper, which wanted a feature on *The Goon Show*. There was an immediate attraction, he said, and he invited her to dinner, the first of scores. He told me he could never understand why she enjoyed their conversations.

'She's a real highbrow – went to university and I didn't.'

The lack of formal education was something that bugged him all his life. I reminded him that his friend, Robert Graves, had written that Spike was 'the most educated uneducated man' he had met.

His response was vintage Milligan: 'What fucking good is that?'

Another of his girlfriends was Roberta Watt, also a Canadian journalist. She was tall and statuesque like Paddy, in contrast to

Liz. Roberta committed the gravest of all sins as far as I was concerned: she fell in love with him. Fatal. I warned him about it but I think her devotion fed his ego. In an effort to prevent things going too far I took her aside and warned her of his black moods, volatile temperament and other girlfriends, of his devotion to his children and belief in marriage. I might as well have been speaking Urdu. She vowed that she wanted to protect and devote her life to him. Apparently, no doubt in the aftermath of one of their rows, Spike had told her that Paddy made him ill. That is as may be, I told Roberta, but he still loves her. She would not accept that he did and confided she would like to have his child. I was horrified.

'It would mean the end of the relationship,' I said, sure it would bring her up short. I was satisfied it had when I heard no more of such nonsense, and he continued to see her just as he did his other girlfriends.

Spike also had out of town girlfriends, even out of the country girlfriends in Australia. These he generally saw when he was on tour. One such was Margaret Maughan, based in Northumberland. Although she claimed to be his mistress she never was, not unless you counted all the other girlfriends as mistresses.

As well as becoming privy to his intimate affairs Spike introduced me to many of his friends, including Sir John Betjeman. Spike and he had a mutual admiration for each other's work and accepted their respective eccentricities. Another great British eccentric was Vivian Stanshall, of the Bonzo Dog Doo-Dah Band. I think their shows reminded him of his days with the crazy Bill Hall Trio. Vivian was outrageous and having dinner with him and Spike was like sitting on top of an unexploded bomb. Spike admired him for not giving a damn about anyone or anything and related with wonder the experience of a hotel manager who had gently reminded Vivian and his band that guests were expected to wear ties in the dining room. They were only too ready to oblige and returned, wearing nothing else.

When Tony Blair used the phrase 'Cool Britannia', Spike retorted, 'How bloody old hat. Vivian coined that way back in '67.' The proof is there as it was the title of a track on one of his albums.

The brilliance and diversity of the guests that joined us at the Trattoo was dazzling. The evening after I met Vivian we dined with Edgar Lustgarten, a brilliant author who read stories on radio and television. Before Spike left the office to record a discussion programme with Lustgarten at BBC Radio's Paris studio (in London) I mentioned that I had always been a fan, and being Spike he invited him to have dinner with us afterwards. Edgar was a generation older than him and his was a brilliant brand of straight-faced humour. Two more dissimilar characters would be difficult to find, but one was the flint to the other's stone and as an audience of one I was dazzled by the sparks of the evening.

A more enduring relationship began within a year or two of my starting to work for Spike. Most years Spike would go to work in Australia and fit in a visit to his parents at their house on the coast at Woy Woy. His mother Florence, or Grandma as I always called her, often came to visit him in the U.K. and she became my very good friend.

Grandma's first letter to me set the tone for those that followed over the next twenty years, containing confidences she knew I would keep. Because I looked after her son she started to refer to me as 'my adopted daughter'. Our letters, often hysterically funny without meaning to be, continued until a week or so before she died. She did not rely completely on the international mail service but always wrote 'S.A.G.' on the top left corner of the envelope to make sure I received them.

'What do the initials stand for, Grandma?' I asked.

'Saint Anthony's Guide, of course.'

Alongside 'S.A.G.' was generally written 'Strictly Private and Confidential'. That was because of references she made to her son – who was to her always Terry – and his family, often far from complimentary. Despite displays of temperament when Grandma was present Spike adored her and she worshipped him. Their love was unconditional and never-ending, which is not to say she could not become his enemy. He could rant 'even my own mother' etc. when she disagreed with him. She could be indiscreet and would often become incensed by what she perceived as the 'freeloaders' and 'scroungers' who paid court to Spike. As a devout Roman Catholic she could find much to disapprove of in her son.

I made sure neither Spike nor his family ever read her letters. Because he showered presents, cars, flats and money on his children Grandma bracketed them with the 'scroungers'. If they were hers, she often declared, they would be made to get jobs and keep themselves. I believe he was so generous to them out of a sense of guilt, as he never forgave himself for the break-up of his marriage to June. Although Grandma always ended her letters with thanks for caring for 'my troubled son' and she knew he was a depressive, she chose to ignore it. Probably this was because she was a no-nonsense sort of woman, fearing nothing and no one. 'Everything can be overcome', she claimed, 'except death.' She demonstrated this by surviving cancer in her eighties and lived to be ninety-six.

I sometimes wondered whether his family background had anything to do with his mental state. If Leo was a fantasist Florence was certainly a one-off. Until she died she always dressed Ascot style for the Melbourne Cup race meeting but never actually went to it. Instead, in all her glory, she watched it on television. 'What could be more natural?' she asked those who commented.

She was a tall, commanding woman. After I met her for the first time I remarked to Spike, 'If I had a vision of one woman who built the British Empire it would be your mother.' Over the years I grew to love her and looked forward to having her to stay.

Spike viewed her visits with more mixed feelings. On the one hand he was delighted she could be with him for a few months, but on the other he was apprehensive because of the rows that inevitably occurred. She always spent two weeks or so with me both to be nearer the shops and to have 'a bit of peace and quiet away from Terry and that chaotic house.' Despite that her devotion to him was total, probably because they were so alike.

I had wonderful times with Grandma. She had such a personality and sense of humour that it was easy to forget she was an octogenarian. She said the first thing that came into her mind, embarrassingly so at times, and once started on any subject would not shut up, no matter who was present or within hearing. Like mother, like son.

Whenever she stayed with me I had to drive her to church for confession.

'Grandma,' I once asked, 'what have you to confess at your age?'

'You're getting just like Terry.'

We went out to dinner with my friends, visited the theatre, and best of all had dinners in the flat when we talked and talked. She liked a sherry or two or three before dinner and then moved on to her favourite wine, Mateus Rosé. She would always try to persuade me to have a glass. When I insisted on Chablis she remarked that I did not know what I was missing. She was a great raconteur and told stories of the amazing life she had shared with Grandpa, of their time in India and Burma, the long voyages back to England on leaves, and the occasion she and the family were shipwrecked. Her voice was worthy of her sergeant major father and could be heard even when she was murmuring a confidence.

If someone asked me what Grandma was like I replied, 'Like Spike multiplied by ten.' But she was more fun because she did not have his darker side. I miss her to this day and have kept many of the cards and letters she sent over twenty years.

One day when she came to see me at Number Nine Spike threw a tantrum. This time it was to do with a filming sequence for *Q5*, the first of the long-running series of comedy sketch shows he wrote with Neil Shand for the BBC. As usual the people he dealt with at the Beeb were idiots. Whenever he asked for a prop it was either wrong or they could not produce it.

'They don't understand me or my work.'

After this outburst he charged to his office upstairs. I could tell Grandma was about to remonstrate with him but advised her not to interfere. That was tantamount to ordering a volcano not to erupt. A few moments later Spike threw his typewriter down the stairs. Grandma's face was stern. She rose from her chair.

'I'll go upstairs and have a word with that young man.' (Spike was then in his fifties.) I persuaded her not to and went up to deal with him. I knew from experience that he would eventually tire himself out, lock the door and go to sleep and by the time he emerged Tanis and I would be refreshed and ready to deal with him. I listened at his door. Everything was quiet so I went back and told Grandma that the emergency was over. I was wrong. He marched back down after me and, oblivious to his mother, started ranting. 'Please God make me anything. Make me stupid, but please God, never mediocre.' Grandma could take the exhortation to God but not what followed. 'Not like all those stupid bastards I have to deal with at the BBC.' She made to rise so I said quickly, 'Grandma and I are going to the park to see the Elfin Oak. If you want to join us there . . .'

He burst out of the office and ran upstairs. Grandma pursed her lips. 'It grieves me to see and hear what you have to put up with.' She sighed. 'But you know he loves you. He's very tortured, you know.' I was about to reassure her that I understood Spike when she stiffened and stared. I followed her gaze to the photographs by my desk. There were several of Spike, Johnny, Tommy Cooper and Eric, but one she did not recognize.

'Who's that?'

'Another tortured soul. Anthony Hopkins. A great actor. I admire him so much.'

Doubt spread across her face.

'He's got a drink problem. Like Spike, he has his demons, but his marvellous talent will out.'

'You wouldn't leave my son to look after him, would you?'

'Tony's in good hands – and I'm not about to leave Spike.'

She smiled. 'That's all right then.'

Later we went to the Trattoo and joined a much calmer Spike for dinner. Beforehand we had drinks and listened to Alan playing brilliantly. He was the consummate jazz pianist, imposing complex rhythms, extemporizing and endlessly inventing as he glided from one key to another. He may have taught piano and composition but Grandma was undaunted.

'You played a bum note there, Alan,' she boomed.

Spike laughed. Nothing his mother did could shock him. Alan smiled.

'You're right, Grandma.'

'No matter. I'll play for you when we've had dinner.'

Alan concealed a wince. Grandma's playing was of the exuberant variety, born no doubt of the necessity of making her music audible to occasionally noisy military audiences, and he guarded his piano jealously from what he termed 'thumpers'. But nothing could have stopped Grandma. After we had eaten she relieved Alan of the piano stool and banged out some of the old evergreens. The day ended enjoyably for everyone, except possibly Alan.

As the day approached for her return to stay with Spike, she suggested the three of us should have dinner together at the Trattoo. 'We'll have a pleasant evening with no tension.'

That will be a first, I thought.

During the meal she said, 'When I went to church on Sunday I lit a candle for your friend Anthony and I'll light another and say prayers for him in my beautiful church in Woy Woy.'

Spike sat up quickly and gave me a knowing look. 'So who's your friend Anthony? And what's he been up to that he needs a candle?'

With as much dignity as I could muster I told him about my hero, Anthony Hopkins. It was no surprise to me that he had not noticed Anthony's photograph. He laughed, mockingly. 'Well, I wonder what he thinks about Mother lighting candles all over the world for him?' Then he started to giggle. 'Somewhere in the States your hero is in some bar or other, smashed out of his mind and wondering how he's going to end up. And then suddenly he knows everything is going to be all right because all over the world Spike Milligan's mother is lighting candles and saying prayers for him.' He dissolved into hysterical laughter. Grandma was furious.

'Don't you ridicule my faith, Terry.' She was very much on her dignity. After a few minutes' silence she looked at Spike. 'I shan't be going back with you tonight as planned. I'll go back with Norma.' So our tension-free evening ended with plenty of it. Grandma, like her son, never surrendered.

Late in 1968 Spike had an idea for a television series, but as he was writing Q5 as well as performing in it he did not have the time to take it any further. The series took a comical slant on racism in the U.K. and featured a Pakistani, played by Spike, who worked in a joke factory in a northern town. Eric Sykes was the boss trying hard to be kind, but with opposition from a black man, played by Kenny Lynch, who did not want 'the likes of them coloured here'. Spike asked Johnny Speight to write it and the first meeting took place between Eric, Spike and Johnny, on New Year's Day, 1969. Everyone was enthusiastic and I arranged an appointment with Frank Muir, then Programme Controller with London Weekend Television (LWT). He thought it was terrific and so *Curry and Chips* was born.

It was to be one of the first packaged shows. We formed a

company, which Spike insisted we call Lillicrap, that would provide the script, the actors, wardrobe and props, while LWT's contribution was to be the studios, director and crew. Frank Muir, with that disarming smile of his, asked if I would like to be associate producer. I could not believe it. At last I had that job in television production. I did not hesitate to accept.

'Right,' he said, 'you'll be responsible for seeing that Johnny produces the script on time every week and for getting Eric and Spike to the studios for rehearsals and transmission.'

If the offer had been made a few years later I would have run a mile.

Some days later a meeting was called. Agents were to be present but Beryl Vertue, representing Johnny, was not there because she and Eric had argued furiously. Then Spike took exception to Eric's new agent, who appeared somewhat theatrically with a camel coat slung over his shoulders. In a loud voice Spike asked, 'Who's the faded Tony Hancock and what's he doing here?'

When an item in the contract was thought to exclude the right of Lillicrap to provide the wardrobe Spike said, 'Let Norma negotiate that.'

Eric's agent muttered, 'Where angels fear to tread.'

'Show the bastard, Norma,' said Spike, in a discreet aside loud enough for all to hear. I went off and came back with LWT's approval.

'What did I tell you?' said Spike.

The meeting crackled with temperament but finally it was agreed who would be responsible for what and we went our separate ways, transmission being scheduled for November.

Then early in the morning of 14 January 1969 Spike rang me from home. He had had a nightmare about his father drowning and being unable to save him. A few hours later his brother, Desmond, telephoned from Sydney. Their father had died.

It was not a complete surprise. When Spike visited his parents at Woy Woy the previous August for their fifty-fourth wedding anniversary Leo had a stroke. Although he was due to return to England he did not want to leave, so I booked a studio in Sydney to enable him to do some dubbing that was urgently required for a film. He stayed on until October, by which time Leo had improved. At the turn of the year his condition deteriorated again, but for some reason Grandma decided against telling Spike and never mentioned it in her letters to me.

Spike locked himself in his office for three days. The sign on his door said, 'Leave Alone'. He wrote in his diary, 'Goodbye to a terrible year ... I sleep at the office as much as possible to avoid the tension at home. It is also the first year without my father. Please God make people nicer.'

Chapter Eight

The read through for the first episode of *Curry and Chips* was not until the autumn, so in the meantime everyone got on with their own projects. Spike was busy with *Q5*, which hit the screens in March. A month or so later he and I were driving to dinner after he appeared on Simon Dee's talk show when Spike suddenly plunged into a downer, for no reason as far as I could tell. I assured him that he had been very funny but he waved that aside. Something else was worrying him.

'Simon's very good but I know he'll self-destruct,' he said. Dee was then very big but proving to be a bit of a problem to the programme makers. I think Spike identified with Dee's predicament and it preyed on his mind. A few days later I found him in the office, still brooding.

'I can't write any more. I don't want to go on.' He fell into silence. 'If the animal kingdom is doomed I don't want to be responsible for it.'

That remark, pulled from some recess of his mind, put him in bed for over a week. Most of the next two months were spent lying on top of his bed at Number Nine, presumably thinking, though what I will never know. He would wait until it was dark and then slip to the Trattoo, sometimes not eating, only sitting next to Alan Clare at the piano. Alan was sensitive to Spike's moods and when things were bad would play his favourite tune, 'Rainy Day'.

Spike's frame of mind had not improved by November. If Eric and Johnny had not been involved in *Curry and Chips* the show would never have reached the screen. But Spike's saving grace was his loyalty to his friends. It took all his strength to turn up for the recordings every Thursday. His state was so fragile that one wrong word from Paddy would have meant no show, not that it would have been her fault. So after each recording he spent the next few days laid up in the office.

Curry and Chips' difficulties did not end with Spike's ill health. Frank Muir had to approve the script every Thursday, but during this period Johnny Speight's alcoholism was at its worst. One Wednesday afternoon I was still waiting at Number Nine for him to hand it in so I decided to go and find him. I trailed around all his usual West End haunts but nobody had seen him. Someone suggested I look for his football friends, none of whom was celebrated for his abstinence. Sure enough I found him with George Best, Ian St John and Jimmy Greaves in a pub in Fulham. Smashed out of his mind, Johnny was playing the drums.

'How about the script?' I said.

'Script?'

'The *Curry and Chips* script.'

'Oh, that script.'

Another riff on the drums.

'It's Wednesday, Johnny. Frank needs it tomorrow.'

Johnny gave the rest of the combo an apologetic look and we went to a table in the corner. He scribbled some ideas on a series of beer mats. That done, he meandered back to the drums and I went back to the office. Luckily Spike and Eric were there and, working into the small hours, they managed to produce a script in time for my Thursday meeting with Frank.

Spike managed to go out most evenings. One night Peter Sellers invited him to dinner at Les Ambassadeurs, one of the hottest clubs in town, and Spike took me with him. Paparazzi crowded the entrance.

'That'll please him,' said Spike. 'He laps it up.'

There is no doubt that ordinarily Pete would have been the most famous person there, but not on this occasion. While I was amused to notice he was a bit put out Spike found it hilarious. For that night the photographers wanted to see John Lennon and Yoko Ono who, to everyone's amazement, were dressed in long, flowing white kaftans (the first time they were seen wearing them, though later they became the fashion). To make matters worse for Pete, John was then Spike's number one fan and made a great fuss of him.

Spike also never missed a cast dinner. There was a Chinese restaurant opposite LWT's studio in Wembley and it became the custom to go there after the recording. I was in charge of the budget and made a rule that each of the ten or so actors and production staff could invite one guest along. I was very strict about it because all too often I had known Spike to invite three people out to dinner and end up paying for ten more. My vigilance on this matter soon became a standing joke. One evening, as was usual before the meal started, I checked on the guests. A man I had never set eyes on was sitting next to Spike. In his inimitable voice, Eric's guest Tommy Cooper asked, 'Who's invited him?'

Spike said, 'Who's the daddy sitting next to me?'

And so it continued round the table, with Johnny, Eric and all the regulars asking the same question. 'Who invited him?'

'Just tell me who invited you?' I asked the gatecrasher.

The table erupted. Eric leaned over and said gently, 'He's a plant. He's Tommy's chauffeur.'

I always tried to get Spike to understand that the greater the expense, the less there was for him. But, of course, he never handled money, apart from loose change for a newspaper or a cake, and really had no interest in it as long as there was enough for him to live on. He knew that he could be too generous so as well as looking after his accounts for him every week by agreement I gave him forty pounds pocket money for incidentals. One day he went to LWT to see Harry Rabinowitz, the musical director for *Curry and Chips*. On his return to Number Nine he told me he had lost his forty pounds in Harry's office and needed more. That lie was not up to his usual standard. I rang Harry.

'Did you find any money in your office after Spike left?'

Harry laughed. 'He had nothing on him when he came here. He arrived by taxi and I had to pay the fare.'

Now then, I wondered, why had there been a taxi in the first place? I had ordered a car to take him and seen him get into it outside the office. I collared Spike. Well, yes, he had taken the car to go to LWT but decided to call at the BBC in Shepherd's Bush and get a taxi from there to see Harry. While he was there he saw a girl from wardrobe crying. She had had her purse stolen and lost her money for the whole week.

'There,' said Spike, who could not bear to see a woman cry, 'I'll solve the problem for you,' and gave her his money. Which was why he needed more from me. Why bother with a long-winded explanation when it was far easier to tell me he had lost it? That was Spike's sense of logic. He had no scruples about lying. Money, savings and banking were mysteries not worth the bother of understanding them as far as he was concerned.

Spike Milligan Productions banked at Barclays in Queensway, around the corner from Orme Court. Spike once found himself without a penny and as I was out of the office he went to the bank. 'Norma has gone out and left me without a penny. I need five pounds,' he told the cashier. 'She'll pay you when she gets back.' It was simple to him. He often went empty-handed round the shops in Bayswater to buy peanut butter, doughnuts, apples, etc., saying, 'Norma will pay you next time she comes in.' To him the bank was no different from any other shop. Mr. Price, the head cashier, who knew me well, cleared it with the manager and gave Spike his five pounds. He later told me that the bank manager dined out on that story.

After recording the last episode of *Curry and Chips* towards the end of 1969 we had a party in the bridal suite at the Royal Garden Hotel, Kensington. The show was good but the social climate was changing and in the end LWT did not commission another series because it was seen to be racist. At the hotel Johnny got very drunk and a strange girl from God knows where came to our table proclaiming her undying love for him. She threatened to throw herself out of the window unless it was returned. We tried to ignore her, but something about her must have struck a chord with Spike. He found her clinging to a ledge outside the window and it took all his powers of persuasion to get her to climb back in. Nobody ever found out who she was or how she got in to the party.

I prayed she would not turn up at the office demanding to see Johnny. If Spike saw her he would offer her a room until things got better. Over the years we housed quite a few lame ducks in Number Nine, a few genuine, most freeloaders. After I had sorted them out and sent the freeloaders on their way, Spike would say, 'You have an awful unchristian streak in you.' This was his catch-phrase whenever I would not give in to him over whatever he wanted. But I needed to keep Spike Milligan Productions together.

On New Year's Eve, 1969, I wrote in my diary, 'Goodbye to 1969.' Spike's entry, succinct as usual, was 'Fucking good riddance.' I was the eternal optimist – Ray Galton sometimes called me Scarlett O'Hara – and sure the Seventies would be better than the Sixties. The beginning of 1970 did not augur well, however.

John Goldsmith, a television producer with Granada, wanted

Spike to feature in a documentary about mental illness and re-enact the period he spent in Friern Barnet mental hospital in 1966. I just knew it was a disaster waiting to happen and tried to persuade Spike to turn it down. At the first meeting with Goldsmith in January Spike warmed to the idea because it could help people. This was a hobby horse of his; he believed that the mentally afflicted had been treated as badly as lepers in the previous century. He swept my objections aside and agreed to do it later in the year.

A few days later newspapers predicted Simon Dee's demise as a chat-show host – obviously a leak because nothing had been announced officially. When it happened Spike commiserated with him and became very low. I realized we were heading for trouble. It was not long coming. In April he wrote to Michael Mills, who was then working at the BBC, telling him he could not go ahead with Q6, which had already been commissioned, because his depressing home life made it impossible to write funny material. He spent much of April in bed at the office and at night he started taking what would have been to most people dangerous doses of sleeping tablets. The tablets worked only for a few hours. Then my bedside phone would ring. It was the familiar voice with the familiar phrases.

'Were you asleep?'

'Yes.'

'Well, you're not now.'

Then he would latch on to one of his pet topics, quite frequently his payment for *The Goon Show*.

'Do you know I didn't get as much as Pete and Harry?'

'But overall you got more with your writing fee.'

'Maybe. But they got eighty guineas a performance and I got only seventy. We should all have got the same.'

'So why didn't you?'

'Because those soulless BBC bastards in suits didn't like me. And they still don't.'

The soulless bastards of 1958 had now retired, I would point out.

'That doesn't make the slightest difference. They haven't changed. They didn't like me then and they don't like me now. They thought we were a strange lot.'

'But you were a strange lot.'

Bang. Down would go the receiver and back I went to merciful sleep until he rang again.

I got to work on Michael Mills and persuaded him to put *Q6* on hold until the black dog had gone to ground. Suddenly Spike started accusing me of keeping *Q6* off the screen. What did I mean by keeping him unemployed?

This meant things were returning to normal. For good measure he decided he was talking to me. He left his diary on my desk opened at the correct date with the message, 'TAKE SLEEPING TABLETS. SLEEP ALL DAY. FOREVER IF POSSIBLE. NO WORK.' That was Spike being subtle.

His temper continued until May but improved when Dusty Springfield asked him to appear on her television show. By then he had spent almost a month lying on his bed, scarcely eating, drugged to the hilt, only leaving when he thought everyone had left Number Nine. Sometimes I was still in my office. When he reached the hall and realized I was there he would creep back upstairs. It would not do for me to know that he was able to go out of an evening.

After the show he became friendly with Dusty and discovered that she too had her demons. In her house there was a room devoted to plate throwing. She would throw dozens at the walls to relieve her tension.

'That's not good, Dusty,' he told her. 'You need help.'

Suddenly he was Dr. Milligan. He said to me, 'I'm very concerned about her and the plates.' What about him going to bed and popping pills, I thought, but kept quiet. His preoccupation with Dusty's condition helped to lift him out of his own depression, that and a campaign to save an old music hall, Wilton's in the East End. It was one of the oldest theatres in London and had been graced by the music hall stars of Victorian days. Spike joined the movement to preserve it and helped enlist the Greater London Council. He persuaded Peter Sellers to star with him in a fund-raising concert and brought in Michael Mills, who arranged for it to be screened by the BBC. Then a few years later they used it to shoot a film about William McGonagall, the worst poet of all time, with Spike playing the man himself and Pete as Queen Victoria, who featured in the poems. Sufficient funds were raised to save Wilton's although I do not know if it still survives. Nonetheless, saving the music hall was a means of saving himself. The sun shone once more and he decided there should be an office dinner for Tanis and me. It was his way of saying thank you.

We had not long said goodnight when my phone rang at two o'clock in the morning. His words will never leave me.

'Always know that if you were in an auction I would be the highest bidder.'

Down went the phone.

The next day we had a meeting with John Goldsmith and it was agreed that *The Other Spike* would go ahead. I still had reservations but, inexcusably, conned myself into believing that perhaps it would not be all that bad. Grandma was in England at the time and she violently opposed the project. We were then in discussion with Ken Russell about a part in his film, *The Devils*, so there was a fair amount of entertaining by Spike at his house in Finchley. She castigated him about the money he was spending on it, her fear that he might end his days penniless, or worse still, in a mental home, 'never to come out'. Yet still Spike's mood seemed buoyant.

He went into top gear. He was writing, he was asked to do an election programme with Johnny and Eric, *Up the Polls*, and the Wilton's project was going well. Things were on the up –

but by then I knew that such confidence could precede a nasty fall. It was not long in coming.

In the summer filming started at Friern Barnet. Spike began to ring me during the night.

'I need more Tryptozole,' he said. To someone who had seen how the combination affected him his behaviour screamed that he was mixing it with Tuinol. There was no point in questioning him because he would lie without a qualm. Then the inevitable happened. On a morning when he should have been filming there was a sign on his office door: 'IN BED. UNDER DRUGS. LEAVE ALONE.' I phoned John Goldsmith and said the re-enactment had got to Spike to such an extent that he was unable to work. There could be no question of a return to the hospital. He did not seem to understand. He told me to get him out of bed, into a taxi and over to the studio. I quoted to him Spike's description of the effects of the beginning of a depression. 'If a man had his leg amputated one day would you ask him to get up and walk across the floor the next?' This made no impression. Within half an hour Goldsmith arrived at the office demanding to see Spike. I told him in no uncertain terms where he could go. Here was a man making a documentary about mental health, yet he seemed incapable of understanding Spike's predicament.

When Spike was well enough to return to work he went to the Granada studios in Manchester to finish recording. After all that had happened John Goldsmith had come up with an inno-vative finish for the programme. News of it came in a late-night call from Spike.

'Norma. They want me to end the show in a strait-jacket. I wasn't put in one even when I was being treated. The idea frightens me and I don't like it.'

Neither did I. 'Don't worry, Spike. It's not going to happen. Go back to sleep.'

'Are you sure it won't, Norm?'

'I guarantee it, so rest easy.'

After I had finished with John Goldsmith it did not.

The programme caused a great stir, breaking the taboo about mental problems and successfully illustrating that depression was an illness and not a mental deficiency. Letters came for Spike by the sack load, over three thousand of them. Most were from people who suffered in the privacy of their homes, either ashamed or afraid to let even friends know of their condition. This one was typical: 'I thought I was alone in this. Thank you for being so brave.'

Soon after Spike's return to Number Nine a huge bouquet of flowers arrived for me with this message. 'I think it's time I sent you some of these. Love Spike.'

Working at Number Nine had toughened me up. One day Desmond Briggs, a colleague of publisher Anthony Blond, asked to be put through to Spike. I had told Tanis he was not to be disturbed so she said he would have to ring again. That infuriated him and apparently he was very offensive. I went upstairs and told Spike Briggs had been nasty to Tanis.

'What do you want me to do?' he said

'I want you to tell him to fuck off.'

'Oh, my God,' he cried, 'I'm red-necked. I've taught you to swear like that. You didn't use that sort of language when you came here. And you a Sunday school teacher.' He shook his head. I ignored him. He must have done as I asked because Desmond Briggs did not ring again.

I was prepared to put up with Spike's moods because that was part of the man. Without them his talents might not have soared the way they did. But I would only take so much and soon let him know when he overstepped the mark. If I thought he had gone too far I would leave the office for an hour or two and let him get on with it, warmed by the knowledge that he would be bawling for me and stirring himself into a temper because I was not there. I usually went for a walk down Queensway or into Kensington Gardens, had a manicure or a hairdo and after an hour or so returned. Then, more often than not, he pretended nothing had happened.

Even when Spike knew he had behaved abominably he still found it nearly impossible to say sorry. He always said it with flowers instead. On one occasion my flat and office were overflowing with them. It started with an argument about the title of a book.

By 1970 Spike had been working for three years on the first of his war memoirs. He suddenly told his friend and long-standing editor, Jack Hobbs, whose small publishing house had printed some of his earlier books, 'I think this is too big for you, Jack.' Wham. Just like that. Later Jack told me that Spike was quite right, but there may have been some soul-searching at first.

Of all Spike's friends Alan Clare and Jack Hobbs were perhaps Grandma's favourites. She and Jack would sit together at the Trattoo listening to Alan. One day she heard Spike talking to Jack on the telephone, and came to me. 'I distinctly heard Terry say "Don't worry, Jack. I'm looking after all of us. You can help me on my book."' She raised her eyes to heaven. 'All these hangers-on. My son's an idiot.' I explained that Jack was going through a bad time, and reminded her that he had published her husband's reminiscences after others rejected the manuscript. So Jack was forgiven after all. But she had to have the last word.

'My son should stick with people like Eric. He's a true gentleman and a good friend into the bargain. What's more he dresses nicely, not like some of the dossers Terry mixes with.'

After the initial shock, Jack did the gentlemanly thing and introduced him to Dick Douglas Boyd, sales director at Michael Joseph, who liked the idea and took Jack on as a freelance editor. He also agreed that the manuscript could be improved. Spike started to work hard on the rewrite of what he said was going to be *It'll All Be Over by Christmas*, which is what his father had said about the 1939 war.

'I don't like the title,' I told him. He glared at me and

disappeared. He came back with an alternative, *Adolf Hitler: My Part in His Downfall*.

'Perfect,' I said.

Two weeks later he decided he preferred *It'll All Be Over by Christmas*. This was the beginning of a battle of wills. It had become his habit to read me each chapter of whatever book he was writing as he finished for my opinion. This time, after each read, I would say, '*Adolf*'s going very well.' I was determined to win. He hated me at times like that because he knew I would not let up. When he finished the second draft he still was not happy with it. To cheer him up I invited him and Paddy to the first night of *Hair*.

David Conyers, as creative an agent as ever, had seen the American production and decided to bring it over through ALS. He asked if I would like to be one of the angels. I did not know what he was talking about and asked if Spike was not one already. He explained the process of backing a show, emphasized that it was a gamble, but I liked the idea and agreed to do it. I went on to do many more musicals, *Joseph and the Amazing Technicolor Dreamcoat*, *Oh! Calcutta!* and *Evita* among the early ones, although of course there were bummers too. I enjoyed the thrill and made a bit into the bargain.

As an angel I had the choice of seats and thought it would be a pleasant evening. But I had chosen the wrong moment. Because Spike was unhappy with *Adolf* he lashed out at me and he took to his bed. This time the note on the door said, 'NORMA HAS MADE ME ILL. LEAVE ME ALONE.'

It was the same as with Paddy; he needed someone to blame. I knew he would soon get over it. Two days later I heard him bashing away at his typewriter. Good. It was probably just the right time to give him the new will he had asked his solicitor to draw up. I slipped a note under Spike's door asking him to ring me.

Spike's friends said I had an innate sense of when to discuss business with him. This reputation was about to take a beating. He called so I went up with the will and Tanis to witness it. Without the slightest warning he exploded. How could I ask him to sign something at such a crucial time? I had stripped him of his creativity and writing ability. 'Over the years you've tried to turn me into a clerk, and now finally you've succeeded.' My behaviour had made him 'unfunny'. He looked despairingly at the ceiling and said, 'Please God make me an idiot so I don't have to suffer like this.' Then he pushed us out of the office.

This was not the beginning of a depression, just a tantrum because his work would not flow. I told Tanis we were finished for the day. She could take her dog for an earlier than usual walk in the park and everything would be back to normal the next morning.

I was wrong. I arrived to find his manuscript in a folder on my desk. He had scrawled a message on it for me.

And on the title page he had written *It'll All Be Over by Christmas.*

I ignored the R.I.P. bit and wrote underneath his title, 'No. *Adolf Hitler: My Part in His Downfall* is so much better.' I took it upstairs and left it outside his door.

I was relieved to hear the clickety-click of his typewriter again. Once he started to work the time of day meant nothing to him. Neither did food. Day and much of the night were devoted to the task in hand. On the delivery date set by Michael Joseph I found the manuscript on my desk with a note. 'Call it what you will, but if you choose *Adolf Hitler* and it doesn't sell it's down to you.'

I opened the file to read the final version and on top of the manuscript was an extra page which had not been there before.

'I dedicate this book to Norma Farnes, my manager, who puts up with me.'

So very Spike.

Adolf Hitler was a bestseller and what was originally intended to be three volumes grew into seven, all of them immensely successful.

With work as fraught as ever it was a relief to get away with John. Two years into our marriage we went for a holiday to Positano, a magical town on the Amalfi coast of southern Italy that cascaded down a hillside to a small beach. Bougainvillea draped our small hotel and evenings were alive with chattering cicadas. Heaven could not be better than this, I thought. But the day came when we had to return home.

'I don't want to go back,' said John. Neither did I but I was touched that he had enjoyed himself so much.

'We've got to go back to work.'

'I don't want to go back to the office. I feel like a prisoner every day when the lift doors close behind me.'

My heart missed a beat. This was not just sadness at the end of a holiday. I knew it because of my experience with Spike. The following weeks confirmed my worst fears.

Depression in someone you love is very different from depression in a colleague. At the end of each day I could slip a piece of paper under Spike's door saying 'I'll be at home if you need me.' It was much worse to go home and find the blinds down, windows closed and the flat suffocating.

Spike understood John's state of mind and tried to help. When John came out of that first depression I knew nothing would ever be the same. By that time I knew better than to believe it was merely an isolated attack.

Chapter Nine

It is strange that two depressives played such a large part in my life. I knew that John needed professional help and Spike tried to persuade him to see his friend Sydney Gottlieb. The South African was no run-of-the-mill psychiatrist. After becoming a specialist in pulmonary diseases he joined the army. When Auschwitz was liberated he was sent there to treat survivors. It struck him that many inmates' illnesses derived from their mental state after years of bestial treatment, so he decided to retrain and became eminent in his new field.

John would have none of it but I went to Sydney myself for advice. I had become the whipping boy and John blamed everything on me. I took his abuse very personally, which I had never done when Spike was low, and it was little comfort to be reminded by friends that John's behaviour was normal for a depressive. I now understood what it must be like for Paddy.

A few months after the first episode John again took to his bed and stayed there for several weeks. He would not talk to or see anyone, including me. I went to the Law Society and appointed a locum. But John seemed unable to accept the fact that I was up and active and he was stuck in bed.

John had refused to talk to Spike but when Spike wrote begging him to accept help he finally agreed to see him. Spike came to our flat and was alone with him for an hour and a half. I never knew what transpired. The next day Spike, Silé, John and I flew to Paris together to watch a rugby game. I could not say which teams were playing, but I do remember that Spike at last succeeded in persuading John to consult Sidney. Despite it all John's condition appeared to worsen, and I found I could not do for him what I did for Spike. I was too emotionally involved.

Three days after returning from Paris I noticed a rash around my middle. I blamed it on something I had eaten but it did not go away and spread to my neck. I have always tried to avoid doctors but vanity won and I found myself one morning at Dr. Stephen Smith's surgery in Carlton Mansions asking for some cream to get rid of it. Such a cream did not exist, he assured me. What I had was a psychosomatic rash caused by trauma. I assured him he was mistaken; I was not subject to such things. 'You are now,' he replied.

I went straight to a phone box at the corner of Abbey Road and West End Lane and let Tanis know I would arrive soon. Then I burst into tears. I knew I could not cope any more. For nearly four weeks John had said, as he stayed in bed and I dressed for work, 'That's right. Get tarted up for your show business friends.' I had humoured him, wearing a plain black sweater and trousers then changing at the office. On the way home I used to pray, 'God, let the lights be on.' If they were, at least he would be up.

John recovered for a time but several months later was ill again. He developed a cycle and each bout was worse than the last. Unlike Spike, there was never a clear indication that he was about to sink into a depression. He would seem all right then one day come home early from the office, go to bed and remain there for days, not eating and barely drinking.

On many evenings when John was low our dear friend, Alex Rudelhoff, would keep me company at the flat. Sometimes John would make an appearance, on one memorable occasion walking across the room and hiding behind the curtains. Alex tried to persuade him to come out but he lurked there until he had left. Then he darted out and, without a word, went back to bed. In 1971 he was admitted to St. Mary's, Paddington.

John's mother was a domineering personality but she seemed to think his illness reflected negatively on her family and could not come to terms with it. The moment he fell ill she would stop visiting him. One evening she dropped a note through the letter box at the flat. 'Just let me know when he is better.' Two days later she dispatched a young American rabbi to see me. He was as puzzled as I was as to what exactly she thought he could do to help. Perhaps it was a method of demonstrating that she had not completely given up on her son although she could not bear to see it. A sort of semi-detached concern, I suppose.

Although his condition eventually improved John and I were drifting apart. Our backgrounds were in stark contrast. He was brought up in the comfort of a middle-class home with all the indulgence shown towards a treasured son. Even as an adult he was incredibly dependent on his mother. He would run up an overdraft. Not to bother, Mother would settle it. And she did. He liked to mock the fact that I had arrived in London with nothing and still held fast to my principles of avoiding debts. At a dinner party he said scathingly, 'Ignore Norma. She wears her poverty like a halo.' It was almost worthy of Spike.

Spike believed John was a victim of his upbringing. To say he took a dislike to Mrs. Hyman is putting it mildly. They only met a few times but that was enough for him. 'Never invite me round when she's going to be present,' he said. 'She uses her money like a crutch and she'll destroy John.'

John had been supportive of my career at first, but as the years went by he disapproved of my dedication to it and could not understand why I was so determined to build my own agency. Spike was full of advice. One day he suggested I should have a baby. 'It'll be good for you. Take two weeks off to have it, then Spike Milligan Productions will pay for a nanny.' I assume he thought a child would save the marriage but it would never have worked. In any case I did not want children and John was happy with his three daughters. Spike persisted for a month but in the end realized he was on to a loser.

Spike's generosity on behalf of Spike Milligan Productions extended to more than offering to pay for nannies. He often offered his services for a good cause and sometimes people would abuse this. As far as he was concerned Bernard Miles could do no wrong. Bernard was a great actor, with a range extending from Shakespeare to playing character parts in films from the late Twenties right until the Seventies, and later created a life peer. During the war, when much of London was ablaze, he became gripped by a vision. He would build a theatre on one of the bombsites beside the Thames. It would continue the thread of theatrical history: an Elizabethan theatre in the round, a style that was in turn based on the Greek amphitheatre.

The project became his overriding ambition and purpose in life, to the detriment of his performing career. The first breakthrough came when the City of London Corporation agreed to lease him, at a peppercorn rent, a blitzed site once occupied by a warehouse at Puddle Dock on the riverbank. All he needed then was the money to build the theatre.

'He did it all by himself,' Spike told me when I first started working for him. 'It took him years to raise the money from all the bastards I can't stand, you know, banks, insurance companies, stockbrokers and shipping lines.'

Bernard's name meant nothing to me and my ignorance must have been evident. 'You can finish what you're doing now later,' he said. 'Come on. I'll take you to the Mermaid Theatre.'

There I met the tall, slightly stooped figure of Bernard Miles, with his lopsided grin and charm that had melted the hearts and opened the pockets of the money men. Spike did not just admire him for his achievements. In 1961, when his pace of work had slackened and he had become convinced that the BBC had decided not to use him again, Bernard offered him a role in *Treasure Island* at sixty pounds a week. Spike's career soon revived, but in all the years that we worked together Bernard only had to ask him to appear at the Mermaid and the deal was done, at the same bargain rate, even if more lucrative offers were on the table.

When I first met him Bernard was going through one of his periodic financial crises at the Mermaid and asked Spike to appear there. He agreed and played Ben Gunn in *Treasure Island* in October 1966. Spike's popularity was such that the run was an immediate sell-out. The following year he went to do his usual stint at the Mermaid. His restaurant bills were often double his weekly wage and I told him he could not afford to work there any longer.

'I owe him,' he said. 'He gave me a job when nobody else would.'

'When will the debt be discharged?'

'Never!'

And it never was. Bernard had only to ask and Spike would appear. When I first complained about the paltry wages it was enough to send Spike into a tantrum. Bernard Miles was a national treasure and it was therefore an honour to appear for him. It took me a while to learn to tread the fine line necessary to avoid annoying Spike and I did not always succeed. When I had the temerity to suggest that Bernard was doing very well out of him, he was furious.

Spike often delighted in giving me a hard time, especially when he was full of the devil, which more often than not he was, when not in a depression. If I was out he would go into my office and muck about with my desk, riflng through correspondence and contracts, writing messages and throwing paperwork into disarray. I would light-heartedly ban him from my office, or better still, threaten to lock the door when I went out, putting the petty cash box out of his reach.

At that time I was still a heavy smoker, about sixty a day. He once said, 'I wish people could see how we behave in this office. You're like something out of *Annie Get Your Gun*, with the pistol cocked behind the desk. I come in, look at the ashtray, and if it's like Mount Everest by midday I go. If there are only three tab ends in it I fire away.'

One day when I was out he saw a Michael Joseph contract on my desk. Now he knew he could not sign contracts or anything to do with Spike Milligan Productions Ltd or the Inland Revenue would come down on him, but he was in high spirits and signed the contract, not as Spike Milligan but Joan of Arc, and popped it in the post. Raleigh Trevelyan, then editorial director and unaware of the SMP arrangements, wrote me a letter asking if Spike could add his signature to that of the Maid of Orleans so that she could receive her advance. Spike found it hysterical but I was annoyed at the waste of time. He must have had a twinge of conscience because the next day he arrived with a plant for my office.

'You have a dress this colour. I thought you'd like it.'

I told him we had had that line before.

'Right. I'll go upstairs and think of a better one for next time.'

This incident was far from unique. Once Spike sent Pat Newman, a BBC producer, a contract signed Mao Tse Tung because that day was the Chinese New Year. Pat knew the SMP set-up and sent it back for me to sign, with a note for Spike saying had he known who was going to sign it he would have had the contract drawn up on rice paper.

Spike's rash gestures could have more lasting outcomes. One evening he had dinner with Dr. Joe Robson, a friend of Spike's.

Robson's son, Jeremy, was going into publishing and Spike promised to give him a book.

'So give him one,' he ordered me.

It was one of those 'Hey, wait a minute, Spike' moments.

'You've got to write one before I can do that.'

'Nonsense! Give him a book. I've promised his father and I'm indebted to Joe. When I couldn't sleep he hypnotized me and I slept. That's the debt so get a book for Jeremy and then it's cleared.'

'But we haven't got any unpublished manuscripts.'

'That's your problem.'

I never knew whether the idea came from Jeremy or Spike, but suddenly it was all systems go to publish *The Goon Show* scripts.

'We', said Spike – I loved the 'we' – 'need six scripts or so and drawings for the book.'

I remember going into the cellar where he kept his scripts, moaning, because everything was covered in dust. Spike had been his usual orderly self, however, and they were all filed by date. I was charged with making the initial selection so suddenly I was an expert on *The Goon Show*. In a different mood he could have gone to the cellar declaring that he had to do everything himself and that he did not get help from anyone. He left it to me because he was totally preoccupied with raising money for the World Wildlife Fund. In the end he just agreed to the ones I picked and his debt to Joe was discharged.

I had told Spike, *ad nauseam*, I am afraid to say, that nobody would buy a book of scripts; Spike did not care whether they did or did not so long as he had done his duty by Joe. Naturally, when it was published the following year, the book became an enormous seller, as did all subsequent collections of scripts. This prompted him to start introducing me as 'my manager, or shall we say damager.'

*

Spike was always a fervent supporter of the World Wildlife Fund. A friend, Cyril Littlewood, was working for the organization and approached Spike to see if he would help raise money. Spike agreed and *Milligan's Ark* was born.

He invited celebrities to draw an animal and write a small poem to go with it. Jack Hobbs was cajoled into editing and publishing the book, with all the proceeds going to the Fund. I thought it a great idea but wondered how much time it would take up because he had promised me he would finish his serious poetry book, *Small Dreams of a Scorpion*, and a children's story, *Dip the Puppy*, for Jack Hobbs's publishing company, M. & J. Hobbs.

He approached Prince Philip, WWF Patron, explaining the idea, and asked him to write the foreword. Then he telephoned John Lennon and asked him to draw an animal – 'any animal, it doesn't matter what.' Lennon agreed at once. 'Anything for you, Spike.' He drew a quirky dog and Yoko Ono drew cats and elephants. Next on Spike's list was Peter Sellers, who sent in a weird bird called a Civil Service heron. Having done all that Spike said he would speak to Eric about a contribution and then threw everything at me and Jack Hobbs.

'Ring celebrities and get them to contribute. You won't have any trouble.'

'They won't take any notice of me,' I said.

'Nonsense. Now this is how it is. If you don't do it then I'll have to stop work on the children's story and halt the poetry book. I'll miss your deadlines and I'll have to tell the publishers that it was all your fault because you wouldn't help me.'

I sighed.

'Okay. We'll do a deal. I'll get all the contributors without asking you anything if you'll draw the cover.' Why, I asked myself, am I having to bribe him to contribute to his own project? At any rate he did produce the drawing.

With the help of Jack and Cyril over the next few months I

persuaded people like Yehudi Menuhin, Dame Sybil Thorndike, Vidal Sassoon, Lawrence Durrell, Elizabeth Taylor, Hattie Jacques, Kenneth More and Stirling Moss. I rang Johnny Speight. 'So that's his lost cause for the week. I'm coming to the office so I'll bring something with me. And then you, Eric and I will have lunch at Bertorelli's.' His drawing was an odd-shaped head, a bit like E.T., which he gave the caption 'Homo Sapiens. The worst animal of all.' We got ninety notable contributors in the end. When the book was complete Spike spoke to Cyril Littlewood and asked him to give me the framed original of the book cover. Such gestures were his saving grace.

Better still, shortly afterwards he summoned me upstairs to announce that he had finished *Small Dreams of a Scorpion*. I was amazed. At the same time he had been working on the children's story, *Dip the Puppy*, and his war memoirs. I returned to my office in a happy frame of mind. But not for long.

Tanis rang me. 'You've got to speak to this bloke, Peter, on the phone. He insists on making a complaint about you. He rang four times while you were in with Spike. I'll put him through.'

'Hold it right there. If he wants to complain about me it's no good him talking to me. Put him on hold while I have a word with Spike.' I rang him on the intercom.

'You must speak to this guy. Apparently I was very rude to him yesterday and he wants to complain.'

'You deal with it.'

'Come on, Spike.' He was in a sunny mood and agreed. Later he told me what happened. Peter had asked me if Spike could make an appearance for a charity. I had said no and explained I had called a halt to accepting more charity work because Spike was overloaded.

'But it'll only take him about half an hour,' Peter protested.

'Listen to me,' I had said. 'I've got about forty people exactly like you, all wanting half an hour of Spike's time. The answer is no.'

Spike heard him out and said, 'Peter, I know what she's like. How many times have you dealt with her?'

'Well, just the once.'

'Only the once. Can you imagine what it's like for me sitting here? I have to deal with her three hundred and sixty-five days a year.'

Peter hung up.

There are many demands on people in show business, and one of the crosses they have to bear is the unwelcome intruder when they are trying to have a pleasant evening with friends. Quite often we would be in a restaurant when one of the diners would recognize Spike.

'Here it comes,' Spike would say. 'Can I shake your hand for all the laughter . . .' Before he could complete the sentence the fan would be at our table beaming, though perhaps a little embarrassed. And sure enough, out it would come.

'Can I shake your hand for all the laughter? I can't believe it's really you.'

If it was a woman normally Spike would stand up and be very polite. If it was a man it depended on his mood: he might shake his hand and then ignore him, to the fan's embarrassment, or say, 'No, you can't. Bugger off.' He hated his privacy to be invaded and could never understand how fans could be so fawning and willing to face a rebuff.

I was bowled over when we walked into the Trattoo one night in 1971 and, after a quick double-take, Spike strode over to a man sitting listening to Alan Clare with the friends we were due to meet. Beaming, Spike said, 'Can I shake your hand for all the laughter you have given me? I can't believe it's really you.'

The man smiled. 'Hello, Spike.'

Spike turned to me. 'He actually knows my name.'

At that my friends, Larry Gelbart and his wife, Pat, burst into laughter. I had had no idea they would bring Groucho Marx with them. They thought I might be unable to keep the secret so had not told me. Quite right, too.

We had arranged to meet Larry with Marty Feldman – he arrived later – for dinner to discuss Feldman's new show, *The Marty Feldman Comedy Machine*. Larry had written for Sid Caesar, co-written *A Funny Thing Happened on the Way to the Forum*, and then came to the UK in the Sixties to make comedy films. Now he was going to produce and direct *Comedy Machine* for ITV.

Larry was bright, witty and charming. If that was not enough, he had the talent to write and produce *M*A*S*H**, to co-write *Tootsie*, and he was also a shrewd negotiator. He and Marty had already persuaded Spike to appear in the show but they also wanted him to write for it. Spike was very busy, and was meant to be working on *Q6* (this was eventually broadcast in 1975), but Groucho was the clincher. Of course, Spike would be honoured to write five minutes for any show Groucho graced with his presence.

All was sweetness and light that night. Spike was thrilled that Groucho was familiar with *The Goon Show*. Groucho was equally honoured that he had been Spike's inspiration. Dinners with Spike were not often harmonious but this was an exception. Afterwards I tried to persuade him to bow out of writing for the show because it would put him under too much pressure, but he insisted.

The friendliness of that evening did not transfer to the *Comedy Machine* studio. Marty fell, breaking an arm, and the tension crackled between him and Larry. Spike, of all people, tried to act as mediator and keep the peace. Two weeks later I walked into the Trattoo to be greeted once more by Larry and Pat.

'How's Marty?' I asked.

'Marty who?' Larry replied.

But despite terrible arguments they stuck it out and the show went on to win awards at the Montreux Festival.

Spike had set aside a month to update his one-man show, which he had launched on a tour of Australia in 1967 and was due to take over there again. Yet after a few manic months, which had seen him publish *Adolf Hitler*, he was exhausted. Instead he became desperately low and withdrew from the world once more.

Chapter Ten

Spike spent a fortnight on his bed at Number Nine before flying out to see his mother and brother Desmond in Australia. There were times when, for all their squabbling, he was desperate to see his mother and this was one of them. The script for his one-man show was thrust aside and I did not press him for it.

Once he was at Woy Woy in October there were no outside pressures on him. If he told Grandma he did not want to see anyone she was better than a Rottweiler at seeing them off. He spent several weeks with his mother and then stayed with his war-time friend, Harry Edgington, in New Zealand. They phoned me one night in high spirits, having just called their old mates at a pub called the Printer's Devil in Fleet Street where they were holding the annual reunion of the D Battery, 56th Heavy Regiment. The lads were 'stoned' and having a great time. And so, at last, was he.

He returned to England on 8 December, quiet and calm. Alarm bells rang. There was a great deal of work in the pipeline but soon after the New Year he went into a downer, not the worst but bad enough. The note pushed under my office door said, 'FUCK THE SYSTEM. IT KILLS YOU IF YOU ARE NOT A BUREAUCRAT OR A CAPITALIST.' What had brought that on?

'It's your bloody piles,' I told him. He had complained about them for years. 'They make you bad tempered and the quicker you have them seen to the better for everyone.' But no, it was Paddy's fault, with her intolerable scattiness and lack of organization. Nevertheless he took my advice and was admitted to the Fitzroy Nuffield.

He wrote in his diary 'Good luck Spike Milligan.' I thought, 'Good luck the nursing staff.'

After the operation he refused to eat anything but 'sunflower seed oil' capsules, as he pedantically put it, for fear of pain. When I visited him Matron Roberts collared me. 'He must eat solids,' she said.

Spike refused but agreed to a compromise: jelly. Matron Roberts was still not satisfied and told him he would have to do as he was told. Big mistake.

'If that woman thinks I'm going to eat and crap broken glass just for her she's very much mistaken. Everybody told me the operation was painful. It's not the operation. It's the crapping and I'm sticking to jelly.'

In a battle of wills there could be only one winner. Poor Matron Roberts. I arrived at the hospital to hear Spike shouting, 'I want my jelly. Get me my bloody jelly.'

A nurse called out, 'For God's sake, someone get Spike his bloody jelly.'

Fit again, he had a busy year with appearances lined up in many films, including *The Cherry Picker*, *The Three Musketeers*, *Alice in Wonderland*, and *Ghost in the Noonday Sun*, scenes of which he also rewrote, as well as the BBC series, *A Milligan for All Seasons*. And Jimmy Verner wanted him to do a U.K. tour. Temporarily at least, his life-long fear of not having enough money to keep his family receded. It was in this mood of optimism that one night we went to the Trattoo. Alan Clare was in great form and Spike had his trumpet ready to play after closing time, when a customer, who had obviously celebrated too heartily, wobbled up to Spike and said, 'You're the comic, aren't you?'

Spike sighed.

'If you're so bloody funny tell me a joke,' the stranger persisted.

Spike eyed him. 'What do you do for a living?'

'I'm a carpenter.'

'Then make me a table,' he said. Collapse of carpenter and laughter all round.

After another evening's dinner at the Trattoo with Peter Sellers we went to the bar to listen to Alan, ordered more wine, and Spike brought out his trumpet while Pete went to his car for his bongo drums. He and Spike were very, very good and Alan loved a session. On these occasions, long after other diners had left, Pasquale, London's best restaurant manager at the time, would go home at one o'clock or so and give the keys to Peppino, our favourite waiter, with instructions to lock up when the music had finished. Sometimes that could be four o'clock. This night, at about two o'clock, there was a tap on the window and Spike looked out. The man indicated he wanted to come in so Peppino opened the door. Although he was small he could be ferocious and anyone unwelcome would have found himself flat on the pavement. But the stranger seemed harmless.

'I was just passing and heard the gig,' he said. 'Can I join in?'

'Yeah, daddy,' said Spike.

He went outside and came back with a double bass. We all looked at each other. Pete asked, 'Where the hell did you get that from?'

'Always carry it – on top of the car.'

The stranger was a natural and as well as joining in soloed

some double-bass standards. My contribution came after a few glasses or more of champagne, when Alan would persuade me to sing 'Send in the Clowns'. I was off-key and terrible, but I knew all the words. Spike said, 'It's her party piece. Leave her alone. She sounds like Blossom Dearie to me when I've had enough Orvieto.'

At about three o'clock, as we were packing up, the double bassist said, 'No one in the world will believe I played a session with Spike Milligan and Peter Sellers. Great! Thanks and good night.'

Spike said, 'I've got to see a double bass on top of a car.'

We walked outside, all except laid-back Alan, who was always prepared to accept anything, and watched the bloke lash his double bass on to his car: a Mini! We never knew his name or saw him again. Sometimes after dinner at the Trattoo, Spike would say, 'I wish he'd come back, just to make sure we didn't dream the whole thing.'

After that session Pete was ecstatic and wanted to show his appreciation to Alan, 'the best jazz pianist ever'. To demonstrate how much he thought of him he had delivered to Alan's flat, without warning, a brand new piano, the very best he could find, and very expensive. Alan was knocked out and effusive in his thanks to Pete. He phoned to tell me and Spike what a dear, impulsive, generous friend he was. Wonderful, I thought. Not so Spike.

'It bothers me,' he said.

'Don't be silly. Pete's lonely and misses the friendship of *The Goon Show* days. The evenings at the Trattoo are very special to him.'

'Hm. There's something wrong. Beware the Greek bearing gifts.'

'You're an old cynic. He's only trying to show Alan how much he appreciates his playing and the sessions at the Tratt.'

But the old sod was right. Some time later, without as much

as a telephone call, a lorry arrived at Alan's flat. They had come for the piano. Pete had decided to give it to Princess Margaret. That it had been a present to Alan in the first place mattered not a jot to him. Alan arrived home to be told by his wife that the gift had made a surprise journey from Holland Park to Kensington Palace, round the corner. Pete never offered any explanation of why he did it. Alan, though dazed, puzzled and hurt, never reproached Pete. But Spike said, 'It's an act of treachery,' and never quite forgave him.

The previous October the BBC had decided to make *The Last Goon Show of All* as part of the corporation's fiftieth anniversary celebrations. Spike was not at all keen on the idea: it had been ten years since he had written the last *Goon* script. But John Browell was asked to produce and direct. Along with Dennis Main Wilson and Peter Eton, he had been responsible for the original *Goon Shows* so already had a rapport with Spike. John came to see him and prevailed. I prepared myself for the usual round of 'Spike will do it if Harry does', 'Pete will do it if Spike does'. Once we got over those hurdles John came to see me about the recording date.

'Right,' I said. 'We'll record on 30 April.'

'Why then?'

'I've learned never to offer them a number of dates or they'll argue and find all sorts of reasons why none of them is any good. Just tell them it's 30 April. Trust me.'

He did, they agreed the date and then Spike chipped in with conditions. It had to be recorded at the Camden Theatre, Harry had to provide the brandy, John Browell the milk, oh, and all the cast had to be the same as before, Ray Ellington, Max Geldray and so on. It looked as though it would go off without a hitch. Until we heard Geldray was out.

'No Max, no show,' Spike declared. 'What's the problem?' It was the usual one with the BBC – money. Max was living in

Massachusetts and they would not pay his airfare. This was just the attitude Spike hated about the BBC, the 'mean bastards.' Spike and Pete offered to forgo their fees so the BBC could afford the fare. 'Right,' said John. 'I'll put that to their Lordships.' This seemed to shame them because they decided that they could afford to fly Geldray over after all. Then Pat Newman and Con Mahoney, who headed Light Entertainment Radio, suggested that Spike and Pete should each put in twenty-five pounds to provide Max 'with his nosh, be it smoked salmon or jellied eels', which could have put the show off if it had not been for John Browell's calming influence. And finally, at the eleventh hour, the BBC said they wanted to film the show. No way, said Spike. For archive purposes only, they promised. 'The bastards won't keep their word. The answer is "No."'

I kept on at Spike and he eventually changed his mind, allowing them to record the show properly. When 30 April came it went smoothly and after all the dramas John and I hugged each other. Pete and Harry thought it a success, but Spike was unhappy with the script. They televised it three years later.

Six months later the Woburn Press published the book of early scripts and were as surprised by the huge sales as I was. (They followed up in 1973 with *More Goon Show Scripts*, then *The Book of the Goons*, published by Robson Books, which Jeremy set up in 1974 after leaving the Woburn Press.) The company could not keep up with the demand, doing reprint after reprint, and neither did they keep up with the payment of royalties. I told Spike but he did not want to know because his friend's son worked at the company. I tried to explain that it had nothing to do with Jeremy and was entirely the responsibility of other people. 'Go it alone, baby. Don't involve me,' he said. 'Don't even tell me what's happening and then if Joe asks me I can honestly tell him I don't know.' I thanked him for his loyalty and support and told him I would consult a solicitor. He did not mention it again.

Proceedings dragged on for months. When the date of the hearing arrived I went upstairs to tell Spike I would probably be out for most of the day. 'Cancel that,' he said. 'I've finished writing a book for Jane's sixth birthday.' It was *Badjelly the Witch*, his fairy tale. It was essential I saw it at once. I told him it would have to wait. He threw a minor tantrum so I explained where I was going.

'Bloody waste of time! What's gone's gone. You'll never see the money. I need you here so do not give yourself a lot of aggravation.'

I bet him £1,000 I would win the case.

He looked at me with that penetrating stare of his.

'No, I won't take the bet. You've got that tenacious look on your face.'

So I went and won back £9,000. Spike was contrite and offered me half, but I told him I was satisfied with my commission. I was not going to ease his conscience that easily. I was more interested in *Badjelly*, which was a beautiful book, hand-written and illustrated by Spike. It was published just as he had drawn it and sold tens of thousands of copies.

His contrite mood did not last long. One day, when he was supposed to be shooting *Milligan in Spring* in Kensington Gardens, part of the *A Milligan for all Seasons* series for the BBC, Spike appeared at Number Nine.

'What are you doing here?' I asked.

'I've come for a slash.'

'There are loos in Kensington Gardens. What's happened?'

'What's it got to do with you?' he snarled. 'You sit there. You don't earn your money. I earn your money.'

So that's how it was.

'No. You generate the money. I earn my own money, and I earn it by sitting behind this desk. I earn it by picking up the pieces when you've stormed out. So earning my money isn't easy.'

He was livid. 'You don't earn it. You just sit there. I'm the one that earns it.'

I stood up. 'Nobody, but nobody is going to tell me that I don't earn it. You know what Jimmy Grafton says about being an agent? "You get the Oscars, we get the ulcers and all the shit that's thrown in with it."'

'You don't even know what shit is. As I said, you don't earn the money.'

'Then you'd better get someone that does.'

He stared at me for a moment, turned and left.

Tanis rushed into my office. I was fuming.

'He's not going to get away with saying I don't earn my money. I'm going, and this time for good.' I waved at the furniture in the office. 'Ninety per cent of this is mine. I'll send someone for it because that's the end. I'm off.'

She looked on helplessly. She knew this was worse than one of our usual spats.

I drove home, called Diana and we lunched at Fortnum and Mason. Tanis rang the following morning.

'What time will you be in?'

'I'm not coming in. I'm going to have a facial, a manicure and a pedicure. I'm going to pamper myself.'

'Oh, my God! This is all alien,' she said (Tanis had picked up Spike's habits of speech). 'He's left the filming in the park. When he came in he said "Tell Norm I'll be back for tea. Get us some doughnuts."'

'He knows what he can do with his doughnuts. I'm not coming back.'

The next day it was Tanis again. 'I'm putting Spike through.'

'No you're not, Tanis. I've finished with all that crap.' I went shopping and wondered what my next job would be.

I rang John Browell that afternoon and said, 'John, I need a job, just to tide me over. I've walked out.'

Darling, wise old John said, 'Look, come to me in a month's

time. You'll be back. You two were made for each other. Nobody will put up with him like you do.'

He was right. The following morning a huge bouquet of flowers arrived at the flat with a card. 'May day! May day! Love Spike.' I wanted to fling them in the dustbin but they were too beautiful for that. He knew my weakness. No sooner had I arranged them than the phone rang.

'Did you get the flowers?'

'They're lovely.'

'Now you've got over the temperament I need you. I'm in the shit here. I've walked out on the *Seasons* and I need to talk to you. If you don't want to stab me in the back let's have a cup of tea together.'

The gall of the man. But what the hell, if I did not do something that would be the end of the series. When I walked through Number Nine's front door Spike was waiting for me. 'Oh *mea culpa, mea culpa*,' he said. 'Oh my God! I'm in sackcloth and ashes.' It was the closest he could get to an apology. I knew I would have to get the series back on track so I picked up the phone. By the end of the day everyone was the best of friends and the *Seasons* was a hit.

While professionally 1972 was an immensely successful year for Spike, domestically he had reached a low point. He and Paddy seemed to do nothing but argue. To some the cause of the rows might seem trivial but to him they were of overriding importance. Her inability to organize the household infuriated him. A fan heater broke down and she ignored it. She forgot to restock the toilet paper. With Spike, should anything need to be mended or replaced he saw to it immediately. By the end of the summer he was taking to his bed in the office with increasing regularity, sometimes for two or three weeks at a time. The notes I found under my door in the mornings seemed ever more despondent. One read, 'God didn't let or get Jane to phone me. She doesn't feel anything for me.' God was Paddy.

I had to cancel shows and appearances. He was distraught when he was unable to accept an invitation from Roger Greenaway to attend the annual dinner of the Society of Distinguished Songwriters. It meant a great deal to him because his first love was music and musicians but he was so ill he could not get out of bed. He wrote in his diary, 'To (sic) ill to go. I'm so lonely.'

Meanwhile, John and I had reached the stage where we had nothing in common. It was time to say goodbye. I went to see my solicitor, and by then friend, David Napley, who had successfully defended Jeremy Thorpe, and he informed me that John was going to claim maintenance, despite his family's wealth. I had never heard of a man being paid maintenance by his wife. David said, 'Don't blame John. Blame Baroness Summerskill. She fought for this equality.'

When I returned to Number Nine Spike noticed I was close to tears.

'What's wrong with you?'

I explained the situation.

'Fuck Baroness Summerskill,' he said. 'I'll speak to David Napley myself.'

'Leave it. You'll only make it worse.'

'Hey. How much worse can it get? He's asking you to give him money.'

Later David told me what Spike had said. 'I will not have my manager upset like this. I want it finalized as quickly and painlessly as possible for her. Just tell me how much and by when.'

A few days later Spike came into my office and said, 'Don't worry about anything any more. I've sorted it out. There'll be no maintenance but there will be a full and final settlement, which David is arranging. Now listen, Norm. Don't start any of your negotiating tactics. Pay it and call it peace of mind money.'

He told me to take it from wherever he had it; I could pay him back over seven years. I could not do that. What if I had a row with him and wanted to walk out? I would not be able to if I owed him money, so I went to the bank and obtained a loan, a sum large enough in those days to buy a small flat.

Spike was furious. 'My manager has become a capitalist,' he ranted, 'borrowing money from a bank. She won't borrow it from me.' It was part of his code for a man to come to the aid of a woman. Three or four days later he came into my office once more.

'I've been thinking about your bread situation.'

'Don't bother. I'll get a night job.'

'Seriously, Norm, why don't you go through my files and collate some of my letters? Ask Michael Joseph if they are interested in putting them into a book. You sort them out, edit the book and keep the royalties. That way you can pay off the bank and we can all get back to normal.' In the end it took me a couple of years to do the job, but the book proved a great success and the proceeds paid off the settlement and more.

When Peter Sellers heard about my divorce he telephoned to console me.

'Remember, Norma, the first time is always the worst.' He was in fatherly mode. 'What you need to do is to get away from it all. Take my yacht, take Bert Mortimer' – his chauffeur, valet, nursemaid and confidant – 'and go to Capri. I've instructed the skipper to go wherever the mood takes you.'

He rang every day for four days, solicitous and anxious that I take up his offer. Given how competitive he could be with Spike I suspected an ulterior motive, perhaps that Spike would be miffed because I had leaned on Pete, and not him, for help. I appreciated the gesture and thanked him but said I would rather stay at work. That baffled him.

That night Spike took me out to dinner. He gave me his solution for how to get over a bad time. 'Move into the Harlequin suite at the Dorchester. Stay three days or so. People can send flowers, you can watch television and be waited on by expert professionals. You'll like that, Norm. And I'll pay for it.'

Both had the same recipe for solving problems: get away and do not think about it. That was not my way. They obviously thought I was mad, but I knew I had to take things day by day and carry on with my life. Life became fun again, although work was never easy. That was its attraction. A battle a day was how I summed it up and sometimes when I left the office I would tell myself, 'I won today.'

When Spike returned from shooting *The Three Musketeers* with Raquel Welch in Spain I reminded him of his promise to write additional dialogue for *Ghost in the Noonday Sun*, the film Pete was starring in in which Spike had a small role. Shooting was due to start in Cyprus the following week. But instead the Inland Revenue occupied his mind to the exclusion of all else. Of course, this situation, like so many others, was entirely my fault.

'You weren't in the office when I needed money. All because you were at the hairdressers, getting a massage or wasting your time – *no*,' he said triumphantly, '*my* time when I needed you.'

Tanis told me what had happened. One day he had needed £200, probably to give to some stray. He raided the petty cash but there was not enough. Tanis tried to persuade him to wait for me to come back, but he just exploded. 'I want my money now.'

As a paid employee of Spike Milligan Productions rather than a director Spike was not authorized to sign company cheques. In his rage he ignored this and ordered Tanis to hand over the cheque book, wrote it out and signed it on the line below which was written 'Company director'. Poor Tanis ran down to Queensway, they paid up, and Spike had his money. When the Inland Revenue got wind of this they pounced. If he had signed a cheque and the bank had cashed it then Spike must be a director after all. Therefore the company was being fined £6,000. When Spike read their letter he went berserk. His face and head seemed to swell and his words exploded between deep breaths.

'I' – gulp – 'am' – gulp – 'not' – a third wheezy breath, and then – '*a fucking director.*'

Director or not, Mr. O'Brien of the Inland Revenue wanted the money.

'All this because you were out of the office,' said Spike. 'By rights you should pay the fine.'

'In your dreams.'

He went to see Mr. O'Brien himself to swear he was not a director. Mr. O'Brien was sympathetic but explained that he had to 'go by the book'. Spike left and returned with his book, the Bible, and put it on O'Brien's desk. Placing his hand over it he said, 'I'm going by my book and I swear I'm not a director.' Spike also insisted that Tanis and I swore an affidavit in front of a Commissioner for Oaths which was then sent to Mr. O'Brien. It made no difference. The fine had to be paid.

My ex-husband once said that work was not a battlefield. I told him to try Number Nine for a day. Ray Galton once described my role as 'a battle with a job tacked on.' True enough, but as Ray added, 'At least it's not boring. The good times are very good and the bad times don't last for ever.' He understood Spike well: 'His generosity isn't compensation for being a bastard. He is generous nearly all the time. Then the illness takes over and for a while the bad, mean side comes out. Real Jekyll and Hyde stuff.'

Spike was not the only *Goon* who could behave like a devil.

Chapter Eleven

I saw Sellers at his worst during the filming of *Ghost in the Noonday Sun*. It was supposed to be a swashbuckling pirate comedy, not exactly your Errol Flynn. Spike returned from filming *The Three Musketeers* with Raquel Welch in Madrid, and was due to fly out almost immediately to join the shoot in Cyprus. Shortly before he left the director, Peter Medak, called to say it was imperative for the sake of all concerned that I should accompany him. This could mean only one thing: trouble.

Whenever Spike flew to meet Pete he and his driver Bert were always at the terminal to greet him. But we arrived at Nicosia airport and there was no sign of either of them. Was it a joke of some sort? wondered Spike. Instead the producer, Gareth Wigan, met us. Spike subsequently dubbed him 'the blue-eyed hatchet man', because he was known to take hard decisions. We went to collect our luggage. We waited. And waited. Spike was near hypnotized by the turning carousel by the time it shuddered to a halt.

'My bag is missing,' he screamed. 'I won't be able to sleep.'

His voice rose a few decibels. 'AND I WON'T BE ABLE TO WORK.'

The missing bag was packed with his remedies: tranquillizers, sleeping tablets, uppers, downers, the lot.

'I'll have to catch the next plane to London. That's what I'll do.'

I knew he meant it. Gareth assured him the company doctor would supply everything he required. Not good enough. He was going back by the next plane. Before he could find his way to the departure lounge an airline representative arrived to say another passenger had mistakenly picked up his bag and it was on its way to Famagusta. Gareth arranged to send a taxi to collect it but Spike refused to leave the airport until it was in his hands.

Four hours later we left for our base in Kyrenia, Spike nursing the bag on his lap, determined not to let it out of his sight. Then Gareth told us the news he had been saving.

'Pete has locked himself in his villa and won't see or speak to anyone until Spike looks at the rushes. He thinks they're a disaster but if you' – looking at Spike – 'think they are funny he will continue with the film. Otherwise he's off.'

So that was it: temperament. Everything was back to normal.

Spike and I went with Gareth to the viewing room. After three or four minutes Spike ordered, 'Stop! This is on a disaster course.'

At that point Medak arrived. He took a look at the rushes and said, 'All you need to do, Spike, is rewrite scenes 113, 179 and 188, and it'll take on a whole different character.' Now if anyone else had said that Spike would have told him what he could do, but he had total admiration and affection for Medak, so he agreed. Medak called a script conference at Pete's villa. Spike outlined his ideas and Sellers beamed his approval. 'Everything will be all right now that Spike's here.' With that rosy view of the future he invited everyone to stay to dinner, and the outlook was both optimistic and enthusiastic.

Except that Sellers did not turn up for the first day of filming the new scenes. Everyone hung around for hours before he phoned to tell Spike he was mentally ill and unable to work. Naturally Spike was sympathetic, but I wondered what Pete was up to now. I had heard that when he arrived at the five-bedroom villa put at his disposal Pete insisted on sleeping in the bedroom that had most of the morning sun. That puzzled me, because Pete normally hated the sun and avoided it whenever he could. But nobody in his entourage knew which bedroom got the most sun. I could hear his reaction. What did they mean they did not know? Had he to tell them everything? All they had to do was establish which bedroom faced east. Nobody knew east from west? Then kindly hand him a compass and he would tell them. Compasses were not everyday items in Sellers' travelling baggage, however.

'Bert,' he ordered, 'go to Famagusta and buy a compass. Now!' It was quite a trip but Bert arrived back with one and Pete discovered which bedroom faced east. Whether he ever slept in it is a different question. So what was bothering him so much now that he could not film?

We got the answer the next day when Pete did not show again and once more phoned Spike.

'I'm being crucified,' he told him. 'It's Miranda.' Miranda Quarry was his current wife. 'She's screwing me for money. It's made me so ill I can't possibly work.'

Nor did he for three days. He had suddenly decided a vase in his Swiss home might be facing the wrong way. That could ruin the villa's vibes. He phoned his secretary, Sue Evans. 'Fly to Gstaadt and take the vase back to London.' Only once the vase was relocated was he prepared to resume filming.

In the meantime Medak had shot around Pete. When he realized how much Spike had improved the script he decided Spike could film during the day and rewrite more scenes of an evening. Medak, I thought, you are pushing your luck.

Filming was on Cyprus's famous twelve-mile beach and on

board an Arab dhow moored off it. The dhow looked beautiful – until it moved. There was a lazy swell and the boat pitched, rolled and yawed in a stomach-churning, corkscrew motion. On the fourth day Pete turned up on the beach. Everyone was barefoot, but Pete, as well as avoiding the sun, had a thing about getting sand between his toes, so was wearing black socks. He also had a plan, but that did not become evident until later.

With the film's mounting problems it was a bonus that Spike fell in love with Kyrenia, the coastline and countryside. He spurned the offer of a chauffeured limousine and instead opted for a self-drive Mini Moke. 'Always have your own wheels,' he told me. This happy mood, the glorious sun, warm sea and wine made him think of matters other than work. One evening over dinner, he said, in what he no doubt considered a throwaway manner, 'Liz would love it here.' What about Paddy? I thought. There was a pause as he gazed into the distance, as if waiting for inspiration. Not a very long pause.

'I know. Let's bring Liz out.'

I do not know how I suppressed a smile. He was trying to give the impression that he merely wanted to improve the life of others. But I knew what was on his mind.

I had always liked Liz Cowley enormously; she was a good match for him and great fun, always prepared to argue the point with him. Spike's spirits improved whenever she was around. So she was flown out and we had a wonderful weekend, with long days on the beach and leisurely dinners of an evening.

The morning after she left Spike fell and cut his knees when the dhow lurched unexpectedly. Now we got the noble Spike, something new to me. Although in pain he insisted on continuing. 'Just get the doctor to clean them up. Medak has enough on his hands with Pete.'

Just as everyone seemed eager to do everything they could to make the film a success the sea became unseasonably rough and seasickness made a mockery of the schedules. First to be affected was Pete's make-up man, Stuart Freebourn. Then the make-up girls succumbed, followed by those in wardrobe. Actors Tony Franciosa and Spike's old pal, Bill Kerr, and the remainder of the cast came next, and Medak and the sound crews were the last to be afflicted. But work had to continue. Spike and I were absolutely fine and Pete had his own solution, having hired a speedboat to stand by the dhow. Between shooting and during the lunch break he would get into this much steadier craft and recline under a canopy to protect him from the sun, leaving the rest of us to cope as best we could. His behaviour made me uneasy. Something was going on in that devious mind of his.

Out it came one evening over dinner. 'The script is being fucked around too much. It's not on.'

Medak did not buy that. He believed the problem was that Pete did not look at the script until minutes before shooting. He then often argued about its content, demanding that Spike rewrite it immediately 'while he waited' – insinuating that he was the one being held up because of the faults of others. Spike backed up Medak and told Pete where he could go.

Everything went back to being normally abnormal but it was not long before Pete tried a new tactic. He had already fired the two original producers and now he had Medak in his sights. Spike did not like that one little bit. Pete then fell ill, too ill to work, and production came to a halt.

He returned a few days later, probably late by design, for a shoot on the twelve-mile beach. The rest of the cast and crew had been waiting for him, sweltering in temperatures of 110°F, for four hours. There are no printable words for what they now thought of the star. Medak described the scene to me:

> He arrived in his speedboat, fell into the water as he got out, and walked up the beach, dripping wet. He drew me away from the crew so they couldn't hear what he was about to say, put his arms round me and said, 'Darling, you know what we

should do. You should quit this film and, as I have director approval in my contract, I'll turn down every director they put up. They won't pay you if you quit but under the terms of my contract they have to pay me in full. So then I'll quit and give you half of my money and the picture will be shut down.' He gave me that conspiratorial look of his. 'What do you think, darling?'

I look at him. The water was dripping off him and there was a look of insanity about him. I pointed to the crew.

'You see all those poor fuckers. They've been building the camera tracks since five this morning in the baking sun, no shade. You turn up four hours late and you don't even have your make up on. You're soaking wet, totally out of your mind and you make this proposal. Now understand this. We both agreed this contract. You are the one that got me into this fucking film and the only way you'll get me out of it is to put on your wig, your false teeth and your costume and let's shoot it.'

He didn't speak to me directly for about three weeks.

Then one day Pete went up to him and once more put his arms round him. Here we go again, thought Medak.

'Darling,' he said, 'in ten days' time, a Sunday, we start night shooting. So the day is free and I've decided to shoot this Benson and Hedges commercial I've told you about, and because I love you I want you to direct me and Spike in it.'

I stare at him and say, 'I can't even get this fucking picture finished because you won't speak to me directly and now you want me to do this commercial on the only day I can rest and sleep. Get some other fucking idiot to do it or do it yourself. It should be easy for you because you know everything better than anyone else.' He just looks at me. Needless to say Sunday came round and there I was shooting this commercial with

him and Spike in Kyrenia harbour with them wearing their
pirate outfits.

The plot of the commercial was simple enough. Pete, Spike and
a cohort, played by James Villiers, were supposed to be breaking
into a customs shed. Pete had to jam a Benson and Hedges
packet into the alarm bell so it would not ring. Medak went up
to him and explained the shot, which had already been agreed
with everyone concerned and storyboarded. The lighting would
reflect beautifully on the gold packet as he held it in his hand.
A wonderful shot.

'Daddy,' Pete said, 'didn't anyone tell you I can't touch a
cigarette packet? I simply can't touch it.'

'You've got to be putting me on. What am I doing here? I
should be fast asleep. It's my rest day, the first I've had after ten
days' shooting,' Medak said. 'But here we are, filming a cigarette
commercial for which you are getting paid a fortune, and now
you say you can't touch the packet.'

Pete said, 'No, I can't. I'm chairman of the Anti-Smoking
League and it's in my contract that I'm not allowed to touch
cigarettes. Dennis [Sellinger, his agent] should have told you.'

Medak was speechless. 'You mean to tell me you are getting
£50,000 and a Merc and you won't touch the packet?'

Pete nodded.

Medak went over to Spike, who was taking his shoes off. 'This
lunatic friend of yours won't touch the cigarette packet and
flash it in the light so I can get a great shot of it. He won't
touch it!'

Spike backed away from him, took a step too far, pitched over
the edge of the harbour and fell into the boat that had been
prepared for the last shot of the commercial, in which the actors
were supposed to make their getaway. Now Spike, from the
boat he had broken, said, 'I can't touch the packet either. I'm
deputy chairman of the Anti-Smoking League. Don't ask me to

do this because I'll have to say no and I don't want to say no to you.'

Medak wondered if he was the one who had lost touch with reality. He said, 'He's getting £50,000 and you're getting £25,000 for a one-day shoot and neither of you will touch the cigarette packet? You both knew this was a cigarette commercial. You're putting me on.'

Spike swore on his life that he was not. In desperation, Medak turned to Villiers. 'These two idiots won't touch the cigarette packet and they are getting £75,000 between them.'

Villiers said he wished they would pay him that much; he was only on £2000 and he could see that disappearing, which was a problem because he needed it to settle his bar bill.

'Where's the bloody cigarette packet?' he asked. 'Show me what to do.'

Medak was grateful to him because he needed his £3000 for his overdraft to keep Mr. Little happy at Barclays Bank in Haymarket. They started to shoot again. Pete, of course, kept his £50,000 and the car, and Spike donated his fee to charity to save three trees in Finchley.

Although filming was not finished I had to return to London on urgent business. The other producers were anxious for the film shot so far to be delivered to them in London, so I offered to take it with me. Spike pleaded with me not to go. 'You are leaving me facing a disaster. How can you do this to me?' In the end *Ghost* was so bad it never went on general release. The cast, crew and director finally wrapped it up and left Kyrenia. It was not long before the Turkish invasion, when the beautiful medieval harbour was bombed and destroyed.

Medak's hair had turned grey in the process of filming. 'It took seventy days to shoot and me five years to recover,' he said. 'Pete and Spike were geniuses. Pete was insane and evil. Spike was slightly touched but delightfully so and with a heart of gold. I loved them both, which must make me more insane than the two of them put together. Afterwards I wondered why I had forgotten to ask Pete about all the dope he smoked. Wasn't that banned in the rules of the Anti-Smoking League?'

Pete went abroad to appear in another film while Spike returned to start rehearsals for *Treasure Island* and at last got around to rewriting his one-man show for a tour of Australia. He was in a sunny mood as everything was going swimmingly, creating a happy atmosphere at Number Nine. He breezed into my office one morning.

'Send this telegram to Pete,' he said. ' "Dear Pete. Please ignore first telegram." ' He grinned. 'You'll see. He'll ring you, not me, to ask what was in the first.'

A few hours later Pete phoned. 'Norm. What was in the first telegram?'

I had difficulty containing myself.

'Pete. There wasn't one.'

There was a gasp. 'Bastard!' He slammed down the phone.

Spike thought it was hilarious. At that time telegrams, which were delivered by hand by a boy on a red Post Office bicycle, were one of his favourite means of communication. The next day from his office he sent one to me downstairs. 'Dear Norma. Money can't buy poverty. Love you. Spike.'

But his mood declined into severe depression, with constant rows at home. In the autumn he flew to Australia and saw his mother and Desmond, then Harry in New Zealand. I hoped he would recapture the happy atmosphere of the previous trip, but Spike was unable to shake off his depression. Instead he would telephone me to rail against Paddy. She was icy cold, and he dreaded calling her from halfway across the world just to be met with indifference, yet he wanted to make up. But as it turned out Paddy was unforgiving.

He was away for several weeks. Because the plane back to the U.K. had to make an unexpected stopover in Singapore, he was in a terrible rage when he arrived at the office so decided not to go home. He was due to go into the Fitzroy Nuffield, this time for an operation to straighten a finger. Poor Matron Roberts, I thought. There was the usual litany of conditions. He wanted the same room as last time because it was quiet; no other would do. If he could not have it then the operation was off, understand? I picked up the phone.

'Hello, Matron Roberts. It's Norma here, remember?'

There was a sigh at the other end. But he got what he wanted and moved into his old room. Before the operation he wrote a message on his left arm: 'Doc, be as economical as possible. I've had a bad year. This is the hand. The other signs cheques.'

After the operation he asked me to take his diary to the hospital, and although the depression was milder he wrote, 'In abhorrent memory of Colonel George Armstrong Custer, U.S. Cavalry, who on this day in 1868 massacred, without warning, the village of Chief Black Kettle and his Cheyennes, men, women and children. November 27th.' As far as I know he had not been reading about the American Indians and the atrocities committed against them, but the anniversary was sufficient to prolong his depression.

Spike ended 1972 playing happy families, inviting Pete and his children to afternoon tea on Christmas Day. That could be lethal. Amazingly, he reported that they all had a wonderful day, and as a bonus he and Paddy had passed the whole day without a quarrel. Nevertheless that was all forgotten by 1 January 1973, when he wrote in his diary, 'HERE WE BLOODY WELL GO AGAIN.'

It did not take an *Old Moore* to forecast that 1973 would not bode well for depressions. Sydney Gottlieb was counselling Paddy and mentioned that it might be a good idea if he were to talk to Spike. Spike had a tantrum at the thought that Sydney might take him to task over his behaviour towards his wife. Guilt? This was followed by another depression and he had to turn down another invitation to the Society of Distinguished Songwriters' dinner. 'Have finally given up after twenty years of struggling to be respectable,' he wrote in his diary. 'Children are lovely. Adults are shit. Stayed awake all night.' Then he locked himself away upstairs.

Whenever Spike was down the telephone calls from his girl-friends poured in. It was like a bush telegraph. How they found out he was depressed I do not know. Liz – I was about to add faithful Liz, but even she would find that hilarious – was generally the first to say she was there if he felt like letting off steam. Other callers included Pat Elstone, another journalist and longstanding girlfriend, Margaret Maughan and Jane Gould. Roberta Watt understood depression because she had suffered from it herself. She appreciated that things could get bad for his carer too, which I suppose is what I was. 'I'm here if he wants me,' she would say, 'and if you do too.' Then there would be calls from another dozen or so peripheral girlfriends, those who were conversational companions.

The depression did not lift and I was not hopeful when BBC Radio asked if he would write a piece for *What Shall We Tell the Children?*. Amazingly he agreed and something beautiful emerged. After that he locked the door of his office and went back to bed. It was three weeks before he rang me downstairs.

'A jazz musician would never start a war,' he said. 'They're not the kind of people.'

He replaced the receiver without any further explanation. However, he still dragged himself to the studio a few days later to shoot a commercial for the *Guardian* newspaper and it was not long before there were the usual signs that he was emerging from his depression. He went home to Paddy. But after a few days he came back in a rage and wrote in his diary, 'I've never been so ill, spiritually, physically, mentally. All I want of live [sic] is peace, love, understanding and it's not. I arrived home to fucking barking dogs!' Spike was paranoid about barking dogs: one bark could mean no work for a week or more. Whenever he was on tour or holiday I had to make sure there were no dogs in the hotel or within hearing distance because a single yap would signal an immediate return to the office. This time Sydney Gottlieb gave him an injection to ease the torment, but it had no effect. The entry in his diary two weeks later read, 'Ill but carrying on – why?'

Then the mania took a new twist. Spike and Eric shared a bathroom at Number Nine. Both had a key, as did I, but nobody else in the office. The bath had been installed so they could use it going to or from the studio, and Spike used it daily when living at the office. One morning he stormed out and shouted downstairs, 'Someone's pinched my shampoo. Who's got it? It's a special one – just for me.' It was not a special one at all; he just had dandruff. Tanis bought it for him at Boots. She was at her desk in reception so I shouted to her, 'Go and get another one.' Spike heard, which made matters worse. 'I won't have it,' he said. 'That was my special shampoo. We've got a thief here and I'm going to find out who it is.'

At that time some of the offices in the building were let to an organization unconnected to Spike or Eric. This made no difference to him. He knocked on each door and demanded that everyone assemble downstairs in the hall for questioning. Incredibly, they all filed in, probably because they had never come across anyone in such a rage. I stayed put. Tanis called out, 'He wants you in the line-up as well, Norma.'

Previously, when anything went missing or failed to arrive on time, be it pens, special paper or some other fad, I would say it was my fault to avoid the lengthy inquisition followed by furious telephone calls to suppliers and the post office. It was the easy way out. For once I was not having any of that.

'I'm not playing silly games.'

'Please, Norma,' said Tanis. 'Just to get it over with.'

'No.'

Just as Spike was working himself into a great rage, Johnny

Speight, on his way upstairs to see Eric, walked into my office.

'What's going on?'

'We're having a Captain Queeg and strawberries day,' I said. 'Leave him and he'll get over it.'

Johnny thought it was hilarious. Spike, the failed detective and inquisitor, had to allow the line-up to disperse, crime unsolved. A few minutes later Johnny rang down from Eric's office.

'I've been on to the Harrow Road police station and they've got two bottles of shampoo there. They want to know if Spike would like to go over to identify which one is his.'

'Johnny, please don't. Just leave it. Otherwise it'll go on all day and things will only get worse.'

Tanis had gone to Boots to buy another bottle. She came back with it just as Dot, the office cleaner, arrived. I heard them talking in reception and then Dot came into my office.

'I threw the old shampoo out, Norma. There was hardly any in it.'

I went upstairs and tried his door. It was locked.

'Dot threw your shampoo out because it was just about empty. There are no thieves in the office so we had all that performance for nothing.'

There was a moment's silence.

'Why don't you all fuck off?'

End of the mystery of the missing shampoo.

Some months later in April he sauntered into my office and suggested that we should have dinner alone at the Trattoo. Normally he would say, 'Let's have dinner tonight. I'll bring someone and you bring a boyfriend or girlfriend – or whoever turns you on.' I had a feeling of unease as I went home to change. When I arrived at the restaurant he was sipping his usual Orvieto and I noticed his was the only glass on the table. So it was to be à deux. He beckoned the wine waiter, Michaela.

'A glass of champagne for Norma.'

As he went to the bar Spike turned and said, 'Roberta is pregnant.'

There were no histrionics, no fury or sense of injustice.

'Is it yours?' I had to ask. It was not what could be described as an exclusive relationship for either party.

He looked hurt and paused. 'I think so.'

'How many months?'

'Five.'

I nearly dropped my glass. Though when I remembered my earlier conversation with Roberta it was less of a surprise to me than it was to him.

'She's told you when it's too late to have an abortion.'

'An abortion is out of the question. I couldn't go along with that.' This was his Catholicism coming to the fore. Just as quickly it left him. 'Paddy and the children must never know about this. It would break her heart and I couldn't face the kids.' I felt like telling him he should have thought of that earlier, but he had enough to cope with. He did not rant or rave. He was shattered.

He studied me for a moment. 'You're not all that surprised.'

I shook my head and told him about the time Roberta had said she wanted his child.

He listened and shrugged. 'I'll need to take care of them. Will you look after that for me and do whatever has to be done?'

'Of course,' I said.

From then on his spirits recovered: he had disposed of the problem by giving it to me. We talked about Roberta. She seemed a warm and friendly girl, I said, but with an air of sadness. He sighed. 'You know, she had a very bad marriage. She's prone to depression. I was merely trying to help.' So that was what he called it.

The help arrived on 2 August 1973 in the form of Romany Anne Jocelyn Watt. I had visited Roberta during her pregnancy after Spike learnt she was in a psychiatric home in Kent. The break-up of her marriage, an acrimonious divorce and then pregnancy had affected her deeply. She remained there for five weeks but seemed fine after she was released, and insisted she did not want anything from Spike but his baby. Once Romany was born she decided she needed his financial help after all. To begin with she wanted to show her parents and friends in Canada the new arrival. She said, 'I wouldn't dare to fly all that way by myself with a small baby in cramped economy conditions.' So she asked for a first-class ticket to Toronto, on to Montreal, then Vancouver, Castlegar, back to Vancouver, returning to Toronto and finally to London. After her ticket was bought Roberta then asked Spike to clear her overdraft. Before we could do so another letter arrived announcing that the overdraft had increased by half. At the bottom of the letter Spike scrawled, 'JUST KEEP FUCKING PAYING'.

That was not the end. She wanted to buy her rented cottage in Fawkham, Kent. Spike was never one to pile up his money in the bank so I had to arrange for a loan. And when the cottage was eventually sold, she said, she wanted him to pay any capital gains tax due. And she would need maintenance. Spike was getting deeper and deeper into the mire. Enough was enough. I urged him to take the matter to court. No, that might upset Paddy and the children and he did not want that. I thought he was being taken for a ride.

The turning point came when we discovered she had tried to cash in the first-class ticket for one in economy. Spike was furious. He considered it to be an act of betrayal. I had been waiting for a breakdown and this was the catalyst. I was only surprised it had not come earlier. This time it was four Tuinol a day, alone in his office, the door locked and a heavy atmosphere throughout the building. It was six days before he appeared. Our solicitor brokered a trade-off and Spike never mentioned the negotiations again.

Not long afterwards a stranger telephoned me. As Spike would have said, it gives me great pleasure to have forgotten his name. He said he was a friend of Roberta's and wanted to come to the office for coffee. I had heard of him and agreed because I needed to know what he was up to. I could not risk Paddy and the children getting to know about Romany.

The man was tall and thin and bearded. He insisted repeatedly that he only had Roberta's best interests at heart; if the story was ever published it would harm Spike, he said, never directly expressing the demand which lay behind his remarks.

'You have to do what you have to do,' I said. Then I stood up, thanked him for coming and told him I would have to finish the discussion because I was busy.

It was a devastating few months. That summer Paddy had discovered a lump in her breast. It was malignant. Spike was distraught. He told me, and so passionately that I believe he meant it, that if he could take the cancer from her body and put it in his own he would. He made sure that she had the very best treatment. She underwent a mastectomy and recovered, and for a time their rows came to an end. But despite his sorrow he continued to take his girlfriends out for dinner and whatever afterwards. I have never come to terms with that.

Chapter Twelve

Jimmy Verner never forgot his first day as company manager for Bernard Miles at the Mermaid in 1963. Bernard had persuaded him to leave a good job at the Old Vic to help prepare for *The Bed Sitting Room*, then in rehearsal. Jimmy arrived to be greeted by the sound of funny noises from Spike's dressing room. Unable to find anyone to talk to, he went in. Spike ignored him completely; he was practising for a scene in which he had to blow a series of raspberries.

The sound man was meant to record the raspberries so Spike could listen to them and decide which was the juiciest. Unfortunately the sound man did not turn up so Jimmy was recruited instead. Having exhausted his repertoire, Spike asked Jimmy to play them back. He did not like what he heard. 'Come back in a couple of hours,' he said. Jimmy came back and recorded some more. Still not right according to Spike. The whole day passed with Spike blowing raspberries and Jimmy taping them.

When Jimmy returned for what he hoped would be the final recording he found Spike dashing round the room wielding a fly swat. 'I thought that was odd because there weren't any flies in the room,' he recalled. He did not realize there was a fly swatting scene in the play. Then Bernard burst into the dressing room with a wild look in his eye and a dagger in his hand. 'There's something wrong with this trick dagger,' he told Spike. Neither of them paid any attention to Jimmy. 'I might as well have not been there as these two eccentrics weighed up the merits of the different raspberries and discussed the workings of the trick dagger. It was surreal. I decided, for reasons of sanity, that I'd have to leave.' After opening night he resigned.

Ten years later, after a successful career as an impresario, Jimmy telephoned to find out whether we would be interested in arranging a tour of *The Bed Sitting Room*. Odd perhaps after his previous experience, but as he said recently, he had either forgotten what had happened or there was an overriding need to make money. We gave him the go-ahead, but I knew the only way it could work, or even last past the first week, would be if Jimmy kept his distance from Spike and allowed me to deal with him.

'If anyone puts any pressure on Spike, for whatever reason, he'll walk out,' I warned. 'You tell me what you want and I'll put it to him.'

Jimmy took me to lunch at Beotty's in the West End and agreed that if a problem cropped up he would hassle me about it and not Spike. He stuck to that and as a result they never, in many years of working together, had a row. As Jimmy found it uncomfortable to have dinner with Spike he avoided doing so, and instead sent him a case of wine every Friday. Spike merely thought of him as 'the chap in the background who puts things on and earns his money the easy way', while in fact Jimmy was accustomed to being very hands-on and must have found it difficult to stand back.

The tour made a great deal of money for everyone concerned. Which is not to say that everything was easy. There were several dramas and tantrums during the tour and Johnny Vivian, one of the actors, described that time as 'Days of Wine and Neuroses'. Jimmy Verner has no idea what sparked them. 'They could have been caused by Paddy, the dresser, a picture on the wall, me, who knows?'

The run started in Southsea and then went to Wimbledon, Oxford, Liverpool, Manchester, Nottingham, Birmingham and Leeds. I went to see it at Liverpool and could tell Spike was tired with the strain of performing two hours a night and writing his second volume of war memoirs for Michael Joseph, *Rommel? Gunner Who?*. He was down when I arrived. He told me he had driven around Liverpool in his Mini before the show and seen a billboard advertising a Judy Garland film. Her smiling face transfixed him for several minutes. Back in the dressing room he was still gripped by the fear that he would end up the same way as Garland, all alone and not a friend in the world. I tried to reassure him but to no avail. He was filled with self-pity. Something else must have happened, but I never found out what upset him.

There was a crisis when the show opened at Nottingham. Spike phoned me the next morning.

'I'm not going on tonight. Sixth row from the front, the third seat is squeaking and I can't stand the noise. It's driving me mad.'

I told him to take it easy, I would have it oiled. I rang Jimmy in London. He had already had a call from his company manager informing him that Spike was refusing to go on.

'Jimmy, for God's sake tell them to get a can of three-in-one and oil the seat,' I said.

'It's gone beyond that,' said Jimmy. 'He insists that every single seat in the house is oiled. There are fourteen hundred seats and six hours to oil them, and I'll have to pay the men to do it. You go to the theatre and I'll tell the company manager to take on three people to oil the seats in the stalls and three to do the same in the circle.'

As I travelled north I wondered whether Spike was already travelling south. Knowing Spike I realized that one squeaking seat could spell the end of the tour. But he was still in Nottingham when I arrived, a happy man. Astute Jimmy had asked that Spike call at the theatre at two o'clock – when he knew the men with the oil cans would be busy. Once Spike was satisfied someone was doing what he had asked he left. As arranged beforehand by Jimmy, the men packed it in after finishing the first six rows. 'Do you know,' he said afterwards, 'the old devil was right. It was the third one in on the sixth row.'

The rest of the tour went off without a hitch and Jimmy went on to arrange five more of Spike's one-man shows from 1973 until the early Eighties.

One constant in Spike's life was his house at 127 Holden Road in Finchley. He loved that spacious Edwardian house in its quiet tree-lined street. When the trees were threatened by developers Spike fought to preserve them, but he knew that the peace of Holden Road would soon be a thing of the past. Developers were dividing the houses into flats, and by the start of 1974 Spike's was the last remaining to be converted. When builders started working on both neighbouring buildings and his precious drug-induced sleep was disturbed by their early morning starts he decided it was time to leave.

That was not the only problem to face Paddy at the time. About twelve months earlier Spike had written a letter and addressed it to himself. 'Post it,' he told me, 'but don't give it to me until I tell you.' Shortly after New Year he called me from his home.

'You can read out the letter I addressed to myself.'

It said, 'Paddy will kill somebody when she's driving her car. Please God don't let Jane be in the car.'

'It's happened,' he said. I knew that Paddy's car had skidded on black ice one morning after she had taken Jane to school, just before Christmas. It mounted the pavement and knocked a man over. Two weeks later the poor fellow died in hospital. Paddy, who had only recently returned from hospital herself, was riven with guilt. I do not believe she was prosecuted in the end.

With their conflicting personalities, it followed that the houses Spike liked Paddy did not and vice versa. As a result of the rows that ensued Spike took to his bed at the office. I was greatly relieved when an estate agent eventually introduced them to Monkenhurst, 'delightfully situated on Hadley Common', according to the particulars. It was a very odd house, combining all the extravagant follies a self-made Victorian businessman would want in his home to demonstrate that he had truly arrived. It incorporated a tower and the unkind would have called it a folly. Only an eccentric could have fallen in love with it. Of course Spike delighted in its large, well-proportioned rooms and huge kitchen and, as he mounted the stairs on that first viewing, each of its four floors revealed more rooms that delighted him. Paddy was not so sure; it was sufficiently large to require two or more staff to run it. But Spike knew he had found his ideal house and they took it. He lavished care, taste and money on restoring Monkenhurst to its original glory and it became a warm, welcoming home for Paddy and the children.

Silé and Jane were now at Channing School in Highgate. From a very early age Jane came to the office every Thursday afternoon for flute lessons with Mr. Horner from the Royal College of Music. All those years and all those lessons paid off handsomely, and now she is master of several instruments and a gifted performer. I saw less of Spike's other children. At that time Laura was attending the Byam Shaw School of Art and turning into an extremely talented artist, so good that she went on to illustrate one of Spike's books, *Open Heart University*. Sean had left school and set up a painting and decorating business with Michael Sellers, Pete's son. I cannot remember who got them the job, but one of their first was to paint Marty Feldman's house in Hampstead. And Spike persuaded George Martin to give them work at Air Studios. Like fathers, like sons, they caused mayhem and mild-mannered George had to kick them out.

The stress and strain of house hunting and the move to Monkenhurst took its toll and for three months afterwards Spike's mood swings were worse than ever. It was during this period that he was commissioned to write an article for *Nova*, a hugely popular magazine, and was behind with the delivery, which was extremely rare for him. I badgered him and eventually he handed it to me on 14 February, the day it should have been at the *Nova* office. I read it at home that evening and found it disappointing. The next morning I left it in his office with a message that a rewrite was called for. I had a meeting in town and when I returned there was a note on my desk which read, 'Prick! I'm a best seller!'

I wrote back, 'You won't be if I let this go out.' My criticism

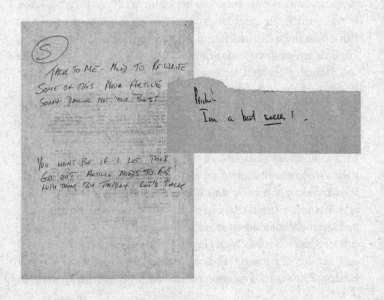

had the desired effect. Two days later another version arrived on my desk, which for me bore the Milligan stamp.

Nova commissioned Cecil Beaton to photograph Spike in his office. I was thrilled to meet this famous man. He had designed the costumes for *My Fair Lady*, a show I had seen eight times, photographed so many great figures of the twentieth century, and had an affair with Greta Garbo, all heavy stuff for me. He arrived wearing a cloak and a large black hat. I was suitably impressed but Spike was not and thought he was a poseur. *Nova* were not impressed either and rang to say they were disappointed with the photographs. Would Spike sit again for another photographer?

No, I told them, he was filming. They liked the article and persisted, reminding me they had paid for the article and a photographic session. I pointed out that Spike had fulfilled his contract; the fact they did not like Beaton's photographs had nothing to do with him. The budget would not stretch to another fee but they offered a case of champagne. Now I knew Spike never drank it but to me it was – and still is – the elixir of life. Spike told me to forget the fee and enjoy the champagne, which was fine by me.

Although I enjoyed the bubbles I was rather a philistine about champagne in those days. As soon as it arrived I opened the case and was disgusted. The cheapskates. Everyone knew that champagne came in a green glass bottle with a concave bottom. These bottles were colourless and with the flat bottoms of ordinary wine. What was more they had flashy gold labels. Obviously, it was some sort of sparkling wine so I put it in the wine cellar at Number Nine, where it would be handy to give as Christmas presents and to long-suffering messengers delivering late night packages. Over the next several weeks four bottles were given to delivery boys. Then I forgot all about the stuff.

That October I was glancing through the Harrods Christmas catalogue when I came across a full page devoted to one bottle of champagne. It looked familiar. After reading the description I went quickly down to the cellar. Disbelief. The advertisement and the bottle in my hand were one and the same. I read the description in the catalogue again. Louis Roederer Cristal. Made especially for the second Czar of Russia, who did not want his champagne bottle to look like any other. The price was outrageous. I ran upstairs to Spike with the bottle and the catalogue.

'Look at this,' I said. 'This is what I thought was the cheapskate champagne from *Nova*.' He knew I had been giving it away and thought it a huge joke. He asked me how many were left and I said there were eight.

'Take them home, taste them and know that Nicholas II sipped the same champagne. But don't get a liking for it or you'll be working the arse off me.'

He got his money's worth out of the story. For years he told his friends, 'The posh bird I have as my manager loves champagne but doesn't know a bloody thing about it.'

The BBC and I had agreed that it was time to put *Q6* back on the production schedule and Spike started to work at a feverish rate with his co-writer Neil Shand. Then something happened that almost put an end to any future television appearances. I came out of my hairdresser's salon one day in May and saw the bills for the evening newspapers: 'SPIKE MILLIGAN ARRESTED'. I grabbed a paper and read the story. Spike had shot a boy.

I knew he had been having trouble with vandals in the garden and on every occasion telephoned the police, insisting that they log his complaint. Then one morning he discovered that the yobs had crapped in his daughter Jane's Wendy House. That was the end. He kept vigil at the bedroom window until one afternoon he saw them at it. Out came his air rifle. Bang. A howl. A hit.

I rushed to the office and phoned him. He had shown them. They would not come back to his garden in a hurry.

'No. Because you'll probably be in prison.'

'Well, I'll sew mailbags badly,' he said.

Given his rifle, I would have shot him myself at that moment. I said I would get a good solicitor and perhaps we could negotiate a deal.

'No thank you. And I don't want a solicitor. I'll defend myself.'

The idea was so laughable I wanted to scream. But defend himself he did, and obtained a verdict a solicitor would have envied. There were strong echoes of his father and the case of the stolen cigarettes. Leo would have been proud of him.

When Spike came before the Highgate magistrates' court he was all confidence. 'Your honour,' he said, 'my garden has been the target for vandals for two years. Every time they've raided it the matter has been reported to the police. They've stolen four ladders, excreted on my steps and my daughter's Wendy House, damaged my work studio and pulled down the fence. As lawful methods had failed I decided to track them down myself. I am not a young man and had no intention of being set upon by thugs. For that reason, and no other, I went to the bottom of my garden with an air rifle. It is only a weak .177 pellet gun and I knew it wasn't lethal.'

Then a police officer said he was appalled at the damage done to the garden, and almost as an afterthought added that the boy had been slightly injured in his shoulder. Spike was given a twelve-month conditional discharge on the grounds of extreme provocation. A grinning Spike left the court and, ever the performer, pointed his hands at waiting photographers, the forefingers extended like an OK Corral gunfighter. Most papers splashed the picture, all with similar captions. 'Dead Eye Spike. The Great White Hunter of North Finchley' ran one.

I was absolutely furious. 'Why the hell did you do that?'

'Now don't get upset. My father was a journalist and I always have sympathy for the lads.' And with that he dismissed the shooting episode.

Far from being tilted into a depression, Spike emerged from the court hearing more or less unscathed. He continued to work on the series and a book he was writing, *Transports of Delight*, and prepared for the June opening of his one-man show at the Adelphi Theatre.

The one-man show had grown out of musical evenings in the Sixties with Paddy singing and Spike reading poetry with Robert Graves, and Spike first took it on tour to Australia in 1967. It changed shape over the years and, as with most things in Spike's life, it involved doing more or less what he liked. If he was on form the show lasted two hours or more, if not he would cut it short without a qualm and blame the audience for not liking him. Although always spontaneous, it did have a loose format. Spike opened by cranking an invisible motor while telling the audience that nothing could go wrong because nothing had been prepared. Then he would tell stories and read poetry until he thought it was time to do his impressions.

Spike's idea of an impression was to take a straw hat from the prop box, lie on the floor, fold his arms across his chest and shout 'Maurice Chevalier' (this was just after Chevalier had died). Or he might produce an oversized tam o'shanter, put it on and talk nonsense for about a minute in an incomprehensible Glaswegian accent. He would do perhaps fifteen of these a night, according to how he felt. He closed the first half by taking out a series of false noses. Putting on the smallest false nose was his cue to sing 'Only a nose, I bring you' à la Rose Marie. As he continued the song he quickly changed the noses, each one bigger than the last. Then he did two minutes with an enormous black hat. He put it on his head, raised his hands and turned it around, as if screwing it on. It was hilarious and he changed the chat that went with it from one night to the next. He kept on twisting and the hat gradually covered more and more of his body until he had disappeared.

The second half saw Spike sitting at a small square table with a bottle of wine – the real stuff – and a glass. He would put on a bald wig, look at the audience and sigh 'Oh, dearie me' in that quavery voice he used for Old Min in *The Goon Show*. This might continue for as long as eight minutes, him sitting in a chair saying, 'Oh, dearie me. I sit all day in this chair saying dearie me.' Then he told stories about old men, always ending, 'Oh, dearie me'. In print it does not seem funny, but because of the way he performed it the audience found it hilarious. Then he read more of his poetry and told stories. Finally the curtain rose on a small combo with Spike on his trumpet playing all his favourite numbers, and at the Adelphi he was lucky enough to have Alan Clare to accompany him. He would do this six nights a week for twelve to sixteen weeks, changing the material every six months or so. For someone so mentally fragile his discipline and stamina could be amazing.

The show was a great success on the number one theatres circuit and one tour, in 1975, was at the same time that Jimmy was staging the failing *Black Mikado* in London. Each Saturday he would send one of his men with a cardboard shoebox to wherever Spike was appearing. Once he had collected the takings, he would whizz back to London so Jimmy could pay the cast of the *Black Mikado* as soon as the curtain went down.

I was uneasy because this particular tour was going too well. It was not normal. Jimmy telephoned one Monday evening to say Spike had not shown up at Bradford for a sound and lighting check. With more confidence than I felt I told him not to worry. Spike would be driving north and had probably been distracted by something of interest to him, but he would arrive eventually. Wrong. Tanis then informed me that Spike was upstairs and had been all day, and probably the night before as well. I went upstairs and told him he had better get a move on as he was due to open in Bradford in a few hours.

He had had a bust-up with Paddy, he said. How could I be

so unfeeling? He was traumatized. I could see this was more than a tantrum, so I telephoned Jimmy to tell him that he would have to return the money to those who had bought tickets. It was a nightmare for him – no show at Bradford meant no cash for the *Black Mikado* – but he bounced back as he always did. A few days later he said, 'I love working with you and Spike but I don't like the menace that comes with it. You I can deal with, and you can deal with him, how I sometimes wonder, probably because you love him over and beyond all his faults.' I think he had it in a nutshell.

On that occasion Spike spent days in the office. The venom poured out. His relationship with Paddy did not work; he found the tension frightening, and she was so disorganized. He simply could not face going home. I toyed with the idea of ringing Jimmy to say his planned month-long run of the one-man show at the Mayfair Theatre in the West End would be off as well. But on second thoughts I decided it would be better to weather the storm and see what happened. Fortunately, Spike's mood did not get any worse and when the time came the show was a sell-out. In the second week of the run he rang me from the theatre.

'Some bastard's pinched my black hat. I can't go on without it.'

No hat, no show.

At that time I had had enough of his tantrums. He could tell the theatre manager himself why he was not going on. I had an appointment with my hairdresser. Soon after I had left Jimmy stormed in. Tanis told him where I had gone. 'She's like him,' he said. 'Always gets her priorities right.'

He tore round to the salon. What should we do? There was no alternative. 'We'll have to get someone to make another,' I said. I have forgotten who it was but a magical wardrobe girl did exactly that and Spike worked with it ever after.

One night Peter Sellers was in the audience. It could have

been the prolonged applause when the curtain came down but suddenly Pete wanted to be part of it. He collared Jimmy and begged him to work something out so he and his old mate could appear together in London. As they would for any good impresario, the box office till tinkled in Jimmy's head and the idea was irresistible. He took them out to Rules restaurant. They were both immensely enthusiastic, but Jimmy, being wise to the ways of temperamental stars, decided to get them to sign an agreement there and then. He had no paper with him so wrote it on the tablecloth and everyone signed it. Then the wine and the stories flowed. In the early hours, as they prepared to leave, Jimmy asked Harry, Rules's manager, to keep the tablecloth; he would collect it the next day on his way to the theatre. Sod's law intervened and after Harry had left for the night the waiters whisked all the tablecloths into the laundry bag, the agreement included. Not that it made any difference because Jimmy could not find a theatre free for when both of them were available. Just as well for his sake. He would have been a nervous wreck with the two of them together. In any case, I told Jimmy I would not get involved with Pete. Spike alone was bad enough.

In the summer of 1974 Spike left to work on the third volume of his memoirs, *Monty, His Part In My Victory*, for a month in Australia. He went off looking forward to seeing Grandma and, inevitably, there was an Australian girlfriend, Beverley George. Beverley had been in love with Spike ever since I had known him and, as with the members of the Bayswater Harem, she seemed prepared to rekindle the affair whenever he chose. He was only too glad to help with her campaign for the Bellbird Sanctuary on the Gosford coast, which was to be officially opened during his visit.

The affair with Beverley continued until he stopped touring Australia in the Eighties. On one occasion she flew to London 'to be with him'. She was an intense sort of girl and I did not want her to get hurt, so I told her about his other girlfriends and my belief that Spike would never leave Paddy. She looked at me uncomprehendingly and I realized that I was wasting my time.

He returned to do another tour of his one-man show for Jimmy Verner, who by this time was accustomed to, if not always prepared for, all his foibles. Before it started Spike had dinner with his great friend Ted Allbeury. They always got on together and Ted rang me the next morning to say he thought Spike looked tired, as if the spark had deserted him.

'People might not suspect it but he's a man who needs to be mothered. Fortunately for him you fit the bill. He's always needed somebody by his side who was a rock. He's lived a very full life and always at a hectic pace.' He paused. 'No, not a very full life, about fifty full lives.'

I mentioned that Alan Clare always maintained there were two people in Spike, while his brother Desmond thought there were four people bursting to get out, all at the same time.

'There's a Spike you can feel sorry for,' said Ted, 'and another you can envy.'

'How about the one you can hate?'

'If you mentioned that to him he would think you were having a bad time or sickening for a cold or something,' said Ted. He asked me what expressions I associated with Spike. 'What the fuck's wrong with you?' and 'Where the fuck have you been?' I told him.

'Not many people would put up with that but then you've enjoyed working with him. And I'll tell you why. It's the same as the exhilaration of riding a very wild but beautiful horse. You stick on and you fall off, but you always get back on again. Fortunately you've remembered to keep out of the way of the hooves.'

I mentioned that only the previous day, in one of his rosier moments, he had said to me, 'You know, you and I have never had an argument.'

Ted laughed. 'Since yesterday afternoon.'

'No. He meant it. Everything at that moment was lovely and in his mind that was the way it had always been.'

New Year's Day, 1975 was a different story. I was recovering at home from late night celebrations when the telephone rang. It was Spike, calling from Number Nine.

'This building is filthy,' he said. It was not, but there you go.

'Nobody is interested in it except me. I've spent two days washing the tiles outside the basement – with Brillo pads! Nothing else would shift the dirt. Ingrained. I've made a decision. I'm going to sell my half of the office.' He banged down the phone.

Happy New Year to you too, I thought. Why the hell had he spent New Year's Eve and the day before at the office cleaning tiles? I arrived at Number Nine the next morning to see a note for the occupants of the basement pinned to their door: 'ALL OF YOU GO AND LIVE IN A DUSTBIN BECAUSE THAT'S WHAT YOU DESERVE.'

Where was Spike? I found him still hard at it. Every cupboard – and there were cupboards on every landing – had been emptied. To him it was immaterial that the contents belonged to other companies in the building. Whatever had been in the cupboards had been chucked out, because in his opinion it was a fire hazard.

'Only I can be bothered to do this,' he fumed.

He had not finished. He hired a skip and tipped everything into it. It mattered not a jot to him that the files and documents could be important to others. I had seen this sort of mania before and knew it to be the build-up to a depression. Or perhaps he was priming to say, 'I'm too ill. Cancel Rhodesia.'

This was a show I had planned at the Seven Arts Theatre in Salisbury, now Harare. If I interfered with the clear-out he was quite capable of calling the trip off so I left him to get on with it. His anger was at its peak when his daughter, Jane, telephoned. She was very upset because her rabbit had pneumonia. Confronted by her sadness, his rage suddenly disappeared. The only thing that mattered now was Jane's rabbit. He rang the vet and arranged to meet him at Monkenhurst – not later but now, immediately! The state of the office forgotten, he tore off home.

Chapter Thirteen

Despite all his efforts Jane's rabbit died and Spike spent several days at home consoling her. Not the best start to the year, but helping his daughter seemed to invigorate him and an energetic, purposeful Spike returned to the office, not a Brillo pad in sight.

'Which hotel have you booked me into in Rhodesia?'

Good, he was going. The Monomatapa, I told him. He approved and then immediately got down to work, making additions and alterations to his one-man show ready for Rhodesia. He also agreed to write a new series, *The Melting Pot*, with Neil Shand for the BBC. Thank God that he was back into the work ethic. But not for long.

Yet again another crisis. He heard that the secretary to the first *Goon Show* was ill with anorexia nervosa. Goodbye Rhodesia, goodbye *Melting Pot*. Nothing mattered but the girl. They had long telephone conversations and Spike set himself the task of finding the best specialist for her illness. He found one in Harley Street and the girl, who lived in Cornwall, moved into Number Nine for several weeks while she received treatment, paid for by

Spike. Only once he was satisfied that he had done all he could was it hello again, Rhodesia, hello again, *Melting Pot*.

The Melting Pot started out as a television show. The idea first came to him in 1974 after he mentioned his concern about the number of illegal immigrants, mainly from Pakistan and India, arriving in England. I thought this was his pet hobby-horse for the week. He had a number of these and enjoyed passionately argued discussions, particularly about the human race, which he hated *en masse* (although I must say he loved more of the opposite sex than most of us). One of his favourite comments on people, for example, was, 'The only thing I have in common with them is that I am a *homo sapiens*.' If passing a large block of council flats he might say, 'Bloody breeding pens. More humanoids to jam the roads.'

Another of his gripes was, 'Yes, we have enough schools, enough hospitals, enough houses, but there are too many people. Bloody overpopulation.' He believed overpopulation due to lack of birth control would be a growing problem worldwide and, just like his concern about the eradication of elephants, whales and rain-forests, this has now become accepted as a global problem. When I asked if he, the father of four legitimate children, was not being somewhat hypocritical in publicly proclaiming that there should be no more than two for every family he paused, but only momentarily. Then came that cheeky, almost evil look of glee, which never failed to make me smile.

'It's okay, Farnesy. You haven't got any, so I've got your two.'

When Romany came on the scene I told him his equation had been blown to pieces. Then came his plaintive, sorrowful expression and his Catholicism surfaced.

'Don't worry, Norm. I'll pay for my sins.'

They were expensive ones.

Spike became seriously concerned about the wave of immigrants from India and Pakistan – and I do mean serious. He could and did go on about it for hours. The situation was getting out of hand, he said, and nobody in the government was keeping an eye on it. I decided to take him on and told him he was exaggerating. For days we went back and forth and his views developed. Now he claimed uncontrolled immigration would dilute the culture of the English. It would be easy to say Spike had a love-hate relationship with the English but that would be an oversimplification. He could be highly critical of them as a race yet he admired English culture: the traditions, the literature, the history, the individualistic ethic and the fierce spirit of its fighting men through the ages.

This was a small island, he argued, and it would soon become overpopulated. He said he had seen it happen to the indigenous population of Fiji, who were facing the loss of control of their government. If illegal immigration went unchecked, he argued, one day in the future England would become a melting pot, its native culture submerged until it became so diluted it would disappear for ever. Total rubbish, I told him.

'It's your imagination taking flight again.'

He gave me a wry look. 'You'll see.'

He never seemed to consider that 'English' culture had changed throughout history due to immigration.

I could tell from Spike's behaviour in the following weeks that these ideas were churning into something more substantial. Then he told me about his ideas for *The Melting Pot*, which the BBC then commissioned. The story opened showing two Pakistani illegal immigrants with the adopted names Rembrandt and Van Gogh, a father and son played by Spike and John Bird, crossing the English Channel from Amsterdam in a stolen boat, desperate to reach their haven. They arrived in England to discover to their dismay that there were scarcely any English people left. Instead, they found themselves living with an Irish Republican landlord; his South African-bred daughter; a black Yorkshire-man; a Chinese cockney spiv; an orthodox Jew; an Arab Muslim who spoke with a Scottish accent, having worked for the Bank of Scotland in Peckham; an alcoholic racist ex-Indian Army soldier, and an Australian bookie's clerk, also a crude racist. It had a strong cast, including Frank Carson, Alexandra Dane, Wayne Brown, Harry Fowler, John Bluthal, Anthony Brothers, Robert Dorning and Bill Kerr. The show was screened in June 1975, and then five more episodes were shot the following year, scheduled for the autumn of 1976. But the BBC got cold feet and the rest were never transmitted. The script was published in book form in 1983.

For the remainder of the year and into the spring of the next Spike worked at a feverish pace, writing articles and appearing in films and on television, and paying his usual visit to Australia. Yet in his diary for 6 March 1975 he wrote, 'No work. Working flat out.' Certainly contradictory, but that was the man. He was bothered that I had not arranged work for the remainder of the year. I had learned from experience that it was not always wise to tell him what I had planned for the future, because if he was busy at that time he usually turned it down. Indeed, the prospect of what faced him later on could trigger a mini-tantrum or develop into a depression. Knowing when to tell and when not to tell Spike about something was, to me, the secret of how to be his manager.

Spike was still desperately worried about his relationship with Paddy. He said he could not live in the turmoil brought about by the disorder of her everyday existence. In April 1975 his diary records, 'Prediction. God help me today. I will say nothing and do nothing to offend. But I will end up being driven from my home by her pressure – tension – and atmosphere of rage.'

I breathed a sigh of relief when he boarded the flight for Rhodesia. On his return he was due to tour his one-man show for Jimmy Verner from 21 April to 7 June, a hectic schedule on the number one theatres circuit, from Wolverhampton to Aberdeen. When he called I decided not to tell him about that or the offer I had accepted for him to record Paul Gallico's *The*

Snow Goose, the story of a disfigured man who lives on marsh-lands and helps injured animals which became very popular and was set to music. He arrived back at Number Nine and once more accused me of keeping him unemployed, reminding me how his children would suffer as a result. Nevertheless, I decided to keep shtum about what lay in the pipeline as, with these mood swings, he was quite capable of cancelling the whole lot.

Sure enough, things were about to get even worse. Suddenly Paddy demanded a meeting with her solicitor, Spike's solicitor and our accountant. She wanted to know the workings of Spike Milligan Productions Limited and how much she had been left in his will. Spike did not explode, he erupted.

He insisted that the meeting should take place in my office. I did not invite his solicitor as I knew between the accountant and me, we could deal with anything that came up. Paddy arrived with her solicitor and Spike immediately accused her of not trusting him. A fine start. She insisted on knowing how the royalties from SMP would be split after his death. Spike was dumbfounded and then appalled. Our accountant, completely disgusted, got up and left. Spike followed him out and I was left alone with Paddy and her solicitor. After half an hour's wait they realized it was hopeless and departed. Spike spent the next two days in residence at Number Nine, dictating letter after letter to Paddy, explaining how he had provided for her, given her marvellous holidays, a more than generous allowance and pro-vided a nanny for the children. Why had she demanded the meeting?

Then he decided enough was enough. Number Nine was where he would live for good. There was no depression this time – just desperation, followed after a day or two by an air of calmness and determination. He invited me to dinner, not a social occasion. He had decided on a legal separation, he told me. Paddy could have the lot: Monkenhurst, the house he loved, and all the books and paintings he had worked so hard for.

'She's castrated me sexually but I won't allow her to destroy my work,' he said. He said he had telephoned his solicitor to arrange a meeting and wanted me to attend. I could tell he was deadly serious.

There was a problem, however. Grandma was due to arrive at the end of June. He asked if she could stay with me for the whole of her holiday, which covered July and August, rather than at Monkenhurst. Of course, I told him, she would be most welcome and I meant it, but wondered whether he should go back to Monkenhurst while she was in England. With a calmness that was alien to him he said that was out of the question. 'I must survive and I can't do that with Paddy.'

His new life at the office meant dinners with a different girl every night – all his old faithfuls, Liz, Pat, Julia, Jane, Valerie, Margaret, Judy, Roberta and several others. To the casual observer it appeared he was trying to carry on his normal routine but I knew that once more he had started to pop the pills. The intake of Triptozole increased and he appeared to me to operate in first gear. He did not ring Paddy and she did not ring him, but she must have realized that this was not merely another of the many tantrums she had dealt with so often before.

Then without any warning Paddy came to the office. She wanted to try again, she said, and had dropped the case. After she left Spike told me he had decided to go back 'for the sake of Jane.' I was delighted, and for Grandma too. As a devout Catholic she would have been devastated at the break-up of a second marriage and there would not have been enough candles in the Vatican to atone for it. Of course the attempt to mend the marriage did not mean that Spike stopped seeing his girl-friends while he stayed at the office during the week.

The workload was heavy so I asked an agency to provide a typist and a tall, well-built young woman called Shelagh Sinclair came to help out for two weeks. After that she returned to her job at the BBC, but was soon recruited to the Bayswater Harem.

Spike was back to his most aggressive form. While I realized that his attacks on me were nearly always an indication of an oncoming depression, that did not make them any easier to deal with. One of the worst happened at the recording of an episode of Q6.

During recordings I always called at the studios in the day to check he was all right. When I was satisfied I would go back to do some work at the office before returning to the studio before the show, taking along two bottles of chilled Gewürztraminer because he liked a glass or two before going on. Spike usually left his dressing room door open with the keys in the lock, but this time the door was locked. I knocked. No reply. I went to make-up. They had not seen him. I went to wardrobe. They had not seen him. I bumped into Duncan Wood, the producer, in the corridor. He had not seen him either.

'He never locks his door,' he said, helpfully.

I looked for the director, Ian McNaughton, a mad, lovable Scot. He had not seen Spike.

'He never locks the door,' he said.

I could have screamed. Sudden realization crossed Ian's face.

'For Christ's sake. He never locks the door. There's something wrong. I hope he hasn't done a bunk.'

I returned to Spike's dressing room. It was still locked. John Bluthal, my dear friend and ally, had the dressing room next to Spike. Hallelujah! His door was open. I put the two bottles of wine into the washbasin and filled it with cold water, leaving a note to say it belonged to Spike.

The recording started at eight o'clock but at seven forty-five there was still no sign of him. I searched for Ian McNaughton and asked him to tell Spike his wine was in John Bluthal's dressing room. Innocent of all this John returned from the canteen, discovered the wine, read the note and, to prevent anyone from pinching it, locked his door.

It was five to eight so I decided to take my seat among the

audience. The warm-up man was doing his bit. And then I heard Ian shout: 'For fuck's sake, will somebody get him a glass of wine.' With that Spike walked on to the studio floor. I knew him so well that I could tell by his walk something was wrong. He gazed at the audience, and then out it came.

'Ladies and gentleman. I have a manager – shall we call her a damager?'

No doubt thinking that it was part of the entertainment, the audience laughed. I did not. I knew something bad was coming. In his most appealing, wheedling hard-done-by manner he said, 'I don't drink very much but I do like one glass of wine before I come out to do the show. Now that's what my manager sorts out. Easy, yes? Bring me a bottle of wine so I can relax over one drink. Nothing else. That's all she has to do – and she can't even do that.'

The audience went 'Ah' in sympathy. There was no way I was going to reveal who I was by telling him where his wine was, not when he had the audience on his side.

'Do you think that's too much to ask?'

It was pantomime time. The audience shouted, 'No!'

'You see, I do my best. I always try to do my best, helping other people . . .' – this was cringe-making – 'but where's my back-up?' Then he launched into a tirade about how his manager always let him down.

I assessed the situation. I was three rows from the front. If I left I would have to walk back up the stairs past the audience. I could imagine his comments: 'Look. That's her. Can't face it.' I would not give him that much satisfaction. But I was tempted to shout, 'Your wine is in John Bluthal's dressing room because your bloody door was locked.'

I decided to keep my dignity. 'You little shit,' I thought. 'Someone else has upset you and I'm carrying the can. And if you think I'm going to play your bloody game so you can humiliate me in front of 450 people you're very much mistaken.'

But then, when the floor manager brought on a glass of wine, he said, beating his chest, 'No thank you. It's all far, far too late.'

With some trepidation Ian McNaughton started the show.

After the recording I went to Spike's dressing room. Meanwhile, John Bluthal heard the Laurence Olivier performance to the audience and, thinking he might save the day, put the two bottles of wine outside Spike's dressing room door. Spike returned, saw the two bottles, and flung them down the corridor. Glass shattered over the floor and wine splashed the walls. It did not seem possible that there could be so much mess from only two bottles. Producer Duncan Wood saw it and said to me, 'For Christ's sake go. You are the cause of all this.' I was stunned.

Duncan had invited the cast and crew to the BBC Club for a drink after the show and in turn Spike had invited everyone to dine at the Trattoo. I went to the bar with John Bluthal and there was a consensus that the tirade had been one of Spike's best performances to date. I had invited Jack Hobbs to the recording and he came to join us. 'Who the hell upset him, and why are you carrying the can?' he said. Tony Crombie, the drummer in Alan Clare's trio, was so upset by Spike's behaviour that he said he would never work with him again, which saddened me because I thought he was taking it too seriously. Spike never showed up.

I left for dinner at the Trattoo. I did not expect Spike but surely some of the rest of the cast would arrive? Only Alan turned up to do his usual stint on the piano.

'Where is everyone?' I asked.

'They're not coming. They'd had enough of him for the night. I told them he wouldn't turn up because he wouldn't have the guts to face you. And I was right.'

I sat next to Alan and the manager, Pasquale, put my meal on a small table beside the piano. Alan played my favourite numbers, such a gentle, understanding friend.

'I've told you before,' he reminded me, 'he's like the little girl with the curl. When he's good he's very, very good, and when he's bad he's horrid.'

The next morning I went to the office early to have it out with him. But the showdown never happened. On my desk was a picture of a vivid setting sun he had painted overnight. At the bottom were the words, 'My God! Please help me. I'm so lonely.'

He had behaved atrociously so what did he expect? However, I forgave him. Duncan sent me flowers and a note, 'I think you're the star.'

Spike wrote to Duncan. 'Just to explain why I didn't come to the bar after the show – I could not have stood all those people . . . I am not like other performers who can turn it on and turn it off at will. I was feeling depressed before the show and I did not feel like meeting anyone afterwards. Anyhow, thanks for the offer. Love, light and peace, Spike.'

A couple of days later I asked Spike, 'What was all that about?'

'Norm. You know better than anybody that wasn't me. It was the illness.'

I knew that to be the truth.

After the last tour of his one-man show Spike started to do mainly universities such as Brunel, Sheffield and Leeds. He worked hard at improving and altering the performances and in a charitable mood he suddenly decided he would give it an airing 'for all the girls in Holloway Prison'. I thought he was joking but he was deadly serious. Apparently he had read in a newspaper that they were short on recreation.

'That's the idea,' I told him. 'They've been put there as a punishment.'

I got his usual 'you have a terrible unchristian streak'.

'Lay it on,' he said, 'and I want you to come with me to see how bad it is for those poor girls.' And that was my punishment.

He was determined to put on a proper show so he persuaded Alan Clare and Dave Start, the rhythm man, to provide some music. I found it strange to be among fans who were murderers, drug peddlers, thieves and useful with a knife, and so did Alan, but Spike was unaffected, chatting with the girls and doing the charming Spike bit. For someone so sensitive, Spike was strangely unaffected. But the experience had a devastating effect on me. I could not speak for a few hours after leaving Holloway. I will never forget the pain and suffering of some of the girls, the stark environment and the ever-present background noise of a large prison.

A few days later I had to put it behind me as I dealt with an enquiry from the States. They wanted Spike to do a commercial for Solo, an orange drink, with Marty Feldman. The money was excellent but the commercial was to be shot in Hollywood. Knowing Spike's dislike of the States it took all my powers to stop him from calling it off. For a time it was in the balance but then Marty arrived in England for a break. He was always good for Spike: they shared the same sense of humour and never bugged one another. He told Spike how much he wanted to do the commercial with his old mate. Bless him! Spike couldn't resist that so we flew to Los Angeles on 27 October and stayed at the Beverly Hills Hotel. The advertising agency arranged a super suite for Spike and a small room for me at the back. I had started to unpack when there was a knock on the door. Spike. I invited him in. He said nothing. Just listened for a minute.

'It's quiet here. Mine's at the front and noisy. Will you do a swap?'

You bet your life I would. The agency was knocked out by what they perceived to be the magnanimous gesture of an English gentleman, and told everyone how he had given up the suite for his lady manager. I did not shatter their illusions.

I was overjoyed with my rooms and overawed by Hollywood. Everything lived up to my expectations and beyond. There I was in this magical town, staying at a famous hotel, which had been home to many stars. As far as I was concerned it was a dream come true. Of course, we were treated like royalty and for the first time I realized how much more Americans respected actors than the British. Wherever Spike went he was fêted. I was also amazed at the quality of service and attention to detail, from the hotel to restaurants and the studio.

The director thought Spike was the most creative guy he had met in a long time. So far so good. It was to be shot at the Key West Studios where, Spike was thrilled to be told, the Tom Mix silent Westerns had been made. He spent hours exploring empty lots.

The shoot passed without any tension, a refreshing experience. Marty and Spike enjoyed each other's company and we shared wonderful dinners, sparkling conversation and lots of laughs. When Larry Gelbart heard we were in town he and his wife, Pat, took us to a wonderful Malibu fish restaurant he claimed served the best clam chowder in the world.

Spike was in one of his 'My manager must have the best' moods, so before we flew back the director put a limousine at my disposal for a whole day. Go wherever you like, he said. Wherever I liked was first Marilyn Monroe's grave, followed by Rudolf Valentino's – I wanted to see if there really were fresh flowers on it every day. There were.

Spike went round telling everyone that he had this crazy manager who, when told she can go anywhere she likes in a limo, spends the day with the dead. The director asked if I had seen Douglas Fairbanks Senior's tomb. I had not but he insisted it was a must and arranged a visit. The tomb was magnificently set in a whole acre surrounded by tall palm trees. I made Spike promise that, if I went first, he would see I was buried there. He said he would, and to prove he meant it he took me back to the Polo Lounge at the hotel, bought me a glass of champagne and a grenadine for himself, and we drank to it.

On our last night Marty turned up for dinner with three

badges on his lapel of what he described as the Holy Trinity: Buster Keaton, Stan Laurel and Groucho Marx. We talked about what a great time we had had. I was so confident Spike could make it in a big way in the States – and therefore worldwide – that I told him I would stay behind, set up an agency and arrange lucrative work for him, big bucks, more than he could ever earn at home. Spike would have none of it.

'I don't want to work here, Norm. I don't like the States and I don't like Americans.'

'But you've had a wonderful time. And what about your hero, Groucho Marx?'

'That's different.'

'And Larry Gelbart?'

'Ah, he's a great writer.'

'But they're Americans.'

'They were born in the wrong country. That's it, Norm. I don't want to work here. Let's go back home.'

So that is what we did, though I was convinced then, as I am to this day, that he could have been a huge success in Hollywood.

We arrived at Heathrow at 6.40 a.m. I went home, soaked in a bath and was in the office by ten. On my desk I found two old pictures and a theatrical playbill, with Spike's name at the bottom.

'What's this in aid of?' I asked him.

'I thought you'd like to see how far I've travelled.'

Everything back to normal, I thought.

While we were away the Q6 series had started. Johnny Speight rang to congratulate Spike on the creativity of the shows, then Eric arrived at Number Nine and went straight to his office to add his plaudits. Everything in the garden was lovely, but for how long, I asked myself.

Chapter Fourteen

Looking after Spike took me all over the world. In 1975 I received an enquiry to see if Spike would take his one-man show to South Africa under the auspices of Gold Enterprises, run by Ronnie Quibell. Previously Spike had refused to appear there because of racial discrimination, but Ronnie came to England and Spike was won over by his quiet charm and delightful family, with at least six children. We decided he would do the tour on certain conditions. The pianist had to be black, the lighting and back-stage crew Cape coloured, and everyone must stay at the same hotels. And he would perform only to mixed audiences. I thought that would be the end of the matter but in Ronnie we had found an extremely adroit operator. How he managed it I do not know. The South African Government was savage in its application of apartheid laws, yet a few weeks later Ronnie telephoned to say he had been able to negotiate every condition stipulated.

I was satisfied but not Equity. If Spike appeared in South Africa he would be blacklisted. I explained the terms of our contract, but they said they had heard all that before. Performers were gulled into travelling to South Africa and when they arrived they found the promised contract had been thrown out of the window. I did not like the sound of that so I got Ronnie to agree in writing that if any of the conditions of the contract were altered Spike could return to England without incurring any financial penalties. When he agreed to that I realized he must be confident he could honour all the conditions. And honour them he did.

Of course Spike could not leave it at that. He took Equity to task. They were depriving members of work in South Africa, he said, because they were not prepared to visit the country to negotiate the conditions we had secured. They went ahead and blacklisted him but Spike lost no sleep over that.

When we embarked on the tour we had no trouble, and over the years Ronnie arranged several more for us. When it came to its close we went for dinner at his magnificent house in Constantia which overlooked Cape Town. The lights of the city twinkled below in the incredibly clear air. Spike loved the warm, relaxed atmosphere when we all gathered round the enormous dining table. I could see the workings of his mind. This was how all families should be. And how he would like it to be at Monkenhurst.

We returned to London on 7 December. And guess what? It was time to work for Bernard Miles. 1975 had been one of Spike's busiest years, with the writing of *Transports of Delight*, the one-man show in the U.K., Rhodesia and South Africa, the commercial in the States, and *The Melting Pot* too. I wondered how he had escaped a mental breakdown. Yet now he was hurtling into his stint of *Treasure Island*, this time at the New London Theatre in association with Bernard Delfont, the impresario and brother of Lew and Leslie Grade. Bernard Miles invited me to the Mermaid's restaurant to negotiate Spike's fee. He gave me his usual line. 'This is all the production can afford,' reinforced by a seemingly apologetic smile. But this time it was not the usual £50 or £60 a week but £500. I told him I would accept £500 but with certain conditions. Delfont was not on the breadline, I reminded him, and I wanted a percentage of the box office. He tut-tutted and doubted whether that could be arranged.

'Let's try,' I suggested. Lo and behold, after a few days our percentage deal was agreed. All went well at first. Then in January Spike came into my office. He looked sheepish and that alarmed me. Angry, depressed or humorous I was used to, but this was a first.

'I've got something to tell you.' That bothered me too, and it must have shown.

'For Christ's sake don't blow your top because I'm in a terrible position.'

My imagination went into overdrive. Did Paddy have evidence of adultery?

'Bernard Miles has asked me a big favour.' He broke off. 'Don't look like that, Norm. The box office is down and he has asked me to take £250 a week for the rest of the run.'

'And of course you said you couldn't make that decision and would have to let me deal with it,' I said.

He shook his head.

'Well?'

'I agreed,' he whispered.

My expression must have been chilling.

'You've got "piss off" written all over your face.'

'And what do you expect?'

'Norm. The box office is down because the children have gone back to school. He's in a mess.'

'Well, Bernard is in the cast so if he cuts his wages by half I'll agree.'

Contrite Spike changed in a flash to furious Spike.

'How dare you embarrass me – asking him to take a cut. How dare you? All you think about is money. You're unchristian.'

'I'm not unchristian. I'm a realist.'

He stormed out. 'Just drop it. Leave it!'

Right, I thought. If you want to be a prat get on with it. I had a percentage deal and would see from that just how much the box office had dropped. The accounts arrived and what do you know, folks? Bernard Miles's salary was the same as it always had been and the takings had not dropped. So I confronted Spike with the facts. Bernard, I said, had taken him for an idiot. Spike tried to make a joke of it, one in questionable taste.

'You were married too long to a Jewish solicitor.'

He immediately realized that was unworthy of him, and I let him squirm. He was furious I had rumbled Bernard, his dear friend, his saviour, the benefactor who came to his aid when nobody would give him a job. It must have hurt but he would never admit it. As he left I made do with, 'You're unreal, Spike.'

The next day he came into my office and handed me his birth certificate, along with a baby photograph taken in India with his mother.

'Unreal? Here's proof of how real I am,' he said and walked out, dignity restored.

I wrote in my diary as the close of *Treasure Island* approached the following month: 'Please let God make this the last one. I have a feeling He won't manage it and I'll be wasting my breath if I ask Spike not to do another.' I was unusually short of optimism at the beginning of 1976. Spike had decided to start the year on a different keel. Two days before the end of the run at the New London Theatre he came into my office.

'Don't book me any more work. I'm going to give some time to raising money for the overpopulation movement and I want to take Paddy to Paris.'

That's rich, I thought. Then I remembered he was due to present prizes for Population Countdown on 30 January. My heart sank. He was due to leave for Australia on 11 February to do his one-man show. And it was not the usual two weeks in Sydney. This tour had been arranged by the Clyde Packer

Organization and would take him to Melbourne, Adelaide, Sydney, Canberra and Newcastle. After that he was supposed to stay with Grandma at Woy Woy and then fly to New Zealand, ending the tour there on 5 June. I decided not to ask him how long he would be staying in Paris. If I reminded him that he was due to go to Australia he could say, 'Well I'm not NOW!' What was the best approach to keep his mind on the tour? Then the answer came to me.

For years Spike had told me wonderful stories of the Returned Soldiers League (RSL) Clubs in Australia, which he loved. I pictured the clubs in Nissan Huts in the outback with entertainers being hassled by the audience. (I got quite a surprise when I first saw one, looking for all the world like the Odeon in Leicester Square, complete with red flock wallpaper.) The managers of the clubs, he said, were a law unto themselves, rough, tough-talking Australians. His favourite tale was about Lovelace Watkins, a great black singer in the late Sixties, who was invited to appear at one of the clubs. I can hear Spike's voice as he would tell it, even now.

Lovelace, he said, got up to do the gig, to be followed by a rather affected male comic, the winsome sort, all ruffled shirt and cuffs. You get the idea. Lovelace finished to reasonable applause, nothing more than that, because the RSL clubs did not feature many black entertainers. Ruffled Cuffs came on and the audience did not like his appearance to start with, his jokes even less. They started to heckle him and the poor man did not stand a chance. Without as much as a by your leave the manager walked on to the stage while Ruffled Cuffs was in the middle of one his jokes. No apology to the comic. He just stopped him as he was coming to the punch line. Now the manager was not the black tie, dinner jacket sort. A singlet was his idea of evening dress, just like some of the audience. He put a hand up to quieten them.

'If you don't give the poofter a chance I'll bring back the

coon.' A pause, while that sank in. They decided to opt for the comic. It seems inconceivable that that could happen, but Spike swore it was true and sure enough, I found Australia was a bit like that in the Seventies.

What intrigued Spike most about the RSL Clubs was an evening ritual that happened 365 days a year. Every night at nine o'clock, whether an act was in full flow or not, the lights were dimmed and then extinguished for the recital of 'The Kohema'. A voice would start, 'Lest we forget . . .', the whole bit, with the going down of the sun and remembering them. Then the lights went up and the act was allowed to start where it had been interrupted. That really touched Spike. Yes, I thought, the RSL was my lifeline.

'Spike,' I said idly one day as he came into my office, 'when I join you in Australia in March don't forget you promised to take me to the RSL Club in Gosford. And you said we'd take Grandma and she could play the pokies [fruit machines].'

There was a silence. He was not fooled for a second.

'You never allow me time for my pleasures. I wanted to start the year as I intended to go on and you've taken it away from me with your "When do we leave, when do I leave, when do you leave" questioning.'

If I did not choose the right moment the answer, of course, was no. It was never straightforward; he would go on and on. A favourite routine went like this: 'The answer is "No". Do you understand English? The answer is "No" and if it's Jesus Christ coming through the door offering me eternal life the answer is still "No".' When that was the response I would tell Tanis to ignore him and I would try again in half an hour. That was enough to remind her that she had to go out. 'I forgot,' she would say. 'I said I'd get him a currant bun in Bayswater.' And she would disappear so she would not be around when I tried again. Sometimes I won and sometimes I lost. On this occasion I got a mini tantrum.

'I can only take my wife to Paris for three or four days and then I have to be back at your bidding,' he said.

He did not say no. Good. Australia was on. Spike and Paddy went to Paris and then he left on time for Australia for what was a very gruelling schedule.

Spike's litany of conditions had not diminished. He would only fly to Melbourne with Qantas, on what he called the 'kangaroo hop', that is, with one stop for refuelling. He had to have a certain seat in the first-class section of the aircraft and insisted on taking along his emergency survival kit. This was in case the plane came down. Naturally, Spike would be a survivor. The first time I saw the kit it creased me. It consisted of a small bag which contained a piece of string; a whistle; a torch; a packet of Elastoplast; a pen knife; a larger knife; and not one but two watches. He wore another two watches on his wrist during the flight, one with English time, the other Australian time, all arranged just so before he boarded the plane. Then two final essentials – earplugs and a black sleeping mask. He wore an eye mask wherever he was, every night, because he said it was the only way he could sleep. I reminded him that all airlines provided first-class passengers with eye masks and earplugs.

'What if they don't? What if the bloke who's supposed to pack them forgets? What if they've run out of eye masks and ear plugs? I'll have to get off the plane before it takes off. I couldn't go twenty-two hours without my eye mask.'

I learned early on to hand him six eye masks before a flight, just to make sure that the lack of one could not be an excuse for not making the trip. After his tour with Ronnie Quibell Spike decided that the very best sleeping masks in the world were supplied by South African Airways, and for years I would telephone them and they would send a fresh supply.

On this particular tour Spike was not opening at Melbourne until 16 February, so he decided to fly to Sydney to see his brother first and then spend a few days with his mother. That always put him in a good mood.

He phoned me from Woy Woy.

'Mum wants to talk to you. I told her you were having a bad time.' I was not but I kept quiet. 'She wants to light a candle for you.'

'Spike! You've only just arrived there. Don't start teasing.'

He laughed. Grandma came on the phone, very concerned about me. I did not know then what she was talking about but found out later that Spike said I had looked very tired when he left England. I wonder why that could have been.

Grandma changed the subject. 'How's your friend, Anthony Hopkins? I know he's getting better because every week I light a candle for him.'

I told her this was getting out of hand. Tony was not a friend of mine. She would not go along with that. Just like Spike, once she had made up her mind that was the end of the matter.

My one and only time with Spike in Australia was free of tantrums. I suppose it helped that he played to packed houses every night. Tom Miller, who arranged the tour for the Packer organisation, was easygoing and honest. There was only one small hiccough. I had arranged for Spike to do an Australian Tourist Board commercial while he rested for a week in March in the middle of the Australian leg of his tour, but then they heard Australian Equity objected. They argued that as Spike had not flown specifically to Australia to do the commercial an Australian actor should get the job. I argued that there was only one Spike Milligan; he was the person the producers wanted and no member of Australian Equity could take his part. Then they said they would not have had any objection if he had flown in from outside the country especially to do the commercial, but he was there primarily for his one-man show and rules were rules. So I decided to follow them.

I asked Spike if he would fly to Norfolk Island during his

week out from the tour and come straight back to Australia to do the commercial. I suspected the answer would be, 'No, forget it, I'm not putting myself through all that aggravation.' But I got another Spike that day. 'Yes, of course I will,' he said. That called for a celebration so we had a wonderful dinner with Desmond and his wife, Nadia. It was a rarity to see Spike so happy. He loved to dine with Desmond, Nadia, their son Michael, then about twelve, and Nadia's parents, Mama and Papa Klun. Spike and I listened to the conversation conducted in an amazing mixture of languages. Nadia spoke to her mother and Michael in Greek; Michael answered in English and Mama Klun in Greek. She then spoke to her father in Italian, which gave the opportunity for Spike to join in. And so it went on and somehow everyone more or less followed the conversation.

I flew to Cairns to survey the commercial's location at nearby Magnetic Island. There were breathtaking white beaches and a tropical blue sea, but no hotel, or not what I would call a hotel. The 'units', as they called them, were the local excuse for hotel rooms and they were basic: a stark room containing a bed, a small wardrobe and a loo. When I checked in the owner asked me how I felt about lizards. I had seen dozens of them before in Spain at my friends' villa, and found them fascinating creatures, so small and harmless. The owner explained that they kept four lizards, geckos she called them, in every unit to keep the flies under control. 'By the way,' she added, 'keep the lid down on the loo or the snakes might come out and wrap themselves round the handle of the door. Someone didn't put the lid down last week and exactly that happened.' I did not bother asking if they were poisonous. Some part of me could not accept I was stopping there.

But I had to see the location. The cameraman was waiting for me and said he would like to film me walking along the beach the next morning. It would be used as a promotion for Spike's commercial. So I was trapped.

That night was the most uncomfortable of my life. The lizards were not at all like their intriguing little Spanish cousins. To start with they were ten times the size. They clapped on to the wall, swarmed up to the ceiling and then dropped back to the floor, over and over again. There was no way I could go to bed. I have very bad eyesight and wear contact lenses. No way was I going to take them out and not be able to see what was going on and where the four herberts were. So I stayed awake all night without so much as a mosquito net to protect me, watching the lizards crawl up and fall, crawl up and fall . . . I was petrified.

And then there was the loo. The lid was down when I arrived and that was the way it was going to stay until I left. I persuaded my kidneys that I did not need to spend a penny. After all, it was only three days. No, I decided in the small, painful hours of that night, I could not stay three days as I was supposed to do before going to Grandma. I would be a nervous wreck if I did. I had to figure a way out of the situation.

I waited until early morning and before there was anyone about, just as light streaked the horizon, I crouched down outside in best Australian outback fashion to do what I had to do. At that moment four huge peacocks surrounded me, squawking and fanning their feathers. Instant constipation. That was it. I went to reception, found the only phone in the place and rang Grandma.

The owner was within earshot so I had to be careful. I said I was sorry I had not rung before I left. I had got her message but this was the first opportunity I had had to call her. Was it urgent? As quick as lightning, Grandma guessed there was something wrong.

'Right. Something's off the rails. You talk.'

Good old Grandma. I said I was sorry Spike needed me so urgently. I would leave as soon as I could reach Cairns to get a flight, and went and packed my bags and checked out.

I went back to Sydney and spent a few days with Desmond.

I phoned and told Grandma all about Cairns and then Spike called. I told him he could go to Magnetic Island but I would not be joining him and explained why.

'Norm,' he said. 'Think how much more exciting it is than sitting in a Number 12 bus going along the Bayswater Road.'

I was unmoved.

At Woy Woy I realized Grandma was even more religious than I had thought. She had an altar in the second bedroom; it was quite ornate with candles and a crucifix. Because it was nearly Easter the altar was dismantled and swathed in black, and she went there every morning to pray for hours at a time.

I had arranged for another break in the tour to enable Spike to record a character's voice for a feature-length cartoon, *Dot and the Kangaroo*, at the Bob Young Studios in North Sydney. It would take a week at the most so he would be able to come to Woy Woy in time to celebrate his fifty-eighth birthday. Grandma was elated. She had missed so many of his birthdays after she and Grandpa emigrated to Australia.

Grandma's routine never altered. She rose at six, had a cold shower, put her hair in rollers for about an hour, then put on her make-up and finished off her hair. So she was ready to go to the shops very early to get all she needed to make Spike's favourite curry. She filled the fridge with food, got all the song sheets out of the piano stool ready to play while he sang. Meanwhile I booked Nino's, a restaurant on the outskirts of Woy Woy, for the evening of his birthday, and hired a car so we would have our own wheels.

As far as Grandma was concerned this was the return of the prodigal son and she loved every minute. I remember so well Spike driving back from Nino's along the coast to Woy Woy. The moon was the biggest I had seen and a dark, almost burnt orange. He and I sang 'Feelings'. Grandma did not know it, but we taught her the words. Spike mentioned that Des O'Connor had recorded the best version of the number. Right, said

Grandma, she would learn it and be better than Des. By the time we got home she pretty well had the lyrics off by heart.

All too soon our time in Australia was over. Spike was scheduled to go to New Zealand for a few shows, and while there he wanted to see his old Army mate, Harry Edgington, again. I said I would go home, but he wanted me to wait and go with him back to England, riding the Silver Bullet train in Japan on the way and seeing Russia. No, I told him, I wanted to go back via Hawaii and San Francisco.

'Everybody does that. It's the plastic route.'

'Plastic or not,' I said, 'that's what I'm going to do.' So we agreed to split. He got to ride the Silver Bullet and see Russia and I saw what I wanted to see. It was no contest as far as I was concerned. I loved both Hawaii and San Francisco and have visited them several times since then.

Back home relations between Spike and Paddy reached an all-time low. He returned to Monkenhurst to find electric light bulbs burnt out and not replaced, a towel rail broken and not repaired and a table lamp broken and not replaced. Anyone but him might have had a mild altercation with his wife about it and had them repaired. But Spike exploded. Paddy dug her heels in, would not accept responsibility for what had happened, and certainly would not apologize.

So no sooner was Spike back in England than he moved into the office and back to the girlfriends. Shelagh Sinclair was seen back at Number Nine, not typing this time, and before long I could see she was falling in love with him. She thought the man could do no wrong and neither questioned nor disagreed with him. Jack Hobbs put it this way: 'If there was a puddle outside Number Nine she would lie down so he could walk over her to keep his feet dry.' That was cruel, and certainly exaggerated, but Spike did revel in never being disagreed with or questioned. So this big, energetic woman became a frequent visitor at Number Nine.

One day Eric Sykes popped his head round my door and said, 'Spike's new girlfriend is sitting in the hall.' Not another, I thought. I went out to take a look. She was huge, about seventeen stone. By this time Eric was walking up the stairs. He turned round with an enormous grin on his face. She was a visitor waiting for an interview.

A few weeks after our return Spike told me sadly that Paddy was going to Malta for a holiday by herself. I believe Spike always remained in love with her, despite all this evidence to the contrary. Roberta Watt once asked me why Spike always went back to his wife. 'He never left her,' was my reply. To many this must seem like standing reality on its head, but Spike had his own set of values, which he would bend to suit the occasion. Although he slept with many of his girlfriends and some of the actresses who appeared in his shows, they were never as important as his wife and children, and he blithely ignored the possibility that such dalliances could threaten his family life.

I think he realized that his frenetic pace of life did not help the domestic situation. It was as if he could not stop, even though I tried to put the brakes on. He had book signings all over the country, a transport commercial, and then he was writing and recording *The Melting Pot* each week. I thought it was a recipe for a depression but it did not happen.

At about that time Peter Eton, one of the *Goon Show* producers, made an appointment to see me about a proposition for Spike, Pete and Harry. He would like to put the three of them on at the London Palladium for a week. Spike could write something and they need do only about ninety minutes. It would be a sell-out. He would be the executive producer and I would be the producer, responsible for the delivery of the script and getting everyone to turn up on time. In return I could have a percentage of the box office. Then he added quietly, 'As well as a mink coat.'

I laughed but was not really amused. This was a bribe. I never had and I never would accept one. Before I could say any more Spike burst in, still in a terrible mood since his return from Australia. He had not seen Peter for three or more years but he might as well not have been there. His face was contorted.

'Where the fuck were you yesterday? I came into the office and nobody knew where you were. You make my life a misery. The whole place is like a monkey tree. You go out and nobody knows where you are or when you are coming back. I get no service from you.'

The ranting continued for several minutes and I let him get on with it. I had heard it all before but Peter had not. In a rage, Spike left as abruptly as he had come in, not once acknowledging Peter, who by this time was trying to make himself invisible. Although he had worked with Spike on the *Goons* he had probably forgotten how badly Spike could behave.

In a mild but incredulous voice he asked, 'How long has he been speaking to you like that?'

'Like what?'

'My God! It's got so bad you don't even notice it.'

'And you are asking me to put up with that for a week,' I said. 'It could get worse, much worse, with Pete and Harry into the bargain. Harry's an angel but I know how bad it can be with the other two when they're together. Spike I can handle, but Spike and Pete together are a whole different matter.'

I told him I would negotiate a fee for Spike's writing and appearance at the Palladium, but he would have to find himself a producer. In the event it never came off. Which is perhaps as well because there were more pressing problems to deal with.

In late March 1976 I was at the Sebel Town House hotel in Sydney, lounging in my housecoat, delighted at the prospect of a Saturday doing exactly what I wanted. I was flicking through the newspapers when the phone rang. Spike.

'Where are you?'

'Come on. You rang me so you must know.'

He did not reply to that and I sensed he was not in the mood for quips.

'I need to see you now. It's very urgent. I'll wait for you here.'

Down went the phone.

This did not sound like a tantrum. It did not sound like a row with Paddy – then he would usually stutter and his voice go very low. What was up? I went to his room and knocked on his door.

'Fuck off!'

'Spike. It's me.'

'Why didn't you say so.'

The door opened. Spike's face was flushed with emotion.

'I've got something to tell you and I don't need you to blow your top. I've got enough trouble without you adding to it.'

I stopped him. 'Listen. I'm not your enemy. Why did you bring me here? Not to give me a bollocking.'

'I don't want you to have a go at me because Margaret Maughan has written to tell me she is pregnant.'

I sat down, or more precisely collapsed into a chair. I had only just got over the shock of Roberta and Romany. I took a deep breath.

'You haven't seen her for months. How far on is she?'

'Seven months,' he whispered.

'Oh, Spike, I can't believe you've done it again.' I told him it was his own fault. He should have known better after Roberta and taken precautions. This met a great tirade from him.

'Let's cool off,' I said.

He shook his head, utterly bewildered.

'It's far too late to have an abortion.'

This prompted another tirade, this time with the 'unchristian' bit thrown in.

'She gets pregnant and she waits until she's seven months

gone to tell you about it. This time you're really going to pay for your sins.'

'I know,' he said dolefully.

All that bothered him was that Paddy and the children must never find out. At all costs it must be kept from his family. On the one hand that made me feel sorry for him, but on the other, I thought he deserved all he got.

'Don't ever spout on to me about overpopulation. You'll have put six on the planet.'

For a long time Spike would not have her name mentioned. I told him the problem was not going to run away and we would have to deal with it. If necessary, I would speak to her and find out what she wanted. At least past experience would help to guide me. What I found difficult to come to terms with was the fact that Margaret had not visited Spike or telephoned him to say she was pregnant. Instead she had sent a letter baldly stating her predicament. Just like that. No breaking it to him gently when she was two or three months pregnant to see what he wanted to do about it. That had a profound effect on Spike and he said he never wished to see the child.

A few weeks after he returned to London Margaret wrote to Spike to say she had given birth to a baby boy. As I opened his mail I told him about it. I got the cold, clinical Spike who had so recently prepared to separate from Paddy.

'I don't want to see any of her letters. You read them as usual, but don't tell me what's in them. You'll know what's going on.' Now while my sympathies were with him, I thought this decision was wrong and told him so.

Spike locked himself away in his room at Number Nine. He stopped writing and seemed about to slip into a depression. On the third day he rang down to my office.

'Norm, have you got a computer? It's just a thought, but if you have will you tap into it to see if there are any more illegitimate kids about? I thought we might just as well get it all over and done with in one fell swoop.' He put down the phone. Good, I thought, we are back on track again. Two weeks later he did a concert in aid of CHUMS, a charity for unmarried mothers!

Margaret sent a photograph of the baby. I rang to tell Spike and he made me promise to throw it away. I did and continued to do so for several years, whenever she sent one – the day he started school and then at different stages of his boyhood. Each time I told Spike a photograph had arrived the response was always the same.

'Tear it up and put it in the bin.'

I tackled him about this and he said it was the only way he could cope with the situation.

'If I don't see his face and never know what he looks like it's easier for me to cope.'

'That's cruel.'

'I can't handle it any other way.'

Perversely, without telling me, Spike got Tanis to buy a silver mug and sent it to Margaret with one hundred pounds for his son's christening. I could not believe it when Tanis let it slip, and asked him why. He ignored me.

'She's called him James.'

'How do you know?'

'I've spoken to her on the phone.'

'You won't read her letters, I have to do that. Why am I doing it if you speak to her on the phone? I don't see the difference.'

'There just is.' He paused. 'I'm waiting for the day when you tell me she wants this and that and until then let's keep it on an even keel – away from Paddy and the kids.

'This child is going to be like the sword of Damocles,' he said, 'It will be hanging over me until the day I die.'

He decided it was best for all concerned to offer her thirty pounds a week. She agreed. Then she wanted James to be privately educated. Spike paid the school fees and gave him an allowance for clothes. In 1987 she asked him to stand guarantor for £10,000 for a period of three months and he agreed. She did not honour her commitment and the bank called in the money from Spike. He always coughed up because he wanted to keep James's existence a secret to spare his family the upset. He was certainly paying for his sins.

Then in January 1992, when James was fifteen, Margaret sold the *Sunday People* newspaper the story of her eight-year affair with Spike Milligan and their 'love child'. Spike was devastated. His children had until that point known nothing of James's existence. He telephoned each one to tell them about the story. Jane, in particular, was dreadfully upset and I felt deeply for her.

On the advice of a friend, Spike gave his side of the story to the *News of the World*. I telephoned Margaret and told her that in view of Spike's generosity over the years I considered her behaviour disgraceful and reminded her of the occasion he had baled her out for £10,000. Her excuse was that she was hard up. I told her she had betrayed Spike and must never again contact the office either by letter or telephone. Then Spike told me she had phoned him at home to offer an explanation. She was short of money and simply had to do it, though she knew his children would suffer as a result.

'The poor woman must have been desperate to do that,' he said.

The outcome was that he sent her even more money.

A few weeks later she pleaded with him to meet James. I told him to exact a promise from her that there would be no photographers present. On that understanding the meeting was arranged. Margaret and her son travelled from Northumberland and stayed at the Mermaid Inn at Rye, where Spike now lived with his third wife, Shelagh Sinclair. Shelagh behaved admirably and agreed to accompany him to the meeting, which went surprisingly well. As they left the Mermaid a camera flashed and a picture of the meeting was published in a Sunday newspaper.

That was the end of Margaret as far as Spike was concerned. He called and told her what he thought of her; when roused, Spike could be brutal. That did not put her off. She wrote saying she had been devastated by his telephone call and had had nothing to do with the photographer being present to record the meeting. Spike would have none of it. He would see James from time to time but wanted nothing more to do with her. But letters of explanation started to come to the office. This time Spike wanted to know what they said so I read them to him. Margaret said she could understand how his wife felt about the stories but she had meant no harm. 'After all, you did choose her instead of me and your baby son.'

'Stop right there,' he said calmly. 'That's the end. Don't ever, ever even tell me she has sent a letter. I don't want you to read them. Put them straight into the bin.'

He never mentioned Margaret's name again to me. James was invited to visit him at Rye but Spike did not approve of his behaviour. Once he brought a friend with him, and they took a couple of girls back to the house while Spike and Shelagh were at a jazz concert. When he returned he found that James had helped himself to a rare vintage wine, a present from his friend John Paul Getty. He was incandescent. After a few such incidents Spike decided 'to cool it', as he would say.

But that was not the end of it. Yet another newspaper carried the story of James's visits, which contrasted his mother's standard of life with Spike's: 'There was champagne and lobster in the fridge.' Wrong. I knew Spike for thirty-six years, Shelagh for nearly thirty and his children from when they were small, and I never saw any of them drink champagne or eat lobster. It was not to their taste. If James had said the fridge contained Gewürztraminer, I would say yes, by the dozen. Again, it was a small slight like this which turned Spike against James. But still the monthly cheque continued while he studied at a polytechnic. In the last decade of Spike's life, when he was ill and had cut down on work, he found it difficult to send James his monthly allowance of £300 and it was reduced to £200.

'Can't he get a part-time job like other students?' I asked him.

'Ah,' he said. 'But they aren't the illegitimate son of Spike Milligan.'

By June 2000 Spike knew he could no longer afford to send any of his children any extras. He was now seriously ill, making a round trip of one hundred miles, three times a week, for dialysis and paying for full-time nursing care. I had sent James his monthly cheque for twenty years and when he did not get one he thought it was my fault. He seemed unable to accept that his father was seriously ill and no longer in a position to support him. He started to ring his father at Rye. At that time it had been decided, because of the seriousness of Spike's illness, to change the telephone numbers to screen calls from charities and fans. He felt under a lot of pressure and wanted to maintain his distance from James. Margaret had not been in touch with me since 1992, but now it concerned money she wrote, 'Whether you like it or not, you are involved because over the years you have always been in charge of payments. It's not like Spike to break his promise.' At eighty-two years old there were days when Spike was too weak to get out of bed and yet the letters did not stop. I ignored Margaret's letter and vowed I would never have anything to do with her again. Nor will I.

After Spike died I read a newspaper article in which James was quoted saying that he felt unwelcome at Spike's funeral and it was painful for him to see the other illegitimate child, Romany, with the family mourners. I have often wondered whether it has ever occurred to him why.

Chapter Fifteen

One day Spike rang me from rehearsals for *The Melting Pot*.

'Where would you like to go to dinner to celebrate our ten years?'

He had not forgotten and neither had I. The anniversary was the following week and we celebrated – where else? – at the Trattoo. There was little time for sentiment. We discussed the Finchley Society and the signing sessions for his third volume of war memoirs, *Monty, His Part In My Victory*. He needed to do more publicity, he said, and asked me to fix an interview with Pete Murray on his BBC Radio 2 show. And so it went on in that vein. I knew this frenzy for work to be a warning. I would just have to sit back and wait until it was necessary for me to phone and cancel this, that and the other.

When the collapse came he spent three days on the bed at Number Nine. I left him for a day or so and then went in. Our dialogue during these moments was always the same. He would be lying down, gazing at the ceiling.

'Spike, what are you doing?'

'Pretending to be a jelly.'

He was due to leave for Ireland to film the fifth episode of *The Melting Pot*. When he announced 'The script is not right', I made no comment. The script had been accepted, the actors had received their copies, and shooting was about to begin. Something else was bothering him. Now it was his co-writer Neil Shand's turn to be the target of his wrath. 'He hasn't got an original idea in his head,' Spike said. 'You show me something he has written on his own. *All by himself*. Show me. He's the most expensive typist I ever had. One-liners. That's all he can do. No ideas. No ideas at all.'

This was totally untrue. It was just a Spike rant. There were times to keep my mouth shut and times to defend whoever was getting it in the neck. I knew that if I said a word now he might well say, 'I'm too ill. I can't go to Ireland', if not worse. The phone once rang during a tantrum and he tore it from the wall and hurled it through the window. So I waited for him to tire himself out, go back to his room, lock the door, sleep and recharge his batteries. Afterwards, no more was said about it.

If I have an unchristian streak then Spike certainly had a cruel one and his friends could suffer as a result. Most close acquaintances were the subject of a Spike rage at some point, with three exceptions: Eric Sykes, Johnny Speight, and jazzman Ronnie Scott. Those acquaintances on the periphery who he saw infrequently, such as Robert Graves, the Labour politician, Michael Foot, and the Welsh rugby international, Cliff Morgan, escaped them altogether. Lucky them.

By October he was due to start writing the seventh episode of *The Melting Pot* and I had the feeling that it could all be off. It was nothing to do with Neil; that outburst had been forgotten. The very next day he greeted him as his 'old buddy'. One day Johnny Speight called to see me as he left Number Nine, and was laughing his head off.

'Your turn today.'

'Thanks for telling me. I thought it was Paddy or something serious like his pens not being delivered.'

'No,' said Johnny. 'It's his "shouting at the world" day and today you happen to be the world.'

Johnny thought it was funny and smiled. He had had fifteen minutes of ear bashing from Spike on how useless I was. I had no conscience about keeping him out of work; he was unemployed because of me; I was fucking up his life; I did not care about him, and if he had turned into a vicar two years ago I would not have noticed. Johnny could do a great impersonation of Spike and he repeated his rant wholesale, including the mannerisms. When Spike worked himself to a pitch his right forearm beat his left breast, a habit which reminded Johnny of Adolf Hitler. I mentioned that their birthdays were very close, and Johnny started marching about my office, playing Spike the Führer, until Tanis and I were in hysterics. At that moment Spike walked in.

Always evil, Johnny said, 'We were just talking about you and Adolf Hitler.'

'I finished that years ago,' said Spike. 'I dedicated that book to you, Norm, didn't I? I've been working on *Mussolini* and I've just finished it.'

I was both surprised and delighted. I had been yapping on about meeting the delivery date for the fourth volume of his memoirs, only to be met with silence. I said, 'Spike, you are a love.'

Johnny laughed. 'I'm going. You two are in a world all of your own. He slags you off to anyone who'll listen, you think he's like Adolf Hitler, and all is forgiven by both of you because he's finished the manuscript. I'm off to the BBC for a bit of mediocrity.'

That was the word Spike and Eric always used to describe the BBC. As poor Grandma had witnessed so long ago, when Spike was having one of his hate sessions with them he always prayed not to be made mediocre. He was never that.

But Spike was soon back on a knife's edge. *The Melting Pot* was suddenly cancelled and only one episode shown. I knew he had started to pop tranquillizers because of what in the office we called his 'clicking', which started when his mouth went dry and his tongue stuck to the roof of his mouth so that each word he enunciated was preceded by a sucking noise. When this happened I would warn Tanis, 'Watch out, he's clicking.' This was not meant nastily, just to caution her to walk on eggshells. There was often friendly banter and repartee between them, but it was essential to know when to shut up.

He then became passionately interested in the work of Erin Pizzey for battered wives and visited the refuge she had set up in Chiswick. He decided to put on a special performance of his one-man show for its benefit, and later dedicated *Mussolini: His Part In My Downfall*, published in 1978, 'to Erin Pizzey in her lonely fight to stop brutal, physical and psychological violence to women and children.' I believe channelling all his energies into helping her and seeing at first hand the suffering at the refuge prevented him from sliding into a deep depression, although work on the rewrites of *Mussolini* was put on hold.

Despite his compassion for broken families Spike was still arguing constantly with Paddy and once more he moved into Number Nine. He was there when I arrived in the morning and still there when I left at night, and I had no respite from him. So 1976 drew to a close on a low. He desperately wanted to go home for Christmas to be with Jane and the other children, but said he was petrified at the thought of the tension at Monken-hurst, so he would stay at the office – alone. A likely story. Stay at the office, yes, but of an evening there would be one of his girlfriends for dinner, etc.

At the last minute he went home after all and it turned out to be a wonderful holiday. Spike's idea of heaven was a happy domestic life, with the family around him, taking afternoon tea and toasting crumpets before a large log fire, and dressing up for dinner in his charming dining room. Spike often said to me that there was nothing better in life than to sit round a dinner table, chatting with friends and drinking good wine, and he meant every word of it at the time. But after a week or two he would need to break free and do what he wanted to do, see a girlfriend or visit Ronnie Scott's Jazz Club.

Every house he lived in had the same dining room, transferred with a few additions from 127 Holden Road to Monkenhurst and, in turn, to the house in Rye. His bedroom was transferred in exactly the same manner. I found that rather strange but he valued the continuity. He was still playing happy families when he returned to the office on New Year's Day. 'Norm,' he said, '1977 is going to be good for us.' I crossed my fingers. He had also brought me a present, a beautiful watercolour of Rome by Brabazon H. Brabazon. It was not like him to remember my birthday.

'Spike, what is it you're going to want me to do for you that I know I'm not going to want to do?'

'Nothing. This is a present. Don't ever sell it without first finding out how much it's worth. I want you to have it. I've treasured it for years and I thought it was about time I gave it to you so you can enjoy it.'

This was Spike at his most generous and sincere. Mind you, years later in 1999, when he was staying at my flat in London, he noticed the Brabazon on the wall. 'Why did I give you that? It's worth something, you know.' A moment later he said, half-joking, 'Go on. Give it back to me.' He looked for my reaction and then added, 'No, I gave it to you because I appreciated all you had ever done for me.'

'At the time,' I said.

'Right on, Norm.'

As it turned out 1977 was to be a terrible year. I had *Q7* reinstated and several other things lined up for him, including a hectic four-day trip to Toronto to do some public appearances, because Penguin Books Canada had had a tremendous success with his war memoirs. There was the usual round of public appearances concerning his numerous interests, from rain-forests to animal welfare, and he agreed to do an interview for Southern Television about what he considered to be the barbaric sport of foxhunting.

When he returned from Southampton I told him that a client and agency were interested in him for fronting a commercial and wanted to have lunch. But he did not want lunch. He gave me his favourite excuse: 'I only eat one meal a day. Why? Because the world's resources are finite and we must all play our part in conserving them.'

I had learnt to ignore that and plugged away.

'There's a lot of money in the commercial. At least you could have lunch with them.'

'No. And don't ask again.'

I rang the agency and told them we could do it, but they would have to fit in with us as far as the date was concerned. I would use the ploy of saying to Spike, 'Think of the handouts to the kids.' Money meant treats for his children. That was always a winner. He agreed, on the condition that lunch had to finish by 2.30 p.m. Done. This had been the case often enough before and I was quite practised at extracting him.

We met at the Princess Ida suite at the Savoy Hotel at 12.30 p.m.

'It'll be the usual peanut and sherry crap until one o'clock and then one and a half hours before we leave,' he reminded me before we walked in.

'Right, Spike,' I said

In fact there were no peanuts; it was an intimate party of eight. Spike's Gewürztraminer was ready in a wine cooler. We were in for a bumpy ride if he said, 'No thank you. I don't drink during the day,' but in with a chance if he accepted the wine. He took a glass.

They had obviously gone to a great deal of trouble and it was an extremely pleasant meal. Spike sat next to the managing director of the client's company and the pair of them swapped stories about the war. He was not going to walk out of this one. So I was able to relax until 2.20 p.m. when I knew I would have to start making the right noises for us to leave. Unfortunately, there was not a convenient pause in the conversation. Spike was laughing away, still telling his army jokes, so I stood up and said in a loud voice, 'I'm so sorry to have to bring this delightful lunch to a close, but Spike has another appointment at three o'clock so we'll have to leave.'

This produced a subdued hush. I smiled at Spike.

'No, I don't,' he said. 'I'm not going anywhere. There isn't an appointment. It's just her.'

I could have killed him. His shoulders started shaking up and down as a trademark silent giggle took over.

'She's like that. She doesn't like me to enjoy myself.'

There was a sympathetic 'Aah.'

Normally, I would have put on a plastic smile and said something like 'That's my rôle in life' or 'That's how it is.' But I had probably had more than a few glasses of champagne and Chablis.

'Spike! Tell the truth.'

I thought he would explain that often he was bored out of his mind at these occasions and expected me to extract him. Instead, he turned to the managing director.

'I thought you would be a prick,' he said, 'so I told Norma to get me out by 2.30 p.m. But I'm enjoying it.'

Everyone laughed and it was half past five before we left the Savoy. Spike got the job and enjoyed that too, and we were well paid for our efforts. If only it could always have been like that.

The next day Spike came to the office looking dreadful. 'Paddy's ill,' he said. Spike said he knew it was serious. I told him not to jump to conclusions. He shook his head. 'I know her cancer has returned,' he said.

In April there was confirmation that the cancer had returned. Paddy was only forty-three. After her mastectomy in 1973 her doctors had said that if she went four years without a recurrence she had a seventy per cent chance of surviving. Spike was devastated. He was convinced she would die. Her mother, too, had died from cancer. Now there was no ranting or raving. Quietly, he said it should have been him. Paddy, on the other hand, was positive and convinced she would beat it. She refused any of the normal drugs on the grounds that they had been tested on animals and consulted a homoeopathic professor, who convinced her that if she followed his advice the cancer would be eradicated.

All was gloom at Number Nine. Spike knew Paddy must not see him in a pessimistic mood, so when he went home he was upbeat. But away from Monkenhurst he desperately sought some hope. He called the surgeon who had performed the operation in 1973 and all the other doctors who had been involved. They were completely opposed to the treatment Paddy was receiving. Spike pleaded with her to see them. Obdurate as ever, she refused, remaining adamant that the homoeopathic professor would cure her. He found it impossible to sway her.

Spike coped as he did with every crisis: he detached himself from the situation and threw himself into his work. He returned to the office, stayed there at night, continued writing, appeared in a film, *The Last Remake of Beau Geste*, and carried on as though nothing was wrong. He spent nights at Ronnie Scott's with Jack Hobbs and anyone else who would go with him, and the Bayswater Harem was called out for dinners at the Trattoo. The routine went like this. Spike would phone Tanis about four o'clock. 'Get me someone to have dinner with this evening.' Tanis knew that did not mean a male friend so she would pick up the book and do a ring round. He really was as casual as that. I wondered how, with two illegitimate children under his belt and the wife he professed to love seriously ill, he could still bear to see these other women.

And at the same time he maintained files in his office, with names and numbers of Paddy's doctors, and information about the treatment they recommended. He made copious notes of what the doctors said and continued to speak to them often, questioning them as if they were before the Spanish Inquisition. Then after the day's medical cross-examination he went out with one of his girlfriends, no doubt having sex to round off the evening.

I found his behaviour distressing and felt compelled to talk to him about it. He was as frank as only he could be. Paddy's illness, he said, had not changed their relationship, which had foundered before her illness. The fact that she was critically ill did not change that. I told him it should change; I thought it showed a lack of respect for Paddy. But on reflection, Spike was never one for humbug.

Then came a late night call.

'Norm, what will I tell Jane if her mother dies? It's haunting me. I can't think of anything else. Paddy is getting worse. Norm, it's going to happen, I know it is.'

He just wanted someone to listen. He talked for ten minutes and then hung up.

Q7 loomed and Spike should have been preparing and revising the script. Instead he wanted to write poetry. Unlike his normal pattern of writing, when he was very disciplined and, once focused on a book, would allow nothing else to interfere with it, with poetry he opened a box file and when the mood took him he would write a poem and pop it in. It might take more than five years to fill one particular file. And so it would go on until one day he would have a blitz on it and write five or six poems in a day and cry, 'There's enough there for a book.' Then I would send it off to Michael Joseph, or Puffin if it was verse for children. This time he went into overdrive, and dashed off four or five poems in an hour. The collection, *Open Heart Univer-*

sity, published in 1979, was finished two days before the *Q7* rehearsals began.

My parents had come to stay so I invited them to a Sunday night recording at the BBC. My father, with his love of music hall, really enjoyed it. Spike could be a charmer and invited Mum and Dad to the BBC Club at Shepherd's Bush, a place he normally avoided. John Bluthal, who was in the *Q7* cast, was appearing with Joe Lynch in a very successful sitcom, *Never Mind The Quality, Feel The Width*, which Dad loved, so Spike arranged that John and Joe would be at the Club that night. Mum was not the slightest bit interested, but I watched Dad turn into a fan with John and Joe, quoting from an episode and joking with them. Then Spike made a huge fuss of him. I was warmed by it, and just a little tearful, because Dad was not well, although at the time I had no idea just how ill he was. He returned to Thornaby and told everyone who would listen what a marvellous time he had had with Spike, John and Joe. Suddenly they were all the best of friends. He so enjoyed it. I cherish the memory of his happy face that night.

For all the trauma of Paddy's illness, *Q7* was going comparatively smoothly. There was also an enquiry to see if Spike would write some poems to go with some of Heath Robinson's illustrations of goblins. I adored Robinson's work and was keen that Spike should do it. The idea appealed to him immediately. The publishers, Hutchinson, sent round some copies of the drawings and I was browsing through them when Spike came into my office. I showed him a rather grumpy, fat old goblin.

'That's Fred Fernackerpan, isn't it?'

Being keen to get him to start work I said, 'He's whatever you want to call him. And I like Fred Fernackerpan.'

Then he displayed what I thought was his genius. He pulled up a chair and sat on the other side of my desk. Without a pause he took the illustration and wrote:

I am a mystery fellow
I'm Fred Fernackerpan
I wear one sock that's yellow
  The other dipped in jam
I walk about the countryside
  I walk about the town
Sometimes with my trousers up
  And sometimes with them down
And when they were up they were up
And when they were down they were down
  And when they were only half way up
    He was arrested.

Spike started to laugh. I read it out and was amazed, then suspicious.

'You've written that before, you old sod.'

'No, I haven't. I thought of it there and then.'

Was he telling the truth? I showed him another illustration. It was a goblin with hands outstretched and a pained look on his face.

'It's Tommy Cooper, isn't it?'

Yes, I thought, so it was. The hand gesture was exactly the same as Tommy's. Spike looked at me, and perhaps he saw there was still doubt in my eyes.

'Okay. How about this?'

Before my eyes he wrote:

I'm a goblin Tommy Cooper
I can do tricks with a hat
I can walk upside down with a barrow
So they made me a water rat.
I can juggle with seventy skittles
Dive through a rubber tyre
I can sleep on the bottom of the Channel

> Did somebody call me a liar?
> I'm a goblin Tommy Cooper
> I fly round the room on a mat
> You ask me how do I do it
> I'll tell you – 'JUST LIKE THAT'.

He completed this in about five minutes. Then he looked through the rest of the illustrations and said, 'I'll really enjoy writing verses for all of them.' Within a week he completed the thirty-eight verses. He paid tribute to Julia Brecht, an actress in all the Q series and his favourite girlfriend at this particular time, in a verse called 'JULIA BRECHTKIN – a beautiful lady goblin', which fitted Heath Robinson's drawing of a very small, heavy-bosomed lady.

When we sent the poems to Hutchinson I rang Tommy Cooper and told him about the verse. He said, 'That's one of the nicest things that's happened to me. I'm really chuffed.' And then he added, 'You know, among all of us Spike's the one with the original talent.' It was typical of the modesty of this hugely talented man, which was one of the many reasons he was so popular in the business. He once said to Eric he wished he knew what it was he did that made people laugh. 'Don't try to analyse it,' he told him, 'don't change a thing.' When the book came out I received numerous phone calls from performers saying how thrilled they were that Spike had written a verse about Tommy.

It was a pleasant change from the atmosphere at the Q7 rehearsals, where Spike was being difficult. His complaints were endless: wardrobe 'haven't a clue', the wig girl 'should be working on a conveyer belt', the dresser needed 'a hearing aid'. It was time for me to intervene so I had a chat with Ian McNaughton, the director.

There was an unlikely chemistry between Ian and Spike because, if anything, Ian had a shorter fuse and could give Spike more than he dished out. Spike's pet name for him was 'Rage', because he got into so many, so there was a pair of them. This combination produced combustible rehearsals but great performances. I asked him if there was anything he could think of to provoke Spike's change of mood.

'Hern,' he said in his heavy Scottish accent, 'I don't know. It's been coming on for days. Everything is wrong. Nothing, absolutely nothing pleases him.' He had suspected it was something to do with the office because Spike had done the usual business of castigating me behind my back, which Ian ignored as he had heard it all before. I left the BBC none the wiser.

By September Q7 had turned into a nightmare. After three weeks my parents decided to return to Thornaby. I so much wanted them to stay, but though both Mum and Dad had retired, London would never be home to them. I took them to King's Cross and waved them goodbye and returned to the office with a heavy heart.

When I opened the door the phone on my private line was ringing. Spike. Forget it, I told myself. I need a little time in my life for Norma and sod everyone else. I sat down, thumbed through a few messages and, while my mind concentrated on what they said, my hand instinctively reached out and answered the phone when it rang again.

A voice said, 'I'll bet you can't guess who this is.'

'Don't play silly buggers with me. I'm having a bad time.'

'It's Jack Clarke.'

I almost dropped the phone. The love of my life! It must have been fifteen years since I had last seen or spoken to him. His voice cheered me up and I told him the call could not have come at a better time. Well, he said, he was coming to London the following week and it would be marvellous if we could meet. The day he named was booked for the annual general meeting of Spike Milligan Productions but I was curious and arranged to see him for lunch. I left a note for Spike on the day, informing him that I had cancelled the meeting and would reschedule it. When I came back I found he had written at the bottom, in big red letters, 'SEX'. I still have that note today.

Jack and I had lunch at the White Elephant in Curzon Street. As we chatted fifteen years disappeared. We were entirely comfortable with each other. A lovely interlude, I decided, when I went back to the office, and a little light relief after dealing with Ian and Spike, but no more than that.

The real world soon intervened. A week later, on 2 October, Spike was due to record the last show of *Q7*. He telephoned me at home in the small hours of the night. He said he had to try to be funny, although that was the last thing he felt like doing. Paddy's cancer had spread to her spine but he had made a decision not to tell Jane that her mother was dying. He would also try again to persuade Paddy to take painkillers offered by their local GP and ignore the regime set by 'the lunatic professor'. But although she was in agony she steadfastly refused to take any medicine that had been tested on animals. Courageous and stubborn to the end, she chose an agonizing death.

Later that day I told him I had decided to visit Paddy. He begged me not to. He had removed every mirror in the house so she could not see what she looked like. He clasped my hand. 'I beg you, please don't go. The shock at seeing her might show on your face and that would be too much for her.' I acquiesced. I still have mixed feelings about it. I am glad to remember her full of life but part of me wishes I could have said goodbye and, maybe, given her a little comfort.

Earlier in the year, in July, when she had known it would not be long before she died, Paddy had taken Jane to New York and Long Island so that they could spend some time alone together and Jane could have an abiding memory of days of sunshine and laughter. She had declined rapidly after that.

Spike was due to fly to Australia in the autumn to do a documentary, *Earth Patrol*, but I told him I would get him out of it. The contradictory old sod said no; he wanted to go. He had spoken again to the doctors who had treated Paddy at the onset of her cancer, and in their opinion she could go on for a year, so he would continue to work. He was due to leave on 10 October, but three days before I found a note pushed under my office door. 'TOO ILL TO GO.'

He was on his bed upstairs. Should I tell the people in Australia so they could stand down or wait and see how he felt? A knock on his door would give me a good indication. If he said 'Fuck off' there was a chance he might change his mind. 'Leave me alone' was not great but it was not an absolute no. Silence was bad. That was what I got this time. I phoned Australia and explained the situation, promising to keep them informed in case he was better in time for filming, which was due to start on the seventeenth. We had a few days in hand. When Spike let me into his office, I discovered he had had an almighty row with Paddy. I could not believe it and said so.

'How can you be like that when she's so ill?'

The selfless days were forgotten and so was his concern for Paddy. He ranted and raved. She was as strong as an ox. Her illness was physical; his was mental and much tougher to take. I reminded him she had cancer and was dying. He did not want to hear it. Paddy was cruel, he said. She did not love him, she was nothing more than an iceberg. She must have said something to trigger this, though what he never said. He was too busy working himself into a fury, screaming and shouting to try and keep the depression at bay. But we both knew it was only a matter of time.

He switched on the electric fires and drew the blinds. I faced a quandary. If I left his office I was deserting him, if I said one wrong word his anger would turn from Paddy to me. I had learnt to sit quietly and listen or, if appropriate, to try to leach him of the rage by having a discussion. Sometimes this succeeded and sometimes it did not. I called Australia to postpone the starting date, then Paddy to say the trip was off. We talked for about an hour. I realized she knew that a depression was on the way, but she kept the conversation to everyday matters. She asked what I had been doing, how was Eric, what were the latest happenings at the office? This was her normal way of coping with Spike but it drove him to distraction, and was one reason he accused her of being an iceberg.

A few days later he came back to life and Australia was on again so I phoned them with the glad tidings. Departure was re-arranged for 20 October on the 10.30 a.m. flight. All systems were go. As he left Number Nine that morning I bade him farewell.

'Goodbye, Spike. Have a wonderful time because that's what we'll have here. A little bit of peace and quiet.'

'Sod off,' he said.

At 12.20 p.m. the door of my office opened a crack. Spike poked his head around it.

'Don't have a heart attack.'

'What happened?'

Well, he explained, he had been sitting in the VIP lounge at Heathrow talking to his old friend, Marcel Stellman, who ran a record company. They chatted away until Marcel's flight was called. As he got up to leave he asked, 'What time's your flight, Spike?'

Time? Looking at his watch was the last thing he would think of doing while having a pleasant conversation with a friend. Of course his plane was already long gone, over the English Channel or France by then. He had been so engrossed that he had not heard the call, two calls in fact.

I did not believe him and suspected he had decided he did not want to go after all. Then I noticed he was travelling much lighter than when he had left the office.

'Where's all the stuff you were taking to Desmond?'

'That's okay,' he said seriously. 'It's on its way to Oz. I'm the only thing that isn't.' He grinned.

'Come on, the truth,' I demanded.

'Norm, believe me. That's what happened. You couldn't write this stuff.'

So what did he intend to do? Because it would be me, not him, on the phone to the client again trying to convince them that he had missed the call.

'I'm going to lie on my bed all day and watch children's television while you get me another flight.' An expression of joy lightened his face. 'Oh, what a bonus day. Norm, send out for some Battenberg cake and I'll have it upstairs.'

Which he did, with a cup of tea, while I rang round the airlines to get him another flight. There was no way I could get him a seat until the next day. Spike said he wanted to celebrate his bonus day by going to the Trattoo with Liz Cowley. It was enough of a celebration for me to have found him another flight. The *Earth Patrol* crew thought what had happened was hysterical. Give them time, I thought.

Marcel rang me the next morning and confirmed that every word of Spike's story was true. 'He's unbelievable. He was as calm as if he had missed the Number 61 bus, you know, there'd be another coming along in five minutes. He said, "Never mind, I'll go and tell Norma. She'll either be furious or die laughing." And off he went.'

Spike loved Australia and Australia loved the rebel in him. So I was not surprised when he phoned to say all was well, the crew having a ball. But he was concerned about Paddy and did not linger, returning to London the moment filming finished. He arrived back in time for the publication of *The Spike Milligan Letters*. The first copy had arrived while he was in Australia and I was a little apprehensive that he might not like it. After all, it was his idea and all his work, really, put together by me due to his magnanimous offer to help me pay off my ex-husband. I was disappointed in one or two aspects of the book but he loved it.

'It's your first book. And with a book you have one editor who can only fuck up about ten per cent of it. Think what it's like with a television script. There's the producer, the director and the actors. You don't stand a chance.'

I told him I had decided to cancel the publication party in view of Paddy's illness but he insisted it went ahead. He did not want Paddy to know how seriously I viewed her condition or me to miss the thrill of celebrating. 'Let's carry on as normal,' he said, so we did our best. I held a small dinner party at the Trattoo. Paddy was too ill to come but rang to congratulate me. Jack Clarke was in London that day and I invited him because I wanted him to meet Spike, though I did not know what they would make of each other. They were poles apart in many ways; Jack was even a Master of Foxhounds. But they got on famously. I do not know how many bottles of wine were consumed over dinner. Afterwards we sat in the bar, talking and listening to Alan Clare at the piano.

Spike was dreading the approach of Christmas, which he knew would be Paddy's last. He wanted it to be perfect for all the family. All work at the office came to a halt as he made his painstaking preparations. After the holiday Paddy declined sharply. The final six months of her life were hell and her homoeopathic diet did little to ease her suffering. Whatever the professor prescribed she went along with. One day she would have to eat nothing but Mexican Yucatan honey, the next it would be two pounds of green seedless grapes, even though her mouth developed sores from the effort of eating them. Her only source of pain relief was to immerse herself in a warm bath.

Eric Sykes once said that at Number Nine we had grown into a family and it was true. I felt close to the Milligan children and wondered how Paddy's death would affect Jane.

Suffering seemed to be everywhere. Early in January Mum telephoned me in distress. My father had fallen downstairs, almost certainly due to a stroke. I left immediately for Yorkshire. He was in hospital and his condition critical, but Mum clung to the hope that he would recover. I rang Spike to tell him I would stay with her. He had few engagements in January but was booked to do *Desert Island Discs*. He wondered whether he could go through with it but I told him he must, otherwise Jane and the rest of the family would wonder why he had cancelled it.

During the afternoon of 17 January my father's condition worsened. I wanted to talk to Spike, but he was not at home or at the office. Tanis said she had booked a table for him at the Ambassadors. I could not believe it. That night my father died so I rang Spike at the restaurant. When he came to the phone he was happy and chatty; obviously he had had a few glasses of Gewürztraminer. Then I told him about my dad and he became concerned and sympathetic. Suddenly I was filled with anger. Paddy was dying and there he was, out enjoying himself.

'What the hell are you doing there?'

Without the slightest qualm he replied, 'I'm having dinner with Shelagh Sinclair.'

I was appalled. I felt devastated both by my father's death and by Spike's behaviour. I told him so but he could see nothing wrong in what he was doing. I found it hard to swallow.

I had seen Jack Clarke several times in December and when he heard of my father's death he offered to take care of the funeral arrangements. Mum and I were very grateful for that. After the funeral I tried to persuade Mum to come and stay with me in London, if only for a visit, but she had always been an independent character and wanted to remain in her own home. So I returned to London with Jack and although I was saddened by the loss of my father there was the thrill of a new relationship, or rather the rekindling of an old one. I had married and divorced in the intervening period and now realized he was the only one for me.

When I went back to Number Nine Spike was in a sombre

mood. He asked me to cancel all his engagements. Paddy had two weeks left to live. She died on 8 February 1978. To spare her the pain he did not tell Jane that her mother would die until the evening before. Her reaction haunted him for the rest of his life. 'But Daddy,' she said, 'I'm only eleven years old.'

I offered to help with the funeral arrangements but he said he wanted to make them himself. There was no depression, no tension, no rages. Even when things went wrong he maintained an unusual calmness. He did, however, ask me to organize the flowers and knew precisely what he wanted: red roses from him, violets from Jane, with a mixed floral tribute from the other children, and a similar bouquet from Jean Reid, Nanny, who had lived with them since Jane was six weeks old. Everything had to be planned precisely: the undertakers must arrive on the minute, the church service should run no later than the designated time, and the cemetery attendants and priest must be in their places for the arrival of her coffin.

Here was a man who always left organization to someone else, generally me, and suddenly he was the man in charge. The prospect before him was daunting. He loved all his children unreservedly, protectively and generously. Now he would have to keep them together as a family. Although only Jane was Paddy's child the other three always called her Mum.

Paddy was buried on 15 February. Spike arrived at the church hand in hand with Jane and Silé, with Laura and Sean behind. I had never seen him look so haunted. I was sitting next to Harry and Myra Secombe. 'Oh, Norma,' said Harry. 'What's happened to my dear, dear friend?'

Chapter Sixteen

Two days after the funeral Spike went into a deep depression that was to last more than two weeks. He did not want the children to see him in that state. So Nanny looked after them with the same devotion she had shown over the past eleven years. Nanny was a Scot, a widow, loving, but never one to brook any nonsense, and she exerted discipline in a family where that quality was in short supply. She nursed Paddy through her illness with great tenderness and sympathy. Now Paddy had gone her rôle was more important than ever and Spike leaned heavily on her.

Spike stayed in his room at the office, sometimes going without food for days. Then occasionally of an evening he would slip out and buy Battenberg cakes and peanut butter. Every morning I slipped a note under the door to say I had arrived and another to say when I went home.

Peter Sellers rang from the States to say he was coming to England and had tried to ring Spike but the number he had was a ceased line. Spike's private number was changed frequently because when he was in a friendly mood he would give it to someone he liked – well, liked at that moment. When he got too many calls he would rail that the world and his dog had his private number and it had to be changed, that day, not tomorrow, but immediately. And so it was. Then some of his close friends might have only the old number, so it was frustrating all round. I gave Pete his new number, but Spike had taken the phone off the hook. Pete wanted to have dinner with him. I promised to push a note under the door to let him know. Still no reaction.

Three or four days later I went into the office and I knew we were back on track. There was a note pinned to his door: 'Leave me alone.' Liz Cowley rang that morning to tell me he had called her the previous evening, saying he needed someone to talk to, so they had dinner at Maggie Jones. I went upstairs, knocked on the door, and said, 'It's me.'

'Who's me?'

'Me.'

'Come in me.'

He unlocked the door. I reminded him Pete was in London. Spike invited me to join them at Pomegranates restaurant. At first Spike was subdued, but as always, Pete cheered him up. They could both be evil and this had not changed. Which is where I came in. Some years earlier I had raved to Spike about Laurence Olivier's performance in *The Merchant of Venice*, when I fell in love with his voice. That was enough for Spike, the man who said 'Never meet your hero.'

'Do you know,' said Spike, 'he has terrible trouble with athlete's foot. When Willie Wyler was directing him as Heathcliff, Olivier's complaints about his foot drove him to distraction.'

'Enough, Spike.'

But he was relentless.

'It got so bad it was suppurating. He couldn't walk across the studio floor.'

Ever after that, when I saw Olivier, I wondered if his athlete's foot was bothering him. Or had he ever had it?

Then it was Pete's turn. He had filmed *The Pink Panther Strikes Again* with Omar Sharif.

'How lucky you were to work with him,' I said. 'What was he like?'

Big mistake.

'You have no idea. His body odour! You would have hated to be near him.'

'I don't want to hear any of that.'

'But it's true,' he said, and warmed to his theme, going into great and graphic detail. Spike was the most cheerful I had seen him in months.

The next morning I asked Spike whether he thought Pete had told the truth about Omar. He grinned cheekily.

'You'll never know, but every time you see Sharif you'll wonder.'

In fact I met him at the Chichester Festival years later and it was not true. But that was Pete. It was typical of the pair of them. If a woman in their company said she admired a particular man, that is, not either of them, they would manufacture a fault in an instant.

Spike was soon back in the old routine, dinner with his 'birds', as he called them, violent squash sessions three times a week at the Lambton Place Health Club in Bayswater, and obsessive days of writing, with hour upon hour spent hunched over his portable typewriter. He was working on a book of serious poetry, *Spike Milligan's Q Annual*, and a children's poetry book, all simultaneously.

'You need to take a break,' I told him.

'Norm, I can't. I'm like Van Gogh. He couldn't stop painting and I can't stop writing.'

He had wrestled with one particular poem. 'Here,' he said. 'I've made some adjustments and I'm happy with it now.'

> We've come a long way
>   said the cigarette scientist
> as he destroyed a live rabbit
>   to show the students how it worked
> He took its heart out
>   plugged it into an electric pump
>   that kept it beating for nearly two hours
> I know rabbits who can keep their hearts
>   beating for nearly seven years
> And look at the electricity they save.

He kept up the same frenetic pace for about three weeks and then late one evening he rang me at home. He had visited Paddy's grave several times and was convinced she was unhappy in her resting place. She was buried close to a wall in Bells Hill Cemetery and deserved much better. Without giving me time to comment he said, 'Goodnight, my sunshine girl.' I wondered if grief or guilt had driven him to visit her grave. Would his concern trigger a depression?

He did not come to the office the next morning, ringing to say he had decided to stay at home so he could meet Jane when she returned from school. Late that evening he called me to say he had visited Paddy's grave once again.

'I've found a much better place at St Pancras in the Roman Catholic section. It's beautiful for her there. I'm going to arrange an exhumation.'

I tried to dissuade him because of the effect it might have on the children, but he would not listen.

The next morning he returned to the office and he immediately started formulating ideas for his next television series, *Q8*. It was as if nothing had happened. He did not mention Paddy's grave again until April, when he announced that the exhumation had taken place.

*

There is no doubt that in Spike Milligan dwelt, sometimes raged, many different people. One of these was the devoted husband and father, another the free spirit who slept with anyone who took his fancy. After Paddy's death, as if determined to put away the sad memories, Spike seemed intent on sleeping with as many women as possible. There was a different one every night and then, after a few months, he started to see Shelagh Sinclair more frequently. I simply could not work it out. In some ways she represented everything he disliked. He was highly critical of people, especially girlfriends, who smoked or drank and whose voices grew louder with every glass. Of course, he went out with other girlfriends at the same time but it was obvious that she had a growing attraction for him.

Neil Shand was co-writing Q8 and one night he and his wife had dinner with Spike and Shelagh. The next day, when Neil arrived at the office, Spike said he wanted to take Shelagh somewhere special at the weekend. Did Neil have any ideas?

'Beachy Head,' said Neil.

Spike thought this hilarious and rang down to tell me. They laughed about it many times, but Spike still persisted in seeing Shelagh.

Then he decided to invite her to Monkenhurst for the week-end. Nanny called me afterwards and said the visit had been a disaster. But she was invited several more times, and after each time, Nanny called me to say how concerned she was. Her main worry was that Grandma Milligan was due to make a visit soon. I advised her to say nothing, because the more people complained, the more Spike would dig in his heels.

A week later I was at the Trattoo with Jack Clarke when Spike walked in with Liz Cowley. After we finished dinner we went upstairs to listen to Alan at the piano and were soon joined by Spike and Liz. Suddenly Shelagh burst in, seemingly slightly the worse for wear, and crying because Spike had not phoned her. He told her to go and she went. The next day I said that having birds burst into restaurants like that would not do his image any good. He was adamant that if she did not change her ways he would get rid of her. 'But,' he added, 'I've got a big problem. Sex with her is the best I've ever had.'

Spike was becoming a cause for concern from a professional point of view because he was not interested in doing anything other than write. He needed to be seen so I persuaded him to appear on a few television programmes, nice and easy. Then he decided to have a dinner party at Monkenhurst with Shelagh and a few close friends, among them Doug Kidgell and his wife. Although Doug had played the drums with Spike and his army band he played Spike's magnificent grand piano very well and I sang all the old songs. Shelagh was on her best behaviour and it was an extremely pleasant evening.

As I was leaving Spike said, 'I'll be in tomorrow. I'm having dinner with Roberta Watt in the evening.'

For a moment I was speechless, but only for a moment. 'Oh, great,' I said. 'Let me know how much.'

He looked at me with those sorrowful eyes. 'That unchristian streak in you just had to raise its head to spoil my evening.'

I heard no more about it. In fact Spike entered a period of unusual calm. And much to my surprise, he and Neil completed Q8 in good time. In August Spike was keen for me to meet Patrick O'Neill, who had toured with him in Australia as schlepper for the Packer organization and was in the U.K. on holiday. 'He has the emotions of a Dover sole but is the best schlepper I've had,' said Spike. O'Neill wanted to become an impresario one day. I was not overwhelmed by O'Neill, and little did I suspect that he would soon achieve this ambition.

Then Grandma arrived but found that the atmosphere at Monkenhurst was not to her liking and came to stay with me. Of all her visits I think 1978 was the most enjoyable. I had some misgivings because I was not sure how she and my mother, who was also staying with me, would get on. I need not have worried.

They were both committed Christians and at that time in Quex Road, North London, half a mile or so from my flat, there was a Roman Catholic church immediately next door to the Anglican church. They walked there side by side every Sunday morning to make their devotions, separating only when they reached the two churches. One day Mum said to Grandma, 'I'll come into your church with you. There's only one God and he cares for us all.' From that moment on they were lifelong friends.

On 7 November she decided to return to Monkenhurst and I took her to the office so Spike could drive her home. We had lunch at a small Greek restaurant at the corner of Orme Court and Moscow Road and afterwards walked to Number Nine. In my office she looked at my new photograph of Anthony Hopkins but did not recognize him. 'Where's the picture of your friend, the one you had next to Terry's?' I explained I had changed the photograph. She said, 'I think he'll be much better now. I light a candle for him every week when I light them for you and Terry.' I told her I had read that he had gone to Los Angeles and joined Alcoholics Anonymous. 'Yes, I know he'll be fine. I'll go on lighting candles for him. I pray that he will have someone to look after him the way you look after my son.' She looked steadily at me. Dear transparent Grandma. In her mind she still thought I might be tempted to leave Spike for Anthony.

Later I told Spike how incredible I thought she was to have remembered the episode at the Trattoo years earlier. He turned to the photograph and said, 'Dear Tony. I thought you'd be pleased to know that Spike Milligan's mother is still lighting candles for you halfway round the world. Do let me know if they are working. Love, Norma Farnes.' I begged him not to mock her in her hearing because he was about to take her home and if there was one wrong word she would pack her bags and leave. I made him promise to behave and for once he did.

Meanwhile, Johnny Speight had an idea for a stage play to be called *Goebbels' Diaries*. Johnny would write it, Spike would play

Adolf, and Eric Goebbels. Everybody was enthusiastic and a meeting was arranged at Luigi's restaurant in Tavistock Street. Johnny was going to bring along an impresario and it would be strictly a business dinner. Spike's no smoking campaign was then at its height and he told me to remind everyone not to light up. If we were in a restaurant and someone lit up nearby he got up and went. What bothered me was that I knew Johnny, an inveterate cigar smoker, would wind Spike up at the table.

'What happened to live and let live?' I asked.

He flew into a rage and I got a ten-minute tirade about nicotine and the danger of cancer.

'If people can't stop smoking for two hours they're addicts and don't deserve to be in civilized company. I don't want to be near them, breathing their lethal smoke.'

A private room was booked and when I arrived Johnny was nursing a large Partagas No. 1 cigar and puffing the smoke up the chimney. Great, I thought, as the room filled with fumes. Spike would probably take one sniff and leave. We waited and waited. He was late, very late. Perhaps an hour passed then there was a telephone call for Johnny. He came back and told us Spike wanted us to join him at Kettners. He had had a row with the taxi driver on the way and got out in Soho. When we arrived he was sitting at a large round table puffing a cheroot with Shelagh by his side, clouding him with cigarette smoke. He had the sort of grin on his face that told me he had had one too many glasses of Gewürztraminer or Orvieto, and Shelagh was enjoying herself. Johnny saw the funny side and gave us five minutes of his earlier antics, puffing smoke up the chimney to avoid offending Spike, who was meanwhile puffing away at Kettners. It was one of those evenings when Spike was in love with the world and joined Johnny in the act. We had a wonderful evening. *Goebbels' Diaries*? It never got off the ground.

The next day Grandma rang before departing for Australia to tell me she was a 'very troubled mother'. 'I've been watching

Spike and his new lady friend,' she said, 'and she's a bad influence on him.' I put in a good word for Shelagh, but Grandma had made up her mind and nothing would convince her to the contrary. She never did change her opinion of Shelagh.

There were more television appearances. Spike and I were both fans of the *Muppet Show*, so when I heard they were filming at the ATV studio in London in November I made arrangements for him to star in it. He was enthralled by the experience. He adored Kermit and Miss Piggy and reckoned Jim Hansen, the creator, was a genius. For once, in his words, he was not 'surrounded by idiots', and everyone concerned was delighted with his performance, including Kermit and Miss Piggy.

Then *Parkinson* was keen to have him and I was satisfied this would not be a problem because he thought Parky was the best interviewer of them all. Great, I thought, no tension. Wrong! On the morning of the show there was a note under my door. 'I'M ILL. CAN'T DO THE SHOW. DON'T KNOCK.' The following day, however, he happily did *Quote Unquote* with Terry Wogan and Anna Ford, falling totally in love with her. 'She's stunning,' he said and wrote her a fan letter. Good, I thought, we're getting back to normal.

Soon afterwards Lord Delfont rang to invite Spike and me to dinner. There was a reason, I thought, but it had not been mentioned. Spike had not seen Bernard for years and was happy to accept. So we went along to the Cavalry Grill at the Hyde Park Hotel, where we were made extremely welcome. The waiters seemed even more intent on pleasing Bernard than Spike, they positively fawned over him. Poor Spike was driven to say something.

'By God, Bernard. They treat you as if you owned the place.'

Bernard coughed and looked embarrassed.

'As a matter of fact, I do.'

We laughed and from then on had a wonderful evening. Spike

ragged Bernard unmercifully about an incident at Eastbourne where he had done gigs for him and his brother, Lew Grade. Spike, then in his early days as a performer, had been told by Lew, 'If you do a good week I'll give you an extra twenty-five pounds.' He did an excellent week but of course Lew never paid up. Every Christmas he sent Lew a card with a postscript, 'You still owe me twenty-five quid from Eastbourne.' When I met Lew I asked him why he did not pay up.

'What! And not get that Christmas card from Spike every year! It's worth more than £25,000.'

As the dinner drew to a close Bernard revealed his hidden purpose. He wanted Spike to appear in a charity show the following year. Spike was happy to agree.

It was now December and Spike decided he would not work again until the New Year. 'I've got to put something back so I'm going to concentrate on saving the elephants.'

He phoned me on New Year's Eve.

'Happy birthday, Norm. Is your life okay?'

I said my love life was booming and all was well. 'What about you, Spike? How's your life?'

'I'll tell you what it's like. It's like the last three hours before Hitler committed suicide. Except my three hours has gone on for thirty fucking years and the trouble is there are no Russians to end the suffering.'

Goodbye 1978.

'Welcome, 1979,' I said to Spike during our usual New Year's call. 'I have a feeling it's going to be a good year.'

'Norm,' he said, 'the one thing I love about you is you're the world's greatest optimist. I'll remind you of the good year in December when I'm saying "Fucking good riddance."'

'No, this time it will be better. I feel it in my bones.'

He was going to tour South Africa again in February, there were more books, and Jimmy Verner wanted to do another U.K.

tour. I thought that recital would prevent the complaint 'You're keeping me unemployed' – for the time being, at least. He prepared to rewrite his one-man show for South Africa, then there was a ray of sunshine. Eric told him he would be in South Africa with Hattie Jacques so we could all meet up out there. Suddenly Spike was all 'love, light and peace'.

'We can visit places of interest during the day, I can play squash and we can swim. We'll have a great time.'

Good. In that sort of mood the rewrite would go well.

'I'll finish it in a few days,' he said.

When he finished he announced he needed a denim suit with very long trouser pockets for his props, and a denim jacket that opened down the front with two large pockets on either side. My heart sank. I insisted he drew the outfits in great detail so I could give it to the wardrobe mistress. I had had too many dramas about outfits not being exactly what he wanted. People – me – could not carry out simple tasks, that was the trouble.

'And I'm the one who has to stand in front of the audience with my head above the parapet when the bloody props don't work.'

I had no intention of being the target for all that. So it was a question of making certain the props were right, and that he had three copies of the running order, because he was quite capable of losing one or even two and then swearing before God that he had never been given one. I would check his wastepaper basket to make sure he had not thrown them away, because there was no doubt who would carry the can.

Chapter Seventeen

Now Paddy was no longer around to shoulder the blame for his tantrums, what or who would be the trigger for 'I'm too ill to go?' The trigger came on 16 January, dangerously close to our departure date. He had had dinner with Shelagh the previous evening and was concerned about her. I tried to calm him and take his mind off it; he was due to do the rescheduled interview on *Parkinson* the following week and have a fitting for the denim suit two days later, and luckily both went off without a hitch. And then a good sign.

'I'll take Liz to dinner before I go.'

South Africa here we come. And then my heart sank.

'I've invited Shelagh to visit us in South Africa.'

I had a nightmarish vision. I could see this leading to rows, which would send him into despair and the show would be off. We flew out as planned and not long after Shelagh arrived that is exactly what happened. The first cancellation was on 7 March in Johannesburg. And what concerned me more was that he too had started to drink too much, though he was aware of it and did something about it.

Shelagh went back to London soon after Eric arrived. I could relax again and reflected happily on the fact that the tour was a sell-out. Then on 16 March Spike suddenly looked far from well. He said it was nothing to worry about; it was 'only physical.' The next day he looked worse so I called a doctor, who confirmed that he had tick bite fever with a temperature of 104°F and said he could not possibly do the show. Spike ignored him and after two hours came off the stage so saturated with sweat that he looked as though someone had thrown a bucket of water over him. The one time he had every justification for not doing the show he did it. There was no show the next day so he stayed in bed but that evening went to the Witwatersrand University to listen to some jazz.

Pretoria was the highlight of the tour as far as Spike was concerned. He had always wanted to visit the Voortrekker Monument and I had to make sure that, no matter what happened, time was found for that. Geoff, one of the entourage, offered to drive us to the monument, several miles out of town. When the pick-up time arrived Spike was nowhere to be seen. He had forgotten all about it and was doing his usual twenty-five lengths of the hotel pool. We got him out and into the car and now we were all set. Then Spike remembered he had promised Dr Sydney Gottlieb, a Pretorian, that he would visit his old school. So we spent some time looking round and Spike was amused to find the young Sydney in a photograph. Now it was late and evening approached, but Spike insisted that we must visit the monument.

'It'll be closed,' said Geoff.

'We'll still go.'

It started to rain and as we drove along the long, straight road across the veldt the sky was split by lightning and thunder drowned the sound of the engine. The rain turned into a deluge and visibility was almost nil. I became extremely nervous but there was no let up. This is how the earth started, I thought, or how it ends.

'Don't worry,' said Spike, 'we couldn't be safer in the car. The rubber of the tyres will act as an insulator.'

Suddenly he was a scientist. I was not convinced. He started belting out, 'I'm singin' in the rain.' Normally I would have joined in but I was frightened. Then suddenly he pointed.

'There it is.' A soft light suffused the stone sculptures depicting the nineteenth-century trek of the Boers into the veldt. There were figures of women and children helping to herd cattle, oxen pulling carts and men on alert against native tribes and fierce animals. It really was dramatic. It was also closed.

'Come on, Norm. We'll have to climb over the railings.' I looked at them. Metal and about ten feet high, or so they seemed to me. I could not think of anything worse.

'Not for me.'

'You'll regret it if you don't. You'll probably never have another chance.'

'Why is it that you're always making me do things I don't want to do?'

The fence looked huge, but he helped and we both climbed over. The lightning still cracked the sky though it was further away, yet strong enough to make the carvings of the voortrekkers even more striking. They brought home to me the tremendous hardships the people had encountered when they escaped British rule in the Cape. We both stood there for minutes on end, gazing at them.

'Aren't you glad you made the climb? You'll remember this all your life.'

I was and I still do.

From Pretoria we went to Johannesburg to end the tour. I decided to have a day to myself and visit the Carlton Shopping Mall. There was an exhibition of paintings in the arcade and my eye went immediately to one by a famous South African artist, Jacobi. It depicted a tranquil scene at Port Edwards with the sea rippling gold in the beams of a lowering sun. I had to have it.

It was about five feet wide and nearly three feet deep, but the problem of getting it into the aircraft never entered my mind. I went back to the hotel and showed it to Spike. He joked, 'It'll have to travel first class back to London while I go economy.'

It went with me when we flew to Bloemfontein the next day and on the two-hour drive to Kimberley, the last stage of the tour. Spike said to the technician, 'Put the painting on the stage tonight. Let the audience look at it instead of me.' They could joke as much as they liked. I had blown all my money on it and wherever I went so did the painting. When we arrived at Kimberley we were all covered in a fine red dust from the unmade road – all, that is, except my painting, which was carefully wrapped.

There were only two nights left and on the last there was a heckler in the house. Spike loved that. It gave him the opportunity to fire quick, unrehearsed retorts and there was nobody better at that than him. That night's heckler brought out all the old chestnuts.

'If you really want me to be funny lend me the shirt you're wearing,' said Spike.

The heckler did not like that and tried several more sallies until the audience told him to shut up. Spike continued the show and got a standing ovation. When the curtain came down the audience refused to leave. So he came back and played his trumpet with asides to the audience. They lapped it up and he glowed in their warmth.

As it was the last night Spike invited the crew and the impresario, good old Ronnie Quibell, and his family to a party at the hotel across from the theatre. Spike had a glass or two of wine in the dressing room with someone he had met in town so the pair of us were the last to leave. Outside the stage door there was a man big enough for a Springbok forward, about six feet seven and menacing. The heckler. He jabbed a fat finger at Spike and said, in a thick Afrikaans accent, 'Hey, you! Are you the guy who thinks he's funny?'

Without a heartbeat's hesitation Spike replied, 'Yes. Are you the cunt that paid to see me?'

Then he took my hand. 'Run, Norm!'

I was dressed for the party and wearing high heels. He dragged me across the road, shouting over his shoulder, 'That's the best ad lib you've heard this evening.'

His response must have stopped the Afrikaner in his tracks because he was still standing outside the stage door when we reached the refuge of the hotel. So the tour ended on a happy note.

We travelled to Johannesburg for the flight back to London the next day and the Quibells were there to say their farewells. Spike saw I was carrying my painting.

'What the hell's that?' he said.

'My picture and it's going with me.'

'They'll make you put it in the hold. It'll get damaged so why don't you just give it away to avoid all the trouble.'

As we walked through the airport to the check-in he told passers-by what an idiot he had as a manager. 'No chance. She'll never get it back to London.' He carried on all the way to the departure gate, but I was persuasive and an air hostess stowed it in a cupboard. Still his quips continued. 'She thinks more of the painting than she does of me', and 'If she couldn't have brought the painting she'd have left me to travel alone.'

'Isn't he adorable?' remarked one of the hostesses. I did not comment.

Jack Clarke met us at Heathrow in his tiny Renault 5, thinking there was only me to pick up with a couple of suitcases. There was a limousine waiting for Spike but he decided he wanted to travel with Jack. I told him he could not because of the painting.

When Jack saw it he said, 'What the hell is that?'

Spike said, 'Jack, you don't want to know. She's schlepped that painting all round South Africa. It can go in the limo. I'm coming with you.'

At this time Jack was new to Spike's eccentricities and could not fathom why he would prefer to travel hunched up in a Renault 5 while an empty limousine carried my painting in state.

Q8 had been screened while we were away and then Spike went to Australia briefly to do a television show. Once he was back he needed to start work on Q9, but Spike was unhappy and things ground to a halt. Peter Sellers bore a large part of the responsibility for this.

Although Spike and Pete's friendship went back many years it had its bad moments. It was tested to the full by Old Min, a 1928 soft-top Austin tourer that had captivated Spike from the moment he saw her. She provided him with some of his happiest times. Quite often he crowded Paddy and the children into her for Sunday picnics, all of them dressed in clothes fashionable when the car was new.

Pete was a total car nut. All the greats of the twentieth century were his: Rolls-Royce, Bentley, Cadillac, Aston Martin and a score of others. He envied Spike's ownership of Old Min more than he treasured his own cars, even more than he could have the most desirable of women, and that is saying something. Over the years he offered ridiculous amounts of money, yet Spike would not part with her and rubbed it in by telephoning Pete on Monday mornings to describe the marvellous weekend he and his family had spent in Old Min. A love of mischief bound them but at times it verged on gleeful wickedness and with Old Min things became vicious.

In 1968 Spike lost his driving licence. He had been working at the ITV studios in Wembley when he met an actress he knew and, surprise, surprise, they had a few drinks at the club upstairs. She asked him to drop her at her flat. No problem. In those days most people thought nothing about driving home after a night out with a bottle of wine or more inside them; however, the breathalyser had just made its appearance. The actress told Spike to turn the wrong way into a one-way street. Unfortunately

P.C. Plod was parked in the street, no doubt having a quiet fag. The policeman stopped them, ordered Spike to blow into the breathalyser and said, 'I'm afraid it's turned green, Mr. Milligan.'

'What do you expect? I'm Irish.'

Whether the magistrate thought that was funny or not he suspended Spike's licence for twelve months. Knowing my man, I insisted on a promise that he would not drive during that period. If he did and was caught it could mean prison, I warned.

'Okay,' he said, not for the first time, 'I'll sew mailbags badly.'

He could not give that promise, he told me, because if any of his children needed him he would have to break it. I had to be satisfied with that. He did not want to be tempted to drive Old Min, so he offered her to Pete for £200. Pete was beside himself, deliriously happy with his old mate, his dear old friend. The classic cars worth thousands in his huge garage were as nothing; Old Min was the thing. A garage was given instructions to make her indistinguishable from new. Seats were covered in the very best leather, the running boards renewed in the original type of wood, the chrome re-plated, the body given an exemplary paint job and the hood replaced.

The year passed and Spike got his licence back. His and Pete's relationship was then going through one of its golden phases; nothing was too good for the other. Pete telephoned from Hollywood. 'Norm. I miss Spike so much I want to give him Old Min as a present. Don't tell him.' I did not and shortly afterwards Old Min appeared outside Spike's house on Holden Road, with a bottle of Dom Perignon on the passenger seat. An ecstatic Spike gave me the champagne – I still have the bottle – and the picnic trips resumed. Such was their magnanimity that when Pete was in London Spike would offer him Old Min on loan. After a weekend Pete would return it with thanks. All very civilized, I thought, but how long would it last?

Not long as it turned out. Pete had a row with one of his girlfriends and rang to say he needed Spike. Would he join him on his motor yacht at Capri? Spike could not go because he was filming a show for the BBC, but Pete insisted. Was not Spike his oldest and dearest friend? Besides, the BBC did not give two hoots about Spike and would drop him whenever they felt like it. His loyalty was not to them but his old friend. Spike was deaf to this: he was contracted to do a job and he would complete it. But nothing was below the belt as far as Pete was concerned.

'How about Old Min?' he asked. He had lavished loving care on the car, had her renovated regardless of cost, not that he was counting the money, Spike should understand.

Spike would not countenance blackmail, at least, not when it was aimed at him.

'Send Old Min back to him,' he ordered and she was duly delivered to Richard Williams, a wonderful mechanic who was the custodian of all Pete's cars.

Months later, when all had been forgiven if not forgotten, they had dinner together. The next day there was a call from an ecstatic Paddy. Old Min, she announced, had reappeared. Pete telephoned me. He knew how much his old and dearest friend loved Old Min, so he wanted him to have her as a present – again. Some time later Pete wondered whether he could borrow Old Min to go on a vintage Austin rally. Of course he could. So back and forth Old Min went.

All this sweet reasonableness, I thought, could not go on. And it did not. In 1979 Pete received great acclaim for his role as the simple-minded gardener, Chance, in *Being There*. For years he had been desperate to win an Oscar and was convinced that his performance would reward him with one. Knowing Pete as I did, I can imagine how shattered he was when Dustin Hoffman won it instead for his performance in *Kramer vs. Kramer*. A few weeks after the Academy Awards Pete was scheduled to do a radio interview in England along with the actress Irene Handl and the producer decided it would be a good idea to have a link up with Spike, who was still in Australia. When they were on air Spike joked, 'Hey, man. You were caught with your trousers down. Hoffman got the Oscar.'

Somehow Pete concealed his fury but he was livid. His secretary, Sue Evans, told me he stormed into his flat in a terrible rage. He made twenty or thirty attempts at writing a letter to tell Spike how hurt and furious he was, how he could not believe that a friend would stick the knife in so publicly. But then, said Sue, he had a better idea.

'I'll pay him back where it hurts most.'

He sent Richard Williams to collect Old Min, and of course everyone at Monkenhurst was accustomed to her being driven away one week and returned the next, so saw nothing unusual in it. When Spike returned from Australia he asked me to have Old Min sent to Monkenhurst for a family outing. I telephoned Richard Williams and asked him to arrange it.

'Don't you know?' Richard said. When someone says 'Don't you know', I do not want to know.

'P.S. sold her.' It was like having ice cubes poured down my back. I was speechless. Richard went on, 'I thought it was unusual because he didn't advertise it. Just sold it and that was that.'

There was nothing for it. Spike had to be told.

'What else have you given away while I was in Australia? Did you give any of my children away? How about my house? Has that gone too?'

After a few minutes of this enough was enough.

'Go and ask your lunatic friend. He's the one with the evil streak. He wanted to hurt you so don't try to take it out on me. You know he's done it so rant and rave at him. He deserves it. I don't.'

I slammed the phone down. A moment later the phone rang again.

'Let's both cool off. If you don't want to stab me in the back shall we have a cup of tea together?'

This was his way of saying 'Sorry'. Although I was tempted

to walk out after the tirade that would have meant a double victory for Sellers. As we sipped our tea Spike suddenly brightened.

'I know what I'll do. I'll find out who bought it and buy it back.'

What he meant was that Tanis would have to find out where it was. She was quite the detective and later that day discovered the new owner in Bradford.

I had an idea that the buy back price would be high because the logbook showed Spike Milligan and Peter Sellers as previous owners. But the asking price was ridiculous. £60,000, the bloke told me, no doubt thinking that Spike was rolling in it and desperate to have the car back, no matter the cost. I tried to haggle but he would not budge. Even Spike baulked at the price. He looked so sad.

'Goodbye, Old Min,' he said. And that was it. He had an extraordinary ability to cut things out of his life and that was what he did with Old Min. She was never mentioned again.

Most people would have ended the friendship there and then and if it had been anyone else Spike would have done so, but he was always prepared to forgive hurts inflicted by his family and Pete was an honorary relative.

So the Q9 box files of sketch ideas remained unopened and the books unfinished. Instead he started to list things that needed to be done at Monkenhurst, absolute trivia, and spent afternoons with Alan Clare or invited Jack Hobbs to the office to swap stories and laughs. Then squash games were back on the afternoon agenda and Ronnie Scott's of an evening. Before long I would be accused of keeping him unemployed, not caring what happened to him, but there was none of that yet. Quite the reverse: my phone rang late one night, the first occasion for some time.

'You are the only constant in my life,' he said. 'God knows what's going to happen to me and God knows where I'll end up. Remember, I dedicated *Adolf Hitler* to you, "my manager who puts up with me." I hope you go on putting up with me.'

I asked him what had brought this on.

'Harry.'

He spoke of Harry for some time. 'He has got it right. If anyone has a fireplace in his life he has. Myra was always at home when he finished a gig, no matter what the time.' No doubt they had their fair share of rows and anxieties over their children, as he had with his, but Harry had been truly blessed when he found Myra. And so it went on. Then he asked if I knew that he and Harry once shared a tiny flat in the early days at Linden Gardens in Notting Hill. The landlord said it was strictly for two people only but they sneaked in Michael Bentine.

'There were only two single beds but Harry insisted Michael slept in his while he curled up on the floor. Harry was the generous one. He thought I was neurotic about tidiness. They were great days. We were all so happy.' This was all said so wistfully.

Spike put down the phone, but by then I was wide awake and pondered over the relationship he had with Harry, completely different from the one he had with Pete. Spike and Harry did not see each other all that often but they talked on the telephone from time to time and there would be the odd funny telegram. It was a quiet but firm affection. Harry, however, was wary of Spike when they appeared together in a show or on television. Sometimes Spike could be cruel. I was present at a function when Harry arrived with Myra. Both were very short and Spike shouted, 'Here come the dwarfs.' It was a hurtful and entirely unnecessary remark, not at all funny and I told him so.

'Don't be silly. You're becoming too sensitive for your own good. Harry won't mind.'

But Harry did mind and so did Myra. He told me Myra was upset and I could tell they both were. Spike was not able to understand this. What I could not understand was why Spike did it because he was fond of them, but sometimes his remarks could hurt. I have never understood why he said it. Perhaps for a laugh. If so it fell flat.

He had only one serious criticism of Harry. After *The Goon Show* had finished all the performers except Max Geldray, the harmonica player, had found work. Spike was trying to find something for him to do so he rang Harry, who was playing the London Palladium. 'Speak to Val Parnell and get Max a job there, perhaps to open the show in the first half.' Harry said he could not because he did not have that much pull. 'For Christ's sake, Harry. You're top of the bill,' said Spike, but Harry would not be budged. Harry was always slightly insecure, so perhaps he did not want to push his luck. That was the only criticism he made of Harry – but he told the story over and over again.

I arrived at the office the morning after this phone call to find a tiny slip of paper had been pushed under my door. On it was only one word: 'ILL.'

Spike was due to meet Jack Hobbs at the office that day, so I rang him but he already knew it was off. Spike had phoned him late the evening before to say he was tormented by nightmares about Shelagh. That night we had booked dinner at the Trattoo with Jimmy Verner to discuss another tour so I decided to go alone. Just as we were enjoying a glass of wine Spike arrived and, strangely enough, we had a constructive meeting and agreed the broad terms of the tour. The evening passed pleasantly, then Shelagh arrived and Jimmy and I left them to it. The next day Spike narrated another concert performance of *The Snow Goose* which went smoothly.

In May, Harry Edgington, his old friend from Army days, was returning to New Zealand after a visit. I was surprised Spike had not seen him all that often and asked why. After all, he had written about this friendship in his war books and often spoke of him in the warmest of terms. Spike let rip. Harry had given him a lecture on the way he brought up his children, indulging their every whim and giving them far too much money. Spike was outraged, claiming he had paid Harry's fare to New Zealand when he and his wife decided to emigrate; to criticize the way he spent his money was a bit rich. It is difficult to conceive that this small difference of opinion, a minor row, could damage a friendship of so many years but it did.

Filming started for Q9 but by then Spike was very worried about Shelagh and the stress had taken its toll. He phoned me from upstairs to say he had asked her to consult Sydney Gottlieb in the hope that he could sort out her problems. I said I thought this was a bridge too far if he wanted to continue the relationship, which obviously meant a great deal to him. No, he said, this was it: if she did not seek help from Sydney the whole thing was over. I disagreed and told him that if he wanted a future in which she played a part he must accept her past because he could not change it. Luckily in the event Shelagh was happy to consult Sydney and this helped set his mind at rest.

Chapter Eighteen

Spike had a short fuse when it came to his cars. One Sunday he phoned me at home to say his car had broken down in St John's Wood. Would I collect it for him?

'Whereabouts in St John's Wood?'

'How the hell should I know!' he said. Down went the phone.

I decided to spend the day peacefully at home and look for the car the next day. After driving round St John's Wood in my own Mini for half an hour or so I found Spike's with its bonnet up. So he had tried to mend it, God help us. I got out and went to put the bonnet down. There was only an empty space underneath. Someone had stolen the engine overnight. I rang Spike. 'Oh, fuck,' he said. 'You'd better get me another car.' He never mentioned it again.

While most of us adopt a measured approach when buying a new car, with Spike it was always a drama. Earlier in 1979 he had had trouble with his Mini, just minor things, there was nothing seriously wrong with it, but nonetheless he left me a note. 'Miss Farnes: the Mini GTX has broken down. Stop all payments. The car is by the side of the synagogue. I want another Mini. If needs be get on to another company. If you can't do it I can.'

I do not know what he meant by 'payments', because SMP bought the cars outright. He had obviously worked himself into a tantrum. I tried the Mini and it started immediately. I went back to Number Nine, but Spike was nowhere to be found, so I left him a note. 'Mr. Milligan: I went to the car to see what was wrong with it. It started straight away. I drove it round the block. One thing: the choke was fully out. It might have been flooded. I rang the garage. What can I do? It's working.'

I was stupid to leave that sort of note when he was in that frame of mind. Nothing or nobody could convince him the car was okay: he would have to have another Mini. This time it was dangerous. He wanted a Mini Cooper S with a Taurus conversion, a supercharged, souped-up motor. Now Spike was perhaps London's most inconsiderate driver, and when he got his new toy he drove round London out of his mind with delight.

Shortly afterwards he was due to appear on a late night live programme at Tyne Tees Television in Newcastle. He would go by plane, stay the night and return the next day. He phoned me early in the morning after the show to report that it had gone well. 'It's lovely up here. Why don't you come north and see your mother for the weekend?' Now what was that all about? It was about him staying in Newcastle for the weekend and driving his new car. He had it all planned. I could drive the monster, hand it over to him, take a train to Thornaby, stay with Mum and return to London by train on Monday morning. Like an idiot I agreed. I drove the space capsule north, and on the way every budding Stirling Moss noticed the wide back wheels and the black windows and threw down the challenge. Car after car expected me to race against them as I struggled to keep the car within the speed limit. I was shattered by the time I arrived in Newcastle.

'Never ask me to drive that car again.'

The reply was vintage Milligan.

'You see, you never know what you can do until you do it. And, best of all. YOU-DID-IT-ALL-BY-YOURSELF.'

'Sod off!' I replied.

The car, like every other aspect of everyday living, was always a problem to Spike, especially when it came to parking. Almost opposite Number Nine was the back of the New West End synagogue with parking spaces for the staff. Whenever Spike could not find a parking space he popped into one of the synagogue's private bays. It drove them mad. One of the staff, a kindly little old woman, would knock on the door of Number Nine and ask very politely if Spike could move his car. One time Spike met her himself.

'No I can't,' he said. 'I can't eat it. What do you want me to do with it?'

She was no match for him. A week later he parked there again and this time a dragon came to Number Nine.

'The rabbi is furious with Spike. He's taken his space and he must move it now.'

I had a spare set of keys so rather than have Spike refuse to move the car and possibly be labelled an anti-Semite, I drove it to Mike's garage round the corner, walked back to the office and told Spike where he could find it.

Two weeks later the dragon knocked on the door once again, this time spitting fire.

'Spike's done it again. This will be the last time. The rabbi has let his tyres down.'

I burst out laughing. She was furious. I asked her to see the funny side of it, this Jewish holy man bending over to let the air out of the tyres of a Roman Catholic's car. It did not appeal to her sense of humour.

'Just move it,' she said.

'How can I when the rabbi has let the tyres down?'

Her reply was magnificent.

'I'm not surprised you two work together. He's mad and you're as bad as he is.'

Mike came to the rescue again and pumped up the tyres and moved the car. When I told Spike he laughed. 'He must be a good rabbi to his flock because he's a human being.' And because the rabbi had shown his human side, Spike did not park there any more.

Spike did a couple of television gigs, but he was most interested in organizing a reading of McGonagall's poems with Jack Hobbs, who had helped him with his McGonagall books. I was against this project because the poet was very much a cult figure. When I first heard Spike talk about him I had thought it was a character dreamt up by him and Peter Sellers. They used to recite 'Bridge over the River Tay' in funny voices. But Jack was a devotee and thought the reading a great idea. I did not because it would delay his next war book, which I had been pushing him to write ever since the fourth volume of his memoirs, *Mussolini*, was published in 1978. Spike was furious.

'I don't feel like writing it. And as long as you nag me there won't be another volume. Then it'll be up to you to explain to Michael Joseph that there won't be any more war books. Anyway, it was only planned as a trilogy originally and now there are four. But you always want more. Well, there won't be any more and that's that.'

I tried to explain to him that he was on a winning streak with the memoirs, which were so popular. He had enjoyed writing them and to say that there would be no more was a big mistake. No. My mistake. He wanted to do other things and McGonagall was one of them. It was time for me to back off. I would have to bide my time.

Location filming for Q9 was to start at the end of July, followed by rehearsals and studio recordings in September which would continue through to mid-October. We also had to fit in a television commercial so I knew there was little hope of any work being done on another war book. I was due to take a holiday while he was filming and before I left a note was pushed under my office door. 'Norma fucks off on hols tomorrow.' I wrote 'bloody cheek' underneath and put it under his office door. He relished these exchanges and if I was in the mood we could keep them going for days. The filming and recording went fairly smoothly – as much as it ever did with Spike. Of course there were his usual rows with Ian McNaughton, and the custom-ary walk-outs – and walk-backs – but in the scheme of things that was fairly smooth, though I doubt 'Rage' McNaughton would have agreed with me. I received only two notes in the three weeks of filming, the first under my office door:

> I'M ILL WITH TOO MUCH
> 1. Idiots at the BBC rehearsals
> 2. Disinterested actors
> 3. Maintaining the house alone
> 4. Organizing the garden
> 5. Shelagh

The second appeared on my office door the next day: 'I need Lomatil.' I got him his prescription and suggested that when he needed drugs he should put the note under, not on my door, as everyone in the offices at Number Nine would be able to read it and know he was ill. He could not have cared less.

'Well, aren't they the lucky ones. They don't need them. Well, I do.'

But this was just routine stuff. The party after the last recording was unusual in that everyone was still talking to one another. 'Rage' McNaughton even admitted he would miss Spike.

Spike was due to gather material for *Get in the Q Annual*, to be published the following year, so I thought a gentle reminder was appropriate. 'Yes, it will be ready on time,' he said. 'By the way, I thought I'd let you know I'm having dinner with Roberta Watt this evening.' Again? But I did not reproach him because I did not want him to go into hysterics. Besides, he was due to do some links for the Chichester Jazz Festival, a four-night live music extravaganza, and I did not want him to cancel.

When Spike came back from Chichester he was in raptures. The jazz at Chichester had been fantastic, he said, and he had a date at Ronnie Scott's Jazz Club the following week to listen to Oscar Peterson. Spike's favourite people were musicians. He loved their sense of humour, especially Ronnie Scott's, and loved all kinds of music. He especially delighted in the Proms, and insisted on having an advance list of the concerts. He would choose one of his favourite composers and take a box at the Albert Hall, invite friends, listen to the music, and during the interval serve chilled white wine and smoked salmon sandwiches.

Perhaps the time was ripe for me to pounce.

'Spike, when do you think you might get down to volume five?' The tantrum was more vintage Milligan.

'That's the end of my war. I'm going to do a children's poetry book and that will be the end of all my writing. I'm going to spend more time at Ronnie's. Warren Vache is due at the Pizza on the Park. I'm going to listen to him and that's all I'm going to do – ever. Listen to jazz.'

Spike entered a new phase. I called this his 'everyone must enjoy themselves' mood. He heard, via the Finchley Society, which was still going strong, that the holy sisters at the convent in North Finchley wanted to see *Bubbling Brown Sugar*, a musical in the West End. Therefore the nuns' outing became the most important project of the week. The 'holy sisters' must have the best seats in the theatre. That meant the house seats. 'And I'll pay for them. Book them a table at the Trattoo for dinner after the show and tell Pasquale, the manager, to give them whatever they want and I'll pick up the bill.' We had to organize the holy sisters' transport to the theatre, then get a car to take them on to the restaurant, and have it wait for them at the Trattoo until they were ready to leave.

A few days before they were due to go one of the nuns phoned to say that something had come up. Would it be possible to arrange the excursion for another evening? Of course it would, said magnanimous Milligan. So I started the whole process all over again. Everything was set. Then another phone call. Something else had cropped up. Could the date be rearranged once more? I told Spike.

'You tell those fucking nuns I'm not a box office or a restaurant manager and I can't go on.'

He had, in fact, done nothing other than issue instructions and it was Tanis who did the schlepping. I almost fell over laughing at the latest description of the 'holy sisters'. Tanis eventually got it together and the nuns had their outing.

Spike's mood of benevolence had not entirely evaporated, however. Now he decided to take Jane's headmistress and her husband out to dinner because he wanted to get more involved with Jane's upbringing. With Grandma on the other side of the world and both Paddy's parents dead Jane had no other adult family but him to look to. He agreed to attend the Christmas Bazaar to raise funds for the school. This was Spike, the family man. But I knew another Spike would make a return and Jane would be left with Nanny. She really was her second mother, which was just as well because he soon returned to the arms of the Bayswater Harem.

When I returned to the flat after a short break with my mother Spike rang me late one evening, full of concern. Had we had a good time, what was I doing for Christmas, where would I be? Taunton, I told him, where I shared a house with Jack. Jack could not leave during the holidays because there were several meets of the local hounds with which he hunted. Then he made a strange remark: 'I think you and Jack are going to make it.' I wondered what all this was about, because with Spike it was the sort of conversation that always led to something else. And sure enough, it did.

A doleful Spike said, 'Norm, I don't like having to do everything, organize the garden and the house. It's not fair to leave everything to Nanny. She has enough on her hands looking after Jane. As well as housekeeper she's taken on the rôle of Jane's mother. I feel I should do more but I don't want to.'

'Do you miss Paddy?'

He paused. 'Yes, I do.' Then he hung up. I phoned him back. 'Do you want to talk about it?'

But in seconds he had collected himself.

'I must make this a wonderful Christmas for Jane. The other kids are older and can cope better but she's still a child. I'm going to make this the best Christmas she's ever had.'

It was my turn to hang up because there was nothing more to say and I was tearful.

Spike and his family had as good a time as they possibly could without Paddy, he later told me. Jack and I had a marvellous few days in Taunton so I returned to the office on New Year's Eve in good spirits. I had to go in to finalize Spike's travel arrangements for his stay in Plymouth the following week, where he was going to play a part in *The Pirates of Penzance* for Westward television. Number Nine was closed until 7 January and I loved being there on my own, no telephone calls, just Anthony Hopkins and me. I said 'Happy Birthday' to him and he said 'Happy Birthday' to me, so we would start the New Year on a happy note, a blissful moment snatched from the normal buzz of the office. I had just settled down when my private line rang.

'Where the fuck have you been? Your mother didn't know where you were, Jack didn't know. Are you in hiding or something?'

He did not wait for an answer. 'Cancel Plymouth!'

I knew it was not a definitive 'Cancel': his voice was too strong, he was angry with the world. When he meant it his voice was no more than a whisper, with a slight stutter, which told me that he was going under and had already taken drugs to block out the pain and help him sleep. This sounded more like temperament. I asked him what was wrong. He was surrounded by idiots, he said. 'Oh, how I hate the human race, oh, how I hate its ugly face. The only thing I have in common with all of them is that like them I am *homo sapiens*. That's where it ends.'

This was a tantrum, so I decided to wait and see if his mood changed. I went to Queensway to my hairdresser, John Burlo, had my hair done, and returned to the office. I was leaving later in the afternoon to travel back to Jack in Somerset and celebrate my birthday and the New Year, but I could not leave without speaking to Spike. What to do? As it turned out I did not have to do anything. The phone rang.

'These bloody idiots made me forget to wish you "Happy Birthday". Happy Birthday, Norm. Are you going to tell me that 1980 is going to be a better year? You'll be bloody wrong.'

So Plymouth was on. I never learnt which bloody idiots he was referring to.

All went well with *Pirates* in the end and on his return I reminded him that he had only three weeks to refresh his one-man show before leaving for Australia. I had strong misgivings about this tour, organized by the schlepper, Patrick O'Neill. It was to last sixteen weeks, taking in all the usual theatres. Patrick O'Neill had convinced Spike he was up to it, though I was doubtful because of his lack of experience. But Spike was feeling magnanimous. 'He has to get the experience from somewhere,' he said, and I had to let him have his way.

He sat down at once to hone and alter his act and was so focused that he managed to rewrite the whole thing in a day. As he was going to be away for such a long time I suggested he go back to Monkenhurst and spend more time with Jane. But he was not in his happy families mood any longer. No, he needed to be at the office. He is going to start on the fifth volume of his war memoirs, I thought. Wrong again. He did have the urge to write, though, and reopened his file on the children's poetry project. He was due to leave at the beginning of February, but a week before, out of the blue, he said, 'Shelagh Sinclair wants to come with me.'

I felt like getting down on my hands and knees to thank God I was not going to Australia on this occasion. Coping with Spike and Shelagh in England when I could close the office door and go home to Jack was one thing, but coping with them on the other side of the world would be a whole different matter.

I said, 'Don't phone me when everything goes wrong.'

The tour went ahead and Shelagh went with him. I was delighted when he phoned to say he had decided to fly Jane out as well. 'She'll love it here and she can see her grandma.' Everything was going well, there was no nit picking, the audiences were fantastic, the weather great. So far so good, I thought. Then Grandma called. She was worried for her son because of his girlfriend. I told her Spike was quite capable of looking after himself. At least Grandma was happy with Patrick. 'He really does look after Terry. Takes his linen to the laundry, even washes his shirts.'

Alarm bells rang. Why would he do that? That was not the rôle of an impresario. I had never heard anything like it. I told Grandma there was something wrong.

'Could you see me doing that?'

Her reply was worthy of Spike. 'Oh no, dear. Spike wouldn't let you do such a menial task. In any case you don't even do it for Jack.'

At lunch time there was a call from Spike, in Townsville, late at night there.

'You asked me not to ring you when things went wrong. Well, I have to. I just need to talk to you. It was so bad in Brisbane the other night that the manager of the restaurant asked us to leave and I thought, thank God Norma isn't here.'

He continued, wallowing in his own misery. After the show he wrote in his diary, 'Did the show tonight. I should get a fucking medal for it. I'm suffering because of everyone else.'

I tried to cheer him up. He would soon be flying to New Zealand to see his old wartime mate, Harry Edgington. He always looked forward to that and their reunions seemed to take his mind off his problems. And he was due to appear at the Opera House in Wellington, which he liked. So things did not seem too bad by the time he hung up. About half an hour later he rang again.

'Is anybody feeding the birds and watering my plants? Keep the French windows open during the day and put the birdseed round the window boxes.'

I assured him that Fred (Spike's favourite pigeon) and his mates were fine and that Tanis was feeding them and watering the plants, as she had done for years; she knew the drill by now.

'Ah, she should know the drill but I remember when she let my plants die.'

True, once she had, and he never let her, or anyone else willing to listen, forget it. When he returned from abroad on that occasion he went into his office, saw the dead plants, and came downstairs.

'I'm good to Tanis and she's let my plants die.'

Soon almost everyone at Number Nine heard his woeful tale. The next item on the agenda was his office.

'Is it getting cleaned? Are you keeping the door locked all the time? Has the cleaner changed the sheets on my bed? Is the door locked to my sitting room? Has the cleaner been in the sitting room?'

I sensed that this could turn into 'I'm ill.' The demons were starting to work and he obviously needed the security of knowing everything was normal in Orme Court. I tried to change the subject, and, I hoped, his mood. Did he remember Eric's comments about the birds? There was no response. One day when

Eric walked into Number Nine he saw three large boxes from Harrods in the hall. He asked Tanis what they contained. When she told him it was birdseed he remarked, 'These birds in Bayswater are the only ones in the world to have their food delivered by Harrods.' At the time Spike thought it was funny. Now there was not a murmur. Then he said in a wounded voice, 'You are all together. You are all there. I'm not.' And hung up.

A few days later he was in New Zealand, but I was surprised when he did not call to tell me what a good time he was having with Harry. I later called Harry and learnt that he had been subjected to Spike's cruel side. From his years with Spike in Italy Harry had experienced his temperaments, tantrums and his mental illness, but he had never been the butt of Spike's nastiness. He was shocked when Spike made hurtful remarks about their friend and drummer, Doug Kidgell, and mocked and laughed at others of D Battery. Until then he had never heard Spike utter an uncharitable word about 'the lads', so he concluded that Spike was undergoing a change of personality. I wondered whether this had been a product of Harry's imagination, fuelled by the less frequent telephone calls since their spat over Spike spoiling his children. But then Harry dropped a bombshell. He said he had told Spike that people were beginning to laugh at him over his infatuation with a woman half his age. 'I came at him very much in the manner of a Jankers sergeant, which I knew he would understand,' he said. I was not surprised to learn that in response Spike delivered a vicious attack on his old mate. The result was the end of a friendship that had spanned forty-five years and as a consequence Spike lost many other old Army friends because the story spread and most people sided with Harry. I felt sad for him.

Spike returned to Sydney and then went on to Hong Kong, only calling me then to complain that nobody ever told him when and where he was to appear. Hong Kong was no exception, he said, the whole tour had been chaotic, never knowing the dates or venues. Then he asked whether I knew the whereabouts of Peter Sellers. Could I get a message to Pete that he would be home in the middle of June so could they meet to have some fun? I thought Spike would have had enough of Pete because of the way he had behaved in selling Old Min, in other words, behaving 'like an absolute shit.' I had been surprised to receive a Christmas card from him, considering all the trouble he had caused and said so. 'That's how he is,' said Spike. 'He wanted to send a Christmas card to you.' That explained everything as far as Spike was concerned. I phoned Pete to tell him Spike would be back in the middle of June. There were telegrams and phone calls but eventually we fixed it up.

Pete was visiting London in July and suggested that he, Spike and Harry, no wives, hangers-on, or girlfriends, should have dinner at Pomegranates. He said he was desperate to have some real fun again. I rang Harry, who wondered what it was all about. What did Pete want? I told him I did not think there was an ulterior motive and called Spike back to confirm that the arrangements were in place for 22 July. I asked how he was getting on in Hong Kong. I had been strongly against the venue, the Sheraton Hotel, and told Patrick O'Neill that Spike was not at his best in an intimate dinner show. But O'Neill was getting his full value out of him.

'I've written a poem,' Spike said, ignoring my question. He read it to me.

> Chinky, chinky Chinaman
> Living in Hong Kong
> Give us a tune
> On your big brass gong
> Velly, velly, goodee
> Me beat out a song
> Me in Chinese hit parade
> Bong! Bong! Bong!

After that performance I said I did not think 'Chinkey Poo Land' (his expression) was doing him much good and gave him six out of ten for the poem. I asked if the audiences had been good and reminded him I needed to see the box office receipts as I had negotiated a percentage of the box office, but nothing had been sent. He said the audiences had not been nearly as good as those in South Africa.

When we spoke the next day he was in a morose mood. The tour had been handled badly, everything was slipshod and, worst of all in his book, 'you never know anything is going to happen until an hour before.' His nerves were shattered. I waited for the final telephone call, the one that would begin, 'I'm ill. I can't go on.' It came after the first few performances.

'I want to come home. I've had enough. I can't go on. Everybody wants a piece of me and there's nothing left.'

He flew back the next day, missing several shows. I was surprised at how tired Spike looked. I did not think he had been paced properly by O'Neill. And I am still waiting for the box office receipts to work out our percentage.

Spike had been given a small part in the film of *The Fiendish Plot of Dr Fu Manchu*, starring Pete and Sid Caesar. He was due on set four weeks into the shoot. There was a fortnight to go when I received a call from one of the assistant directors.

'Have Pete and Spike had a row?'

'Plenty of times, but not recently and I would certainly know if they had.'

Four days later the director, Piers Haggard, telephoned me. Did I know why Pete did not want Spike in the film? I could not believe it and did not have the heart to tell Spike the truth, so I said his part had been cut because the film was overrunning. He took it philosophically and shrugged. 'I'm like a taxi driver. I never know where my next fare is coming from.'

The three Goons were due to meet at Pomegranates on 22 July.

That morning Sue Evans rang me. Pete had collapsed in the Dorchester with a massive heart attack, his second, and had been rushed to the Middlesex Hospital.

'It's serious, Norma. Please tell Spike.'

Spike was filming in Twickenham. I managed to get through quickly to give him the bad news. He was sceptical. Pete had a habit of feigning illness when he wanted to cut loose from his obligations.

'Which film doesn't he want to do or which location doesn't he want to go to? Or which wife is asking for too much money?'

'He's in intensive care, Spike.'

'Yeah! He could arrange that. Give me a progress report during the day.'

I did and the news was not good. After filming Spike went to the hospital and I saw a shot of him arriving there on the nine o'clock television news bulletin. Visitors were banned but they admitted Spike to his bedside. Pete died two days later on 24 July 1980.

When I arrived at the office the next morning I read the note on his door. 'Don't disturb.' He stayed there for two days. On the third day I went in to see him. He talked about Pete as though he was still alive, as he always would through the passing years, just as he did about his father. I made sure Spike never knew about Pete's final betrayal over his part in *Dr Fu Manchu*.

On the day of Pete's heart attack, I had a meeting with Jimmy Verner to arrange another tour for Spike. It passed in a haze. Afterwards I remembered we had agreed on a four-week tour, starting at the Mayfair Theatre in London on 31 July. My antenna told me Spike would not do it. Our relationship was not too good at that point because the money for the Australian tour was still outstanding. He had done something like sixteen weeks' work, yet had been paid for only the first three. By September the money still had not arrived and I deviated from my normal practice of keeping any bad news about business from him, because I had been so against the project and wanted him to know what the outcome was when he got involved with inexperienced people. Of course, Spike did not want to know.

'I've delivered. I've earned my money. Now it's your turn to earn yours.'

I was not going to let him get away with that. I told him that if he wanted to get back to amateur status he was going the right way about it. He stormed out of the office, an indication that he knew I was right but could not quite handle it. Sometimes he was transparent. He came back to see me in the afternoon.

'When is Pete's memorial service and are you coming with me?'

'8th September', I told him.

'Poor bastard. That was his birthday and now they're burying him on the same day.'

'Spike, he died in July. He was cremated at Golders Green Crematorium. You were there. This is a memorial service to celebrate his life.'

'Why would they want to do that? He had a bloody awful life. He told me the happiest days of his life were when we did *The Goon Show* and it was downhill from then on.'

We went to the service at St Martin-in-the-Fields off Trafalgar Square. Jerry Crampton, the stuntman, a favourite of Pete and Spike, was an usher. He showed us to our places on the second row. In a loud voice that echoed round the church Spike said, 'Hi, Bruce! Are you okay?' Bruce Forsyth smiled. I recognized two or three others in the same row from *Dad's Army*. Next to me was an old man in a camel hair overcoat. He smiled as I took my place.

During the service Harry Secombe sang 'Guide me, O thou great Redeemer', a hymn Spike called 'Bread of Heaven'. When Harry reached that particular line it was too much for Spike and he burst out laughing.

'Norma! If I die before Harry promise me one thing. Don't

let him sing 'Bread of Heaven' at my funeral. Pete will be looking down on us right now and having hysterics. Go on, Norm. You have to promise me.'

I said I would if he behaved. He was now enjoying himself and started having an imaginary conversation with Pete and paid no attention to the readings. I suddenly realized he was deeply upset and hiding it. When the service came to an end we filed out, Spike talking to Lord Snowdon, who had been sitting across the aisle, with the old man who had been sitting next to me following behind. We walked out of the church to the flashes of a host of photographers' cameras. I had never seen so many. My God, I thought, Spike is popular today. They must think he will be the next Goon to meet the grim reaper. I turned and saw the little old man suddenly tall and erect. It was Laurence Olivier. I had been sitting next to one of my idols and not known it. I now witnessed a perfect demonstration of star quality. As soon as he saw the cameras he turned it on, finding the energy to transform himself into the man the public would recognize.

'Spike,' I said, as we made our way to our car. 'I thought that was all for you. Do you realize it was for Olivier? I sat next to Larry and didn't know it.'

'Did you ask him how his athlete's foot was today?'

Even such a smart alec remark could not spoil the moment for me.

Spike did not return to the office for days. I had to cancel the tour with Jimmy Verner. We had dinner and I told him Spike was in a fragile state and on the verge of a depression. It would be crazy to start looking at dates and venues until this spell was over. Philosophically he said, 'Days of Wine and Neuroses. Let's turn to Plan B.' That meant he would keep out of Spike's way until I told him the show was on again.

Spike was also due to start work with Jack Hobbs on a children's poetry book, but if that had to be postponed there would be no harm done; Jack was even more experienced than Jimmy with Spike's unpredictability when he was ill. Jack arrived as planned on 18 September. Spike did not show so we discussed what Spike should work on after the poetry book was finished. He still had not started volume five of the war memoirs, and Jack agreed that Spike might lose the readers who had been so enthusiastic over the first four. I told him not to mention it to Spike. Then out of the blue Jack suggested I should write a book called *Ups and Downs with Spike Milligan*. He drew the cover, with Spike and me in an old-fashioned lift, the sort with a trellis gate. At that moment Spike walked in, at least an hour late.

'What the hell are you doing here, Jack?'

I took one look and realized this could turn nasty. I reminded Spike that he had arranged to meet Jack, and explained that in his absence we were working on an idea for a book on my ups and downs with him. Spike was still agitated and insisted there was no entry in his diary about an appointment with Jack. I had turned into an agent for MI5; everything was being kept secret from him. I went upstairs to his office and returned with the evidence. 'There!' I pushed the diary in front of him. In his own writing there it was. 'Six o'clock. Work on book of poems. J. Hobbs.' He did not comment. Then he glanced at Jack's draft book cover and said, with an impish smile, 'This book on ups and downs. Are you in a good mood with me? If you aren't tell me when it's coming out and I'll visit Mum and Des in Australia until the flak's stopped flying.'

I smiled. Later Jack told me he could understand why I could never be annoyed with Spike for very long. We all ended up the best of mates at the Trattoo and Spike arranged another date to see Jack in a few days' time. But two days later it did not surprise me in the least to see a note on Spike's door: 'LEAVE ME ALONE'. It was a Friday. I knew from experience that if the depression was not too bad he would make an effort to go home to spend the weekend with Jane. If he were still in his office on

Monday I would have to cancel the television appearances I had lined up, with Granada and then two days' reading for *Jackanory* at the BBC. Thankfully when Monday arrived he had gone home and the work went well. On the Thursday I asked him if he would like to find a bird and join Jack Clarke and me for dinner. He looked at me sheepishly. He said he would love to have dinner with Jack and me but he already had a date. Bring her along, I said.

'You wouldn't want that. It's Margaret Maughan. Would that be all right?'

It certainly would not. Where the hell had she come from? He explained that she had telephoned and wanted to see him. Frankly, I could not understand why he agreed.

'It'll be about money,' I said, and got the usual rejoinder about my 'terrible unchristian streak'.

When I saw him at the office the next morning all I said was, 'Well?'

'£250,' he said, and that was the end of it.

I was puzzled as to why he had agreed to see her after all she had put him through and I guessed it was guilt. He was very big in that department, it was one of his saving graces.

We were back on track. I call it that because there was a sense in the office that everything was behind us – temporarily no doubt – so we could move forward. It was a positive feeling.

Jack Hobbs came in at the end of September and Spike had come up with a title for the children's poetry book, *Unspun Socks from a Chicken's Laundry*. He was in good spirits, with Grandma at home in Monkenhurst and the tension running low. He agreed to do the Thames Television charity *Telethon* and to attend a rally for Compassion in World Farming at Trafalgar Square – he was always in a good frame of mind when he thought he was helping the planet. Grandma was to return to Australia two days after the rally so Spike invited Harry and Myra to dinner the evening before. Grandma liked Harry very much. He always visited her in Woy Woy when he toured Australia and they had built up a warm friendship. They had a lovely evening, and Spike was triumphant the next day when he came to the office and handed me the final manuscript for *Unspun Socks*. Lovely. Time to pounce again.

Spike had already agreed to read *Adolf Hitler: My Part In His Downfall* for an audio book by EMI, and was about to go on holiday. First I congratulated him on finishing *Unspun Socks* and then said, 'After your holiday you have a couple of free weeks. Do you want to start the fifth volume of the war memoirs?'

Without pausing for breath he said, 'Okay, Norm. Let's check our diaries. How about I start around 16 November?'

Done. I applauded myself on my timing.

I thought the year was going to end happily for me. Not that I expected him to start work on the memoir when he said he would, but at least he had acknowledged that there would be another volume. My euphoria was short-lived. When he came back in December he suddenly decided he would clear out his office, all the cupboards and even his wine cellar, which had always been sacrosanct. This basement room contained not only his wine, but floor to ceiling shelves of his original manuscripts including all the *The Goon Shows*, with drawings done by each of the Goons while they were in rehearsals. Now they would all have to go. I told Spike he would regret it but he would not listen and sent all the scripts to be auctioned by Christie's. I found it very sad, like selling a piece of family history, yet Spike had no apparent emotions about it. He said the only time *The Goon Show* would be mentioned again was when he died, and that was all that he would be remembered for. People would say, 'Spike Milligan wrote *The Goon Show* and died.'

By then I had learnt that when he was in that sort of mood the best thing was to let him get on with it. He had no regrets. When the time came, in April the following year, Elton John bought all the scripts for £14,000. I was glad they had gone to a real fan and Spike too was pleased.

'They've found a good home,' he said, 'and they'll continue to be surrounded by temperament. I have a feeling that Elton's like me.'

When the scripts were gone we drank the wine.

I had received an early Christmas card from Bernard Miles and did not like any of it. He had written, 'To Norma, who carries cheerfully a GREAT BURDEN. Reward will be received in the hereafter. Love from Bernard Miles.' I suspected it was to soften me up for another request to play the Mermaid at sixty pounds a week.

'Have you been in cahoots with him about something?'

Spike laughed. 'Right on, Daddy.'

All I could do was sit and wait.

When the time came he did the show, for his sixty pounds a week.

1980 was drawing to a close. I said to Spike, 'How we survived it I don't know.'

On New Year's Day 1981 Spike telephoned me. How nice, he was going to wish me a happy new year. Silly me. He did not even say hello.

'My father said M was the thirteenth letter in the alphabet so was unlucky and that we had been born under a black star.'

I asked him what was so unlucky about his life. It had not gone the way he had wanted, he said. He should have stayed in Italy and married Toni Pontani. I reminded him that if he had done that there might not have been *The Goon Show* and a lot of people would have been deprived of a lot of happiness.

'Fuck them. What about me?'

Then he remembered he had forgotten my birthday (for a change). He brightened and invited me out for a slap-up dinner that night to celebrate. He invited Jack Hobbs and Jack Clarke, and brought along Shelagh and his daughter Jane. Jack Clarke could not believe how attentive he was. He heard Spike say to the restaurant manager, 'It's my manager's birthday. She's a champagne girl and she must have the best in the house tonight.' At this stage Jack had not seen any of his tantrums and thought Spike the perfect host – as indeed he was when he felt like it. That evening saw Spike at his best.

The following morning I rang to thank him for a wonderful dinner. His reply stunned me.

'Shelagh doesn't think you do enough for me.'

Well, this had to be nipped in the bud. Was he going to take the same route as Peter Sellers, which Spike had deplored. After Pete married Lynne Frederick she systematically got rid of all his friends, 'all those who had been loyal to him and the ones Pete liked', as Spike said at the time.

'Spike. Tell her from me to try the Archangel Gabriel.'

He laughed, said 'Right on, Daddy', and put down the phone. It was never mentioned again.

Chapter Nineteen

After four days at home Spike came into the office, walked behind my desk and out came the old chestnut.

'I bet I can kiss you without touching you.'

'We've played that game three or four times before and I know the pay-off.'

'Go on. Indulge me.'

So I played the game all over again. 'Okay. I'll bet you a pound you can't kiss me without touching me.'

He then planted a kiss on my cheek.

'But you touched me.'

'I know. Here's a pound. It was worth it.'

He was in a good frame of mind and had decided to work all day on guess what – the fifth volume of his war memoirs. All things come to those who wait, I reminded myself. It is just that some of us have to wait longer than most. My elation was shattered by a telephone call from Jack Hobbs. He had been speaking to Spike and it was all systems go for the Scunthorpe book.

'What the hell is that?'

He and Spike, he said, had been tossing an idea about between them for a book called *Indefinite Articles and Scunthorpe*. Of course they had. What about volume five? Was I going to have to give up on it? Jack said he could not envisage the day when I would give up on anything. I accepted defeat, reflecting that if it was going to prevent 'You are keeping me unemployed', then bring on Jack Hobbs and *Scunthorpe*.

Spike and Jack got on very well. Jack generally arrived at the office about eleven o'clock and they worked until lunchtime. While Jack went to the pub Spike and I caught up on business, and he made his telephone calls, and when Jack returned they started again, generally finishing about six o'clock. Some days they did nothing but laugh and talk over old times and sometimes the pair of them went to see Alan Clare to while away the afternoon. Other days they surprised me by the amount of work they produced. Of course there were arguments. If Jack cancelled or was late there would be the usual tirade of 'he's no good'. I had a soft spot for Jack and always defended him. Punctuality was not part of his nature but when he was late for a meeting with me he always brought a small bunch of flowers, which meant total forgiveness as far as I was concerned. But sometimes 'I'm sorry' was not enough for Spike.

On one occasion Jack was over half an hour late. Spike called the whole day off. I told him that was unreasonable: Jack had to travel from Walton-on-Thames, and although he could be late, we could always be certain he would show up. I should have kept my mouth shut. Spike went into a beauty.

'Do you remember *Monty, His Part In My Victory*? Do you?'

As if I could ever forget. It was 1975. Spike had finished writing it and Jack had been at Number Nine for most of the day, editing. Drained, he left in the evening with the completed manuscript, the only copy, and caught a taxi from the office to Waterloo station. On the train home he decided to look at the manuscript. It was not there. Can you imagine? He hunted in all his bags, up and down the carriage, to no avail. He did not know what to do. He knew there was a first draft but Spike had rewritten it twice since the original version and the only copy had presumably been left in a black cab running around London. The next morning Jack confessed to me what had happened. He had had a sleepless night. When he rang the Hackney Carriages head office first thing it was closed, so he rang Waterloo, just on the off-chance that he had dropped it. But he knew he had not. He rang the cab office again. It was open but the script had not been handed in. Then just before midday he got a call from Michael Joseph. There was a manuscript waiting for him at reception. He went to pick it up and there was a note from a London taxi driver, Mr Moy. Jack had been his last fare and when he arrived home in Brighton he saw the manuscript in the back of the cab. Mr Moy happened to be a fan and had read *Adolf* and *Rommel* so recognized the script for what it was and had taken it to the publisher.

Imagining the scene, I decided not to tell Spike, but at the launch party he saw what Jack had written in the preface, thanking 'Mr Moy, a London taxi driver, who returned the manuscript of the book to the editor with no claim for reward and without whom this book would not have appeared.'

'What's all this about?'

He laughed when we explained – but he never let Jack forget it.

Spike was in the middle of his tirade about Jack's unreliability when Jack walked in. Even by Spike's standards he executed an amazing turnaround.

'Jack! Where the fuck have you been? I've been waiting to tell you this story. I was talking to George Melly. He had been in some pub or club in South London and went to the gents. Now this is a true story, Jack. I promise it isn't one of mine. Anyhow, George is in the karzy and there is the usual machine with French letters and at the bottom of the machine there is a metal strip with the words, "To British Standard Specifications." Some joker had written on the machine in large black letters, "So was the Titanic!"'

It creased Spike and Jack too. Spike said the guy would probably never again write anything so witty, and Jack remained unaware of the venom that had poured out about him only minutes before he arrived.

Then it was time for one of his lifelong favourites.

'Norm, if you don't want to stab me in the back shall we have a cup of tea together so we can talk things over with Jack and all of us know where we're at?'

So that day saw the start of the book, *Indefinite Articles (Culled from his Newspaper Cuttings) and Scunthorpe*. What about my fifth volume? Try, try and try again. And I would after *Scunthorpe*.

While Spike and Jack worked together Spike was in an unusually good mood. It gave me the opportunity to rearrange work that had been cancelled, to do some P.R. with anyone he had been cruel to or upset, and to map out what he was going to do in the future, at least, what I hoped he would do in the future. So it was time to see Jimmy Verner to discuss the tour that had been cancelled.

I rarely saw Jimmy downcast but he was now. Everything had gone wrong for him, and he was not even dealing with Spike. He went serious on me. Had I considered the effect Spike's tantrums were having on my personal life?

'You've been away too long, Jimmy. You must be mental not to remember that everything is my problem, whether it's a tour, a book, a girlfriend or a television show.'

I wanted to cheer him up so invited him to dinner the following evening. Jimmy was on form again when he arrived at the Trattoo – the fact that Spike was not there made him happy – and we were on course again for a tour of Spike's one-man show in the autumn. I had also lined up several television and radio gigs, one of them a trip to Dublin for a show with Fergus O'Gorman, so when his attention was not taken up by *Scunthorpe*

I did not get the usual 'You're keeping me unemployed. I'm not earning enough money to feed my family.'

Then in February we heard that Roberta Watt had died from complications following a gallstone operation. She was only thirty-six. Romany was brought up by her grandparents in Canada and they did a wonderful job. A few years before Spike died she wrote saying she would like to meet him; she wanted nothing more from him. She stayed with him for two weeks and was delightful. I met her for the first time at his funeral and had a weird sensation. Not only was the accent familiar but she was the clone of Roberta. She was a sunny natured girl with old-fashioned courtesy. I do believe she adored Spike.

It was just a matter of time before the next bombshell. When it came a few weeks later it was atomic.

The phone rang as soon as I arrived at the office on Monday morning. 'The office is a disgrace. I've said it before but you all live in filth and this time I mean it.' This was a force ten tirade. The tiled wall in the well of Number Nine was filthy; he had spent the whole weekend scrubbing. It had taken a whole day and two boxes of Brillo pads just to reveal the colour of the tiles. I reminded him that we had had another Brillo pad episode not so long ago. This time, he said, it was different. The yard was filthy, so bad he had had to buy a tough new broom and Domestos to clean it.

'I will not allow you to turn me into a janitor.' Then the big bang. 'I want to sell Orme Court.'

I had assumed he was phoning from home but a few minutes later he clattered down the stairs and demanded a meeting with Eric Sykes.

'I want to sell my half. Where's Eric? Get a solicitor and sell it. Now.'

Oh no, I thought, not in this mood. The drill was to let him get it out of his system until he was so tired he would go to bed and sleep, but this time he was relentless. I had to find Eric. He exerted a calming influence on Spike and was always there when I needed him: he was my rock, and so he is to this day. But Spike beat me to it. When I managed to get hold of Eric he told me Spike had been on the phone and was adamant he was going to sell his share of Number Nine. He had got the bit about Norma turning him into a janitor. 'What brought this on?' asked Eric. I told him I had no idea, but Spike had been furious about the yard in the well of the building. 'Something else has triggered it off,' he said, 'and he was getting rid of his anger on the yard.'

But he had not got rid of it. A week later Spike asked for a meeting with Eric and me. He was going to sell, he told us. Eric told him he was stupid and pointed out that the money he got for it would be given away within a week, so what was the point? He tried very hard to change Spike's decision but he was not having any of it. Eventually Eric asked our accountant to have a word with Spike and explain the idiocy of it. He agreed and a further meeting was arranged with him, Spike, his solicitor, Eric and me. Eric begged him to change his mind, explaining that when they both stopped writing and performing they would have Orme Court to fall back on and they could sell it then; now was not the time. But because Spike was working and earning none of this made any sense to him. Then it was our accountant's turn. He explained the disadvantages of selling when the market was low. After all this I was certain Spike would see the light. Not a bit of it. Spike was adamant. He wanted to start the process of selling at once.

It made no sense to me. He neither wanted nor needed the money from the sale. His office was his sanctuary. Where was he going to write? Where would he sleep? Where would he take his birds? I decided to leave it for a week and then try to have a sensible conversation with him. Perhaps Nanny would know the real reason for the sale. She always knew what was going on at Monkenhurst and in the family. But he had not mentioned it to her. 'What will he use for his bunk hole?' she asked.

That was a polite way to put it, I thought. I had it out with him, but all he said was, 'I want out and that's final.'

'Where will you go?'

He looked astounded. 'Go? I'm not going anywhere. I'm staying here. Where would I go? Are you trying to put me out? I was the one who brought you here and now you want to evict me.'

I was sitting in his office. I laughed so much I nearly fell off my chair. I recalled Alan Clare's advice. 'Go to Harrods, buy a white flag and hang it on your office door.' It was time to surrender. The whole thing was unreal. He sold his share of Orme Court and, as Eric had predicted, he gave the proceeds to his children and whoever else he thought needed money at the time. In weeks it had all gone. The only thing that had not was him. He stayed at Number Nine and insisted on paying rent for his office. Eric did not want to accept it. Spike insisted. Eric was equally insistent he did not want it. In a compromise that could only have been hatched by the two of them, Eric very reluctantly agreed to accept half the going rent.

I expected that in the aftermath Spike would have regrets or sadness, but he was as unsentimental about the building as he had been over the scripts. His only interest at the time was a girl called Diana Keyes who had written to him from Hillend Hospital, St Albans, I can only assume, in a psychiatric wing. In one of her letters, which came with wonderful drawings of wild horses, she said she had neither a mother nor a father. She also wrote to me and some of her letters were heart wrenching. Spike convinced himself there was nothing wrong with her and that she had been 'locked away'. He spoke to the hospital and they agreed she could visit us. A car was sent for her and she came to the office several times and stayed with Spike at Monkenhurst.

Diana was very thin and hyperactive, and looked about

eighteen though she was in her early twenties. She had spent more than half her life in hospital. I warned Spike he was on dangerous ground because she was obviously unstable. She started to call me 'Mother' and spent weekends at Monkenhurst, poor child. Nanny rang to tell me that Diana was disoriented. She did not know what to make of the vast house and the people in it, and then she started to wet the bed. Spike dismissed that as a mere trifle and told Tanis to buy a rubber sheet. That meant the problem was solved as far as he was concerned.

He convinced himself that Diana was well enough to leave hospital and fend for herself and persuaded the authorities that she was capable if given a little help. He got her a flat and signed his Army pension over to her, confident that she could cope with ordinary everyday life, but I was not so sure. What if she met a boy and it ended in tears? No problem, he would get Nanny to help her. She was the most sensible person he knew. So that was another problem solved by Milligan. Diana's visits to Monkenhurst continued for several years until it was sold and then I believe she saw him several times at his house near Rye. I often wonder what happened to her.

All of this took up a great deal of his time. God forbid I should ask him whether we could try to earn a living. The page layouts for *Unspun Socks* arrived and he hated them so much he refused to discuss it. I had to tell Michael Joseph to delay publication; Spike was extremely busy but would be able look at the layout the following week. I wondered why everything in my life at the moment seemed to be 'next week'. They also sent the layout of *Scunthorpe* but that seemed to be all right. Then came a late-night phone call.

'I've finished my limerick book.'

Marvellous. What limerick book?

'If you can't keep up with what I'm doing that's down to you.' He swore blind he had told me about it but he had not. 'I write them and you sell them.'

'What about the layout of *Scunthorpe*, dare I ask?'

'All done. You'll find it on your desk when you go in tomorrow.'

I decided not to mention the layout for *Unspun Socks*. Sure enough when I went in the next morning the *Scunthorpe* layout and the limerick manuscript were on my desk. They were good, and I said there were probably enough for a book. He wanted to know how many he had done. Ninety-three, I told him.

'Hold it right there. I'll do a few more and call it *101 Best and Only Limericks of Spike Milligan*.'

Within half an hour he phoned me. He had done the other eight. His spontaneity and creativity always amazed me, as did the way he could sit and pound away at his typewriter. Johnny Speight, an early convert to computers, came in one day when Spike was mid-flow.

'Spike, why don't you buy a word processor?' he said.

Spike looked up at him and said, 'I am a word processor', and got back down to it.

When Spike rang to say he had written the rest of his limericks he said to me, 'That's finished. I'm now unemployed.'

It was not as bad as 'You're keeping me unemployed.'

Pounce time. 'Spike! I've just re-employed you. How about starting volume five?'

I could not win.

'You must not mark time on me like this,' he said. 'I need a breathing space and time off. You give me no time for pleasure.'

Spike had a breather and the *Unspun Socks* layout was altered and approved. Then it was time to start filming *History of the World* for Mel Brooks. It was easy-peasy as he and Mel were on the same wavelength. 'It's a pleasure to work with someone who knows exactly what he is doing, unlike that no talent lot at the Beeb. Not one of them with an original thought.' Spike and Mel enjoyed hilarious dinners together and on the last day of shooting he rang me from the set.

'I've finished *Sir Nobonk*.' This was an idea he had been tossing around for some time, a children's fairy story about a knight and a dragon. When he first told me of the idea I said, 'Oh, very original.' He did not like that but it acted as a spur: he had to show me what he could do. Well, he had finished it on set while waiting to be called. I told him I had only just finished the limerick book.

'Norm. I've said it before. I'm like Van Gogh. He couldn't stop painting and I can't stop writing. It's becoming a disease.'

When it came to be published it was generally agreed that *Sir Nobonk and the Terrible Dragon* was a wonderful book, beautifully illustrated by Carol Barker, although I never cared for it and thought her illustrations were much better than his writing. At the time I was getting increasingly anxious about volume five and, though I tried to sound pleased about *Sir Nobonk*, I felt now was as good a time as any to tax him about it. He claimed it was all in his head. I told him that if he left it much longer there would be no point because he would have lost his readers. He was not at all concerned. I left the office very dejected. The next morning there was a note on my door.

'I'M UPSTAIRS. LET ME KNOW WHEN YOU COME IN.'

He was waiting for me. How I dreaded those occasions. But this time there were no screams or swearing, no blaming the world for his ills, just, 'Norm. I'm exhausted with life. I can't go on. I want to die.' He was very, very tired. He handed me a sheet of paper. 'I wrote this last night for my father.'

> Why did you go Dad?
> So much left undone
> So much unsaid
> You never finished the story
> There was so much wine left
> Did you order too much

Or did we drink too little?
Mum had put fresh sheets on the bed
So why did you go
in the middle of the song
The tune was so good
we wanted to hear the end
Why DID you go?
There was so much love
the fridge was full of it
If you were not coming back
Why did you send your suit
to the cleaners?
You know tonight there was
Gunsmoke on the telly
Tomorrow we were going to walk
up Blackwall mountain.
Why DID you go?
And what about Mesopotamia?
What did happen at
the battle of Shaiba?
I've arranged the muskets
in the gun room
So why DID you go?
We are waiting . . . waiting.

Spike's father had died in 1969 so I asked him what had brought
this on. He said he had been playing it around in his head for
some time. But did not want it to be published yet. (Many
years later he had it privately printed on his favourite paper.)
This was not the Spike I knew. His sombre mood continued for
another week, a lacklustre Spike with no interest in anything.

I left for a week's holiday. Nothing much could go wrong in
that time because most of the week he was just going to write
in his office. There was only a photo call for EMI for the release

of his album, *Adolf Hitler, My Part In His Downfall*, and a small drinks party afterwards. Unusually, he had agreed to endure the 'peanut and sherry crap'.

Before the shoot Spike caught a cold and it affected his throat so much he could scarcely speak. Whenever this happened he went to bed, put on his woolly hat and stayed there until Doctor Milligan told him it was safe to get up. He had an obsession about getting a high temperature. According to him, when he had malaria as a boy in India he once had a fever for two weeks and the memory had lingered. Well, that was his story.

When I returned from holiday there was still a frog in his throat. He said he had telephoned EMI and told them he could not make it. I knew then that he must have been ill because he hardly ever cancelled any arrangements himself. That should have been the end of the matter, but a week later EMI billed us for the cost of the drinks party on the grounds that it was our responsibility because Spike had not attended. Spike was furious at this injustice. The organizer either had no compassion or thought he had lied about his illness. I told Spike to forget it. The bill was only for about £150. I would just settle it. This was the wrong thing to say.

'Who's the head of EMI?'

'Your friend Bernard Delfont.'

'Get him on the phone. He needs to know he's got a pernicious, small-minded little toad of a man working for him who hasn't an ounce of compassion.'

'He's probably never heard of him.'

'Well, he will now.'

Spike spoke to Bernard and then wrote him a letter. We never heard about the bill, or the publicist, again.

The next day I received a bouquet from Spike. His note read: 'NORMA. WELCOME BACK. WHERE THE BLOODY HELL HAVE YOU BEEN? SPIKE.'

Spike had a hectic month ahead: a British Leyland commercial;

television interviews in Newcastle, Bristol and Southampton; several charity fundraisers, and he was due to present an Award for Ladies of Television. He also had to prepare for another tour of Australia so it was imperative I keep everything calm. Even a ripple could jeopardize the trip. At such times I would say to Tanis, 'Remember, "Yes Spike, no Spike, three bags full Spike" and then he'll be on his way to Oz.'

The ripple came when he asked why Ronnie Scott had not replied to a letter. It was the sort Ronnie would appreciate as they often held long, bantering conversations on the telephone. They had first met when Spike and Ted Allbeury found a common interest in jazz and started going often to Ronnie Scott's Jazz Club. One day, Ted told me, they were in Frith Street on the way there when they passed an old dear sitting on the pavement surrounded by carrier bags.

'You're Spike, aren't you?'

Spike agreed he was.

'Where are you going?'

'We're going to listen to the jazz at Ronnie's.'

'I've always wanted to go there,' she said, wistfully.

Spike didn't hesitate. 'Come with us,' he said and helped her up, taking her carrier bags, stuffed with old clothes and shoes. As they walked to Ronnie's they realized the old lady carried a high scent, and it was not one by Estée Lauder. Gentlemen both, they allowed her to go in first, and as she drew aside the hanging curtain on the door she came face to face with Ronnie. He was about to tell her what she could do and where she could go when Spike leaned over her shoulder.

'She's my guest.'

Spike was one of his best customers so Ronnie was not going to offend him. He ushered them to an out-of-the-way table in the hope that nobody would see her. He was far from pleased but Spike could not have cared less. They bought her a few glasses of wine and she dropped off to sleep. At the end of the evening they said goodbye with a few quid to help her on her way. The whole gesture was typical of Spike, thought Ted. 'The old dear had never been to Ronnie's and as far as he was concerned she had to be given the chance to go there,' he told me later. 'He was just the man to do it. I found him a naturally likeable man and he was like that with everyone he met.'

Really! What planet had he been living on?

Spike was always a demanding customer. After another visit to his club Spike wrote this letter, addressed to Ronnie Scott Jazz Esquire:

> Dear Ronnie, Dear Pete, or anybody who is listening,
>
> What can I say about that evening at Ronnie Scott's listening to Buddy Rich? I have a theory now, that if the people who were sent to extermination camps during World War II had been given a choice they would say 'Do you vant Auschwitz or that fucking awful table that Ronnie Scott gave to Spike Milligan at the Buddy Rich concert?' Please let me know next time I have bought a ticket for Auschwitz as the next Buddy Rich concert gets nearer and nearer, the queues for Auschwitz are getting longer and longer. In fact, I think one of the people in the queue is Buddy Rich. He can't stand it either.
>
> Let me put it this way. If that table was a suit I would look like a fucking cripple. Whoever invented that table invented a guide dog for the deaf.
>
> Do you know that Ringo Starr hangs around outside John Lennon's apartment wearing a bullseye over his heart? He is determined to make it somehow.
>
> Look Ronnie, you really could have gone the whole hog. Why didn't you put that table in the centre of the door leading to the dressing room? Think of the fun it would have been nurgling.
>
> I await your usual fucking silence.

How can you both become members of the Wig and Pen Club?

As ever

Spike Milligan

As a result Spike got a permanently reserved table at Ronnie's, complete with earphones so he could listen to the music and not be distracted by the noise of conversations and waiters.

Spike wrote letters like this to all his closest friends. After Marty Feldman went to Hollywood he occasionally became homesick and often wrote to Spike. It was a miracle that some of the envelopes got through the postal system. When Marty was living at the Château Marmont Hotel he wrote to Spike saying, 'If you don't write, I will. If you don't answer my letter, fuck you. I won't bother to write in the first place.' On the back of the envelope he had written for all to see, 'From a man posing as superjew Feldman, last seen sitting by a pool in a flash hotel getting angry about being rich.' Spike replied: 'OK. Love Spike. P.S. Don't say I haven't written to you.'

After a few days Spike discovered Ronnie had not been in touch because he had gone into a terrible depression, brought on, Spike said, 'by woman trouble'. He was 'doing the drugs too much, they'll kill him.' Fortunately, Ronnie recovered and Spike started preparations for Australia. Then he wanted to see his old house, 127 Holden Road, and was obviously thinking a great deal about Paddy and his past. I told him he would be wasting his time because it had been scheduled for demolition soon after he moved into Monkenhurst.

Before he left for Australia I reminded him of the quotation he had sent to a school newspaper some years before.

'Copulation equals population equals pollution. Answer: birth control.'

With a half smile he said, 'No time for pleasure, Norm.'

'Keep it that way.'

After the previous year's fiasco this trip was for three weeks, solely to promote a book and appear on *Parkinson* in Sydney. He returned in time for the big social event of the year, the wedding of Prince Charles and Lady Diana. Grandma, a fervent Royalist, was more excited than Spike when she heard he had been invited. According to Desmond she told everyone she met, 'Terry has been invited to the Royal Wedding, you know.' But her Terry had not been behaving himself. Newspapers quite rightly asked him how he could accept the royal invitation when he openly condemned Charles's passion for foxhunting. Spike had several replies to that but I liked this one: 'We all have rights. It's Charles's right to go foxhunting. I have the same rights and I don't like what he does, but he's my friend and I'll go to the wedding.' Prince Charles was not the only huntsman Spike called a friend. Jack Clarke was still a Master of Foxhounds but we went on a holiday together and dined almost every week.

Two weeks before the wedding Spike had a phone call from Buckingham Palace. Charles would like to see him. It was not a question of whether he could be there or could a suitable date be arranged. He must come at 12.30 p.m. on 14 July. I told Spike it could be worse. It could be the Tower. Once more he had opened his mouth at an inappropriate moment. As far as Prince Charles was concerned, too much was being made of the foxhunting bit. Spike agreed so it was not mentioned again.

Spike, this Irish rebel who had refused to take an oath of allegiance to the Queen, loved every single minute of the ceremony. He dressed in a grey silk hat and morning coat and emerged from his chauffeured car outside St Paul's Cathedral to glad hand it with the fans. He lapped up the pageantry. For once the English were in his good books. 'The English are the only people in the world to get it right.' I asked what he would remember about the wedding. Without hesitation he said, 'The music, that sound and the singing. To have been in St Paul's for the ceremony is something I will remember for ever.'

The high did not last for long. In August he brought me back to earth with a jolt. I found a note on my door. 'CANCEL EVERYTHING. CANCEL MY LIFE.' Eric brought the note to me. 'Here, he's hiding behind you again. What is it he doesn't want to do?' He was right. When Spike was in this mood it was like working with a time bomb. Yet again I had to cancel Jimmy Verner's tour. Jimmy was okay about it. All he asked was, 'How do you keep on doing this sort of thing for him? Obviously you like him beyond all his faults.' I suppose that summed it up.

We were booked to go to Johannesburg for a commercial. While there I had arranged to meet Ronnie Quibell to discuss another tour. I wondered whether cancelling his life meant cancelling South Africa. It did not. The trip went well and he behaved impeccably, not a harsh word.

A few days after our return we were walking through Kensington Gardens to visit the Elfin Oak when, without any preliminaries, he said, 'Shelagh thinks we should get engaged.'

I said, 'What do you think? Will you or will I tell the Bayswater Harem?'

He laughed. 'She's a good Catholic.' He and Shelagh got engaged on 24 October and my concerns about the Bayswater Harem were short-lived. Nothing changed. On 23 December he told me he was having dinner with Liz Cowley.

'You should be at home with Jane getting ready for Christmas.'

'I'll see to all that tomorrow,' he said.

While he went home on Christmas Eve to be with Jane, Jack Clarke and I went to the Meridiana Restaurant where Alan Clare was then playing, having left the Trattoo. It was a wonderful evening and as a bonus Alan's wife, Bloom, a professional singer, was there too. I told Alan about the engagement and the continuing Bayswater Harem. He used the same expression as Spike had applied to Peter Sellers. 'That's how he is.'

*

In one respect 1982 was the same as ever. Fan letters continued to pour in at the rate of about five hundred a week. In the early days he insisted on replying to each one, which drove Tanis, typist in addition to all her other duties, crazy as she thought half of them should be dumped. Some were from fans and others from people asking his advice on a myriad of subjects. People sent their treasured possessions, anything from sepia family photographs to an old seventy-eight record of Beniamino Gigli for Spike to listen to. Another sent a Richard Tauber record, which arrived broken. Spike did not know how to tell the owner what had happened.

Hundreds of letters came asking him to attend 'my husband's birthday party' or 'our wedding anniversary', and more came enclosing a blank birthday card, asking Spike to sign the card to their husband or wife, or some other friend or relation. There were sad letters from people with depression, some having not left their houses for months; at times two or three letters arrived together because the writers had waited for someone to call and post them for them.

There were also begging letters and I remember one in particular from the early Seventies. The writer, an elderly woman, needed some money to go on holiday. She explained that she and her husband were elderly and had not been on holiday since 1945. Their ambition was to spend a week in Blackpool. Something about the letter grabbed Spike so he sent them £100. A week later another letter arrived asking for a little more because, she explained, it was so long since they had been on holiday that they needed to buy new underwear. As you can imagine, Spike thought this was hysterical. I asked him not to send them any more cash because the requests could be endless and he would never get rid of them. He agreed so I wrote a polite letter saying the £100 was the end of the matter. She then sent us an ambulance driving licence to show what she had done during the war. When that did not get her anywhere she sent her engagement ring with a request that Spike should buy it. I returned these letters with the ring and presumably she got fed up, but I have often wondered who she was and whether they had the holiday in Blackpool in their old underwear.

One day Spike decided to stop replying to the letters because it was getting out of hand. Of course there were exceptions and one of these was Groucho, real name Alan Matthews. Out of all the hundreds of thousands of letters Spike received over the years, Groucho was the only fan to whom Spike wrote personally, maybe three or four times a year. I also wrote to Groucho and to this day we still correspond and see one another as friends.

When he was twelve a friend had misfired an air rifle at him and as a result Groucho lost his right eye. He wrote many times to Spike and in one of his letters mentioned the accident. This touched a chord with Spike and he replied, beginning a correspondence that lasted many years. When I arrived at Number Nine it was in its early days and something about Groucho intrigued me. His spirit shone through his letters.

He had trained as a plumber but his ambition was to be a pop star. He played guitar in a group that was popular on Tyneside and got his nickname after he decided to follow the example of an old comedian he had met at a club and wear a 'grouch pouch' containing enough money to get home if a job did not pay up. He was earning good money as a session musician and engineer, and though his group was not destined for the top, the outlook was good. Then in May 1978 he was walking with his brother along the banks of the Tyne at Hebburn. His brother spotted a small boy struggling in mid river. The ebbing tide meant the current was swift but Groucho, a strong swimmer, kicked off his shoes and dived in. The boy kept disappearing under the surface of what was then a filthy river, full of chemicals as well as raw sewage. Groucho pulled the boy above the surface and fought his way, clutching the child, to a nearby jetty. They gave the boy mouth to mouth resuscitation, but by the time an ambulance arrived the child was dead. Groucho was taken to hospital to have his stomach pumped and his remaining eye developed an infection. Within six months he was completely blind.

Groucho told me later that for twelve months he sat in an easy chair at home, traumatized by what had happened. His wife was pregnant and realized she would have to be harsh to make him fight back. 'I've got one baby coming. I can't manage two.'

She taught him how to be useful round the house, and he learned to touch type. Spike and I encouraged him as best we could. According to him the most important thing I ever did was to tell him in a letter, 'Groucho! Get off your arse and do something.'

He learned Braille and then became a blind athlete, winning three gold medals. He climbed the Matterhorn and, with a companion as his eyes, drove a Jaguar to a blind person's land speed record of 110 mph. Soon he was teaching Braille to blind children. In 1991 he got a job with a local council and, with skills learned as a recording man in the old days, he produced newspapers on tape for the blind of the area. This grew into a project to help disabled people, mostly blind, to get back to work, but after a decade he and his partner were told their services were no longer required. That was two years ago and he phoned to say he and his partner were thinking of starting a business to help companies to train and employ blind and disabled people.

'Go for it,' I said.

Two years later they employ forty-two people and have a turnover of £2.5 million. How about that for guts. He reckons it would never have happened if he had not received encouragement and help from Spike and me at a time when Denise was shouldering the massive burden of dealing with a baby and a man who, on the face of it, had given up on life.

*

1982 started on a high note for me personally. Jack and I had our house near Taunton but he was anxious to return to his beloved Yorkshire moors and we looked for a place for some time. In 1981 we found somewhere we both liked in a valley on the banks of the River Esk, a salmon river. It was a stone house in a state of total disrepair because nobody had lived in it for ten years or so. We had workmen in it for almost a year but we were at last able to move in during the autumn of 1982, so for me the year marked a milestone in my life.

Spike and Neil Shand had been writing *There's a Lot of It About* for the BBC, which was effectively *Q10*, and doing the odd television work so I thought things were going relatively smoothly. A late night call shattered that illusion.

'Ronnie's ill. He's in a bad way so I've arranged for him to see someone.' Within a week Ronnie was in the Montagu Clinic. His condition was drug related. 'Ronnie hasn't got any money so I've agreed with Pete King [his business partner] that the club will pay half and I'll pay the other, so just pay it,' Spike told me.

Ronnie was out after three weeks but in less than a week had to go into the Regent's Park Clinic. Spike was paying his share, and, you have guessed it, the club did not pay theirs. When the bill had reached £4,500 I told Spike it had to stop. He could not afford that sort of money. Not only was he paying for the world's supply of sodium amytal, but he was also paying Ronnie's Benson and Hedges bill and Ronnie smoked more than Stromboli. When I told him the club had not paid their share he said, 'He's my friend. I have to look after him. Just pay it. Don't tell me how much the bills come to. Just see they are paid.'

Fortunately for Spike's finances Ronnie came out of the clinic at the end of March after seven weeks' treatment and Spike continued to go to the club to eat spaghetti pomodoro, drink Orvieto and listen to musicians like Warren Vache.

*

Spike's cruel streak had nothing to do with his illness. His tirades against the world before he went into a depression were completely different from the vicious attacks he directed at anyone without reason. This was the nasty Spike Milligan I disliked. I understood, or tried to, the tirades as he sank into depression, but not the vicious personal attacks he made on both friends and enemies. Normally this mood did not last for any length of time, maybe a week or two, but in the early part of 1982 it carried on for several months. He was rehearsing, filming and then recording *There's a Lot of It About* for the BBC at the time, and how the actors and crew tolerated him I do not know. They were all familiar with the usual litany of 'nobody is any good, everyone is incompetent, I'm surrounded by no talent actors'. These tantrums were normal and would be over in half an hour, but this time the abuse was relentless. He was in turmoil and lashed out at everybody. I had to cancel lots of work, including yet another Jimmy Verner tour.

After the show was completed at the end of June we had ten days before we were to fly to South Africa for another commercial. Shelagh wanted to go with him and Spike complained about having to buy her a ticket because, he maintained, he could not afford it, which was not true. This was my opportunity. I do not think I could have survived his appalling behaviour, away from home and Jack. I told him there would be little for me to do in South Africa as I had made all the arrangements so Shelagh could have my ticket. What a bonus! I could now go to Yorkshire and become clerk of works for a week, without having Spike bellowing down the phone every few minutes. The kitchen was being fitted, the bathroom suites were due for delivery and Douglas Readman and Arthur Beadle, in my opinion two of the finest interior designers in England, telephoned me from Saltburn to say the swags and tail drapes were ready.

I returned to London in the hope that South Africa would have produced a 'love, light and peace' mood. Spike had flown his daughters, Jane and Laura, to South Africa to go on safari. This would normally put Spike in good spirits, but not on this occasion. There were no pleasantries when he walked into my office. He asked if the launch of *Sir Nobonk* was still on. Yes, in two days' time. That sent him into a rage. After that, he exploded, he would be unemployed. I reminded him of the cancellations I had had to make before he left for South Africa. I would now put them on again, including Jimmy Verner and the much-delayed tour of his one-man show. Then in his next breath all became clear to me. Because I had not got him any work he had found it himself (that was a new one). So he would be going on tour round the U.K. with his one-man show for Patrick O'Neill.

Chapter Twenty

I could not believe he was prepared to do business again with Patrick O'Neill after all the problems on the previous tour. I asked him if he had forgotten the letter I had written to him in March 1980, detailing these problems. He denied any knowledge of it. I was so annoyed I found the file, unearthed the letter and read him the first few lines: 'I know you do not get involved, ever, with business, but I want to explain the situation re the Pat O'Neill non-payment. You can believe whoever you like – that's your right – but I am setting the record straight as far as I am concerned. That's my right.'

He took the letter from me and read out the closing lines. 'As ever, Norma (a little irritated by the whole fucking business).' He laughed. Yes, he remembered, and added, without a trace of irony, given his own fondness for filing, 'I hate those bloody files you keep.' But Spike was determined to press O'Neill's cause. 'He's promised it won't happen again and he'll pay me every week,' he said.

I wondered what the hell he had got himself into this time. I told him that Patrick had better come to my office so I could sort it out. I needed to draw up a contract before this lunacy went ahead. 'Oh, we're not going to bother about contracts. The deal will be the same as last time,' said Spike. After a heated argument I reminded him that Spike Milligan Productions had the exclusive services of Spike Milligan and he could not work without their agreement. He stormed out and I hoped that would be the end of it.

Two days later Patrick O'Neill rang to make an appointment to see me. The day came and he did not turn up. He made another appointment, but did not turn up for that either. Spike informed me that O'Neill did not want to come to the office. 'What do you want me to do?' I said. 'Have a meeting outside Bayswater tube station?' So yet another appointment was made and this time he turned up – with Spike in tow.

'What the hell are you doing at this meeting?' I said.

'I've come to support Patrick.'

I knew he was not joking. I said I was not his enemy and he had got it the wrong way round. 'I'm negotiating for your money.'

'I'm supporting him against you,' he repeated.

This was crazy. Then I had a brainwave. I guessed the meeting was about Patrick not wanting to pay Spike a guarantee, which he had not wanted to do for the last tour. I had to use words Spike would understand, and from experience I knew what they were. 'He does not want to pay you your wages.'

What a transformation. He looked at me and then looked at Patrick. The survivor in him then emerged.

'Oh, Pat. That's not right. I need my wages. Sorry, lad, I did my best for you.'

Spike got up and left my office. Patrick followed. I turned to the photo of Anthony Hopkins. 'That's the most surreal moment you'll ever see. You like comedians. That is a comedian.'

I got my guarantee and the tour went ahead. It was a disaster.

Spike phoned from Dublin and at some length explained that there was a noisy air vent outside his room and he could not sleep. He had taken the sheets and blankets from the hotel and now his bed was in his dressing room at the theatre. Nobody was looking after him. 'I warned you I wouldn't pick up the pieces if things went wrong and that you'd have to rely on Patrick to sort it out.'

He banged down the phone. A minute later it rang again.

'The worst thing in a human being is a lack of compassion. You've got it in abundance.'

The next day there was the usual bouquet of flowers. The note read, 'WITH LOVE. HOPE THIS MAKES THE DAY BETTER FOR YOU. LOVE SPIKE.' Ironic, I thought. He was the one who tried to upset my day. Spike sent me flowers throughout our time together, not only when he was feeling guilty but also when the occasion struck him. I still miss them, not the flowers so much as the accompanying notes. However, this time the flowers did not herald a real change as his vindictive mood continued.

Whenever Spike got involved in business it ended in disaster, simply because he did not understand anything about it. Now, prompted by some wild misunderstanding, he vented his ignorance and aggression on his editor, Jack Hobbs, who had become one of his best friends. Shortly after the O'Neill tour, without any warning or consultation, he wrote to Jack Hobbs and Dick Douglas Boyd at Michael Joseph, 'I would like to reassess my relationship with Jack Hobbs and Michael Joseph.' The reason, he explained, was because Jack had earned royalties from *Sir Nobonk* when the illustrator, Carol Barker, should have been the recipient. This was completely inaccurate, incidentally. I wondered what had started this vicious nonsense. Spike did not understand the meaning of royalties or contracts. He and Jack had worked together since 1968 and nothing like this had ever been mentioned.

Jack replied saying the letter had come 'like a bolt from the blue'. He explained that Spike had got the situation totally wrong. Spike Milligan Productions had a contract with Carol Barker and the royalty split was agreed by her agent. He had a contract with Michael Joseph, 'one that does not affect your earnings. I take no part of your royalty nor do you pay me in any way.'

I reassured Jack that the whole thing would die down, although I was taken aback by the vitriol of the language in Spike's letter. But I was wrong. Spike told me he was going to form his own publishing company, Monkenhurst Books. His daughters, Silé and Jane, would run it, and in future they would publish all his books. 'You'd better sign on at the Finchley Labour Exchange,' I said. Normally, that would have raised a laugh and I would have got the usual Milligan face saver – 'I'm putting the phone down. You put the phone down and we'll both cool off. I'll ring you later.' But this time he was furious. One of our coldest exchanges ensued.

Calmly, I asked him what was wrong. 'You've been unbearable for months,' I said, and reminded him how viciously he had treated Jack Hobbs. 'I want no part of that. It seems you want to go it alone so you'd better find another manager.' From now on I would pay Eric the rent for my office because I needed a base, and this would avoid having to change my stationery. The words came out as smoothly as if they had been rehearsed. I felt as if somebody else was speaking.

Remaining, for once, equally calm, Spike said that he needed me to be a director of Monkenhurst Books so I could run the business.

'That's not going to happen,' I said. 'I want nothing to do with the company and I won't help in any way.'

Very quietly he said, 'This time you mean it, Norm, don't you?'

'Yes.'

He put down the phone.

The following evening I took a very upset Jack Hobbs out to

dinner. Strangely, he repeated what Harry Edgington had said. 'He's changing. His personality is completely different from what it was. A few years ago he would never have sent such a letter to me.'

Four days later Spike wrote a long letter to Jack in an attempt to justify his appalling behaviour. It ended, 'Anyhow, I desperately want to see you again, have dinner and a laugh. I will not feel happy until I see you again as a friend.' I had asked him to apologize to Jack, but Spike could not climb down and just say sorry. That day Spike chipped away a tiny bit of the affection and friendship I had for him.

Then the inevitable occurred. Monkenhurst Books was stillborn. Spike admitted that it had been a failure and wrote to Dick Douglas Boyd to say he wanted to hand everything back to Michael Joseph. He seemed angry because Jack would not help him, adding, 'He threw a huff and decided not to have anymore to do with me. So fares the human race in friendship.' How about that for hypocrisy.

I continued as Spike's manager but I never forgot his treatment of Jack Hobbs, a sensitive, gentle soul. Eventually they made it up but things were not quite the same between them. Jack and I continued as normal, going out for dinner and listening to Alan Clare on the piano, the three of us swapping outrageous Milligan stories and laughing so much. Spike was the loser.

While all this was going on there was some light relief. We arrived at the office one day to find it had been burgled. Some quite valuable pieces were missing, including a costly, framed Persian rug, office equipment and cheque books. But Spike was not interested in any of that.

'The bastard has stolen my trumpet.'

Everyone in the building heard, and everyone had to be equally concerned. The same refrain was repeated throughout the day. It was his beloved trumpet, the one he had played in dance bands in the Thirties and during the war. He had once stolen cigarettes to buy a trumpet and this one was much better. He would spend hours playing it as he sat on the bed in his office, and 'Laura', 'Body and Soul' and 'Rainy Day' provided the regular soundtrack for Number Nine.

Spike wanted his trumpet back, and work, family, friends, none meant a thing until he could put it back to his lips once more. That 'dear old trumpet' was not quite as old as all that. A man from Boosey and Hawkes told me long ago that so many parts of the instrument had been replaced that little was left of the original, and if Spike thought he was playing the one from the Thirties he was very much mistaken. But now was not the time to disillusion him. When the police failed to recover the trumpet within twenty-four hours it was 'What do we pay them for?' and so on. Spike became the super sleuth of Bayswater. He pestered shopkeepers, tramps, pickpockets and the ladies of the street, all of whom normally passed the time of day with him, and asked them to let him know of any thieves operating in the area. He asked ex-cons, wide boys and those operating on the fringe of legality to tell him if they heard anything on the grapevine. To ease their memories he offered a reward of £1000. And every day he badgered the police at the Harrow Road station about it until a Sergeant Bennett came to see me.

'Ask him to lay off about his trumpet, miss, please.' He looked exhausted and I knew the feeling. I described the tatty blue cardboard case in which the instrument was kept and sent him on his way.

For almost three weeks Spike refused to discuss anything other than his trumpet. If anyone managed to get through to him to talk business they were cut short.

'Don't you realize someone has stolen my trumpet, the trumpet I've had since I was a lad, the trumpet that went through the war with me and the one I've played every day of my life?' (An exaggeration but so was the man himself.) 'And you have the temerity to try to talk business with me.'

I was getting very anxious because if the trumpet did not turn up the mania could distil into a depression that would spoil every project I had planned for months to come. Then one day a policeman, not poor Sergeant Bennett, arrived with photographs of an instrument case. It was the very one. Spike had caused so much kerfuffle at Harrow Road and elsewhere that the boys of the Met, who thought the world of him – he had done many charity concerts for them – had put the word out to every station to keep an eye open for his trumpet. So when there was a call to attend a disturbance at a house in Warwick Road an alert copper noticed a scruffy blue case and there was Spike's trumpet. Stashed in another room was the Persian rug, along with some of the stolen *objets d'art*.

Suddenly, instead of the police being 'useless buggers' they became 'grand lads', and those involved were invited to dinner at the Trattoo. That night they established a house record for the number of bottles of wine drunk at one party, and that is not taking into account the bottles of beer and spirits.

After the next day's hangover had faded I heard the strains of 'Rainy Day' coming from his office, and so normality, if there ever was such a thing, returned to Number Nine.

In December Spike opened his one-man show at the Lyric Theatre in Hammersmith. Within days of opening Spike rang to say Patrick O'Neill was short of money. Could Spike Milligan Productions lend him some so he could honour his commitment at the theatre?

'No, Spike. He's your friend. You lend it to him.'

Happy Christmas, Spike.

Maybe 1983 would be different. But within weeks I had the evidence that nothing would change. Despite my advice Spike had made the loan to Patrick. His excuse was that there was no alternative: the performance had been advertised so it would reflect negatively on him if it did not take place.

'I don't want to know any more. And spare me the details,' I said.

'You are my business manager. You need to know where my money is. I've let him have £10,000.'

'Of your own money. That's a personal loan and has nothing to do with me. I look after your business affairs. And what's more, I was against this tour in the first place.'

I reminded him that there was a busy year ahead of us and I needed to concentrate on business. He was furious and marched out of my office. On 11 January he was due to do a Kellogg's commercial and I consoled myself with the thought that this would make up for the money due to us from the Lyric, money I knew we would never get. The commercial was a great success so on 24 January, in Spike's presence, I wrote in my diary that he had promised, once again, to start on the fifth volume of his war memoirs. Two days later I opened my diary and alongside the entry found he had written, 'SO?'

A few days later Equity telephoned to say that Spike had broken their ban on actors working on commercials. I had to attend the meeting because my signature was on the contract. The attitude of the officials made it a nightmare. Spike was a high-profile member and his breach was very damaging to the union. They decided that the only course was for Spike Milligan Productions to return the fee. I told them they could tell Spike they wanted the money. Anyway, I had not had a letter informing me of a ban and was unaware that one existed. The officials said they would convene a council meeting and let me know of their decision. I demanded evidence of the date of the ban and the date they had informed their members. They said the ruling had been made on 17 January. I had signed the contract on 10 January and the work was completed the following day; it just so happened that the commercial had been televised after the ban was enforced, but that did not put us in breach of it. Collapse of complaint but I was annoyed by Equity's autocratic behaviour.

I usually kept anything like this from Spike but foolishly I told him about the meeting. 'One of them acted as though he was Adolf Hitler and I was a rabbi's wife.' Spike wrote to the general secretary, Peter Plouvier, who had not been present, and we heard no more about it.

Then came a chink of light. Jack Hobbs was brought back on track after he agreed to a meeting with Spike to discuss the war memoirs. Afterwards Spike wrote to Michael Joseph, Jack and me to say he would make a start in June after his tour of Australia and New Zealand. While in Australia he sent me a telegram on 16 April: 'I'm 65 today. Remind me to die or get a bus pass.' I sent him a card:

ABOUT 80 BIRTHDAY CARDS WAITING. IF
a. I send them it'll be 'wasting fucking money on postage.'
b. I do not keep them for your return it'll be 'What do you
   mean? I wanted to see the cards from my fans.'
c. If I do keep them for your return it'll be 'Why did you
   keep these? My fucking birthday was two months ago.'
PLEASE TICK. ERIC SYKES SAYS, 'WHERE APPLICABLE'.

Spike phoned as soon as he received the card. He loved it and, laughing, he said, 'Oh, Norm. What have I done to you? It sounded just like me. Through all the tension you've managed to keep your sense of humour. I'm right, you are my sunshine girl.'

Yes, I thought, for today anyway. He would be my sunshine man if he kept his promise to start volume five in June. Of course when he came back he did not start on it. He was having trouble with his eye and decided he needed an operation. Operations were meat and drink to Spike. About one a year became par for the course. He went to see an eye surgeon, Eric Arnott, and after the consultation at 7 Queen Anne Street Spike returned to the office. What was the verdict?

'It's the worst building I've ever seen.'

'Never mind the building. What about your eye?'

Spike brushed that aside. He had the operation, which was successful, and then wrote to Mr. Arnott about his building. Mr. Arnott protested that it had won the Queen's Award for Architecture. Spike wrote back. 'That does not mean a thing. She wears glasses as well.' He was far more in sympathy with Prince Charles's opinions on architecture.

Later he was told he needed another operation on his eyes. He decided he wanted to speak to Mr. Arnott again for reassurance. Luckily for Mr. Arnott his phone was not working so Spike sent him a letter. 'This is to report that both telephones in the Queen's Award for Architecture building are out of order. Would your secretary please phone me?' Mr. Arnott did not call back, but Spike decided to ring me again late one night. Without preamble he said, 'Listen. I'm not going to worry about my eye. Nelson did all right and he got Lady Hamilton.'

He was out of the office for a while. I wondered what was keeping his attention. On 28 July he phoned in the afternoon.

'I've just written in my diary, "SHOOT MYSELF". Put it in your diary.'

'If you're going to do it, do it at home and not in the office.' He laughed and hung up. I thought no more about it. The next morning, just before noon, I phoned him at Monkenhurst to say that Michael Joseph were putting on the pressure for the fifth volume of the memoir and wanted to know if he had started it.

'I told them you hadn't.'

'Not *now*.'

'If not now, when?'

'Can't you ever leave me alone? I'm getting married today. Shelagh wants to get married on the same date as Princess Diana did and that's today.' He put the phone down.

The slightest puff from Puff the Magic Dragon would have

knocked me over. I knew he meant it. My first thought was about the South Africa tour contract I had signed. Oh God, I prayed. He was meant to leave in the middle of August. Please God, no honeymoon.

I tried to collect my thoughts. Earlier he made out he had got engaged to please Shelagh, but had never mentioned the possibility of marriage. Spike was aware that not all his close friends approved of the relationship. Later I discovered that apparently Spike had told nobody outside his immediate family about the wedding.

He phoned me the next day and asked if my diary was in front of me.

'Yes.'

'On today's page write, "Reload Pistol!" That's what I've written in mine!'

He was due to go to South Africa on 15 August but the week before he phoned to say he could not. I expected to be told about his honeymoon plans, but then he explained his reasons. He could not stand the piped music that was played as passengers boarded the plane. It gave him a migraine and he could not possibly fly with a migraine. This ranked high among the bizarre excuses he made for refusing to do what somebody else wanted. In all the years, over all the flights, he had never complained about the music. What if the airline switched off the music? I tried the regional manager but got nowhere, so I persuaded Spike to write to Mr. Fran Swartz, the head of South African Airlines. Back came the reply with a crate of South African wine. Certainly, he said. This seemed too good to be true so I double-checked with Mr. Swartz's office and within days he had sent a telex to his London staff with a copy for Spike to take when he boarded the plane.

I never told Ronnie Quibell about this performance. There had been enough trouble for him before Spike flew out, when Spike had suddenly insisted that he needed a road manager, also a first. Ronnie had been against this because it was unnecessary and expensive, but he understood how to handle Spike and agreed.

'Spike,' I asked, 'do you have anyone in mind or shall I start asking around to see if anyone would like to accompany you on the tour?'

He was so transparent.

'No. I've already got somebody in mind. Patrick O'Neill needs the money and he knows my props. He'll do. I'll phone him.'

Of course, I knew that Spike had already made arrangements with Patrick. Poor, poor Ronnie Quibell.

'Spike. Listen to me. I know you've just got married, but are you having an affair with Patrick O'Neill because that's what it looks like?'

He laughed. 'Patrick's had more women than I have.'

The tour went ahead and, predictably, Ronnie complained several times to me about Patrick's behaviour and extravagance. In early October, a month before he came back from South Africa, Spike rang for what I knew was a conscience-easing session. He said he would definitely start the next instalment of his memoirs when he returned and therefore I could go ahead and sign the book contract (not that I had any intention of doing so until I was satisfied he was really going to get down to it). And by the way, would I set up another British tour of his one-man show with Jimmy Verner? He said he was dying to come home. He had had enough.

It was only when Spike returned to England that Ronnie wrote to him to say there would not be another tour as far as he was concerned if Spike were to insist on a road manager. Spike's guilt got the better of him and he insisted on sharing the loss that Ronnie had incurred because of Patrick.

The British tour started in November and Spike worked right up to Christmas. Although he did not start work on volume five, I thought one out of two was not bad.

I thought 1984 would be better because one thing was sure, it could not get much worse. It got off to a roaring start. Jack Hobbs came to the office once a week to help me with my second book, *More Spike Milligan Letters*, which I published later that year. What is more, Spike started on the fifth volume. Then he told me that Shelagh did not think he needed to go to an office every day as he could write just as well at home, so he gave up his office at Number Nine. I thought he would miss the stimulation from Eric, Johnny and the others who visited the office; Spike needed it. Then he revealed his safety net: could he rent Room Fourteen, one of the small rooms on the top floor, and use it as a bedroom? There was a stipulation. Nobody, except those in the office and Jack Hobbs, must know about it.

Jack rang. 'I hear the Bayswater Harem has started again.'

He laughed when I replied, 'It never went away.'

I was seeing less and less of Spike now. There was another tour of his one-man show to Australia in the summer and not without the usual tension. The day before his departure he rang. 'I think I'm too ill to travel.'

Right, I thought, that did not sound too serious, and with a little cajoling he went and returned in September, an unhappy man. I never found out the cause, but he told me to erase every booking from his diary. His mood worsened when he discovered the BBC had cancelled the sequel to *There's a Lot of It About*. He complained to Equity without telling me. It was a straightforward decision by the BBC not to put it out and I had negotiated a cancellation payment while he was in Australia.

'You did not do a very good deal,' he said.

'Sue me.'

'That's what I'm going to do.'

This was the sort of challenge with Spike that I relished. He never listened to reason and, acting on all the wrong information, went for it for all his worth. As with all his tantrums it fizzled out when I told him to see Equity again. I would make an appointment for him and he could take along the necessary files. He met them but I never heard another word about it. Welcome home, Spike, I thought. Everything was back to normal.

But then tragedy struck Number Nine. Eric's manager was killed in a car accident, leaving behind a wife and young daughter. Eric was deeply saddened. After a few weeks he realized he would have to make other arrangements. He asked me to look after him. I said I had enough on my hands with Spike, but agreed to bank his cheques and pay his bills until he found another manager. In the end that never happened. We had always been close friends, and he had often been a calming influence on Spike. So I became his manager and, almost twenty years later, I still enjoy looking after him.

The day after the publication do for *More Spike Milligan Letters* Jack Hobbs had an appointment with me and brought along a bouquet with a note, 'To Norma. Late, contrite, inadequate congratulations on the book from one who's always late, contrite and inadequate. With much love, Jack (Hobbs, not Clarke). The other one's always early, in control and more than adequate.' He was in my office when Spike walked in and jumped to the wrong conclusion – that Jack was in the office because of volume five. He started shouting. He would not be hassled like this. Everyone wanted a piece of him and there were no pieces left, so there would not be a fifth volume if everybody hounded him.

I used one of his expressions. 'Just hold it right there. Jack's here to see me. Nothing to do with you.'

Then we had Spike at his best. 'The bloody letters books are finished. Why should he be here if it is not for volume five?'

Very quietly Jack said, 'I'm here to discuss with Norma her new book, which I'm going to call *Ups and Downs with Spike Milligan*.'

That was too much for Spike. He raged out of the office.

'There are no bloody ups. Those days are gone. The only thing left now are the downs and she can put me into one of those very easily.'

I shouted after him to come back as he had an interview with James Jonathan Moore of the BBC. Too late. He was in his car and on the way back to Monkenhurst before I reached the front door. Jonathan was an old friend so all was well and I rearranged the interview.

Then came another late night telephone call.

'Before I die I would like to do a pantomime.'

I had had this before and reminded him that I had to be satisfied he could accept the discipline of being at the theatre every night. It would not be like his one-man show when he could change it at will. Yes, he understood that and wanted to do it. So he took a part in *Babes in the Wood* at Chichester and enjoyed it because he was among children, which always brought out the magic in him.

Chapter Twenty-one

At the close of 1984 he started writing *Floored Masterpieces and Worse Verse* and, at long last, completed the first draft of volume five, to be called *Where Have All the Bullets Gone?* Seven long years after *Mussolini* it had become a reality, and both books were published later in 1985.

Meanwhile, in 1984 Shelagh's friend, Pauline Scudamore, had asked Spike to co-operate with her on a biography she was writing, an academic biography and critical appraisal of his work, to be used as a reference book in libraries and universities. When he mentioned it to me I rang Spike's editor at Michael Joseph, Jennie Davies, and explained the project which, because of its nature, I assured her could not possibly interfere with *Where Have All the Bullets Gone?*, which was due out the following autumn. I agreed to an interview with Scudamore, and it was then that I realized the biography would be entirely different from the 'academic' description I had been given. I telephoned Spike and told him it was going to be just another biography; matters should be put on a business footing and he should receive a share of the royalties. Of course, I was being ridiculous. 'Utter rubbish,' he said.

I rang Jennie once more to tell her I had been misinformed by Spike about the nature of the book. Its publication date was of even greater concern to her because Michael Joseph was throwing all its weight behind Spike's book, was already committed to spending money advertising it, and she had made a presentation to an enthusiastic sales force. I wrote asking Scudamore to let me have the name of her publisher and the publication date. When she did not reply, I asked Spike to contact her.

'Do you want me to be an author and make money for us both or do you want me to be a business man? You have a choice. Don't ask me any more about the biography.'

'Sorry, Spike, Michael Joseph need some answers.'

Eventually, he wrote to her. Two days later he informed me that the pressure was off: the book would not be going ahead. I rang Jennie with the good news. And there the matter rested.

Months went by and in the spring of 1985 Jennie invited me to a meeting. I was ushered into Michael Joseph's board room. Sitting round a large table were the heads of department, but none wore their usual smiles. The accusations came from all sides. Had I seen the *Bookseller*? On the front cover was Michael Joseph's advertisement for *Bullets* with a big picture of Spike. But then further inside there was a large advertisement from Granada, announcing the publication of Scudamore's biography – eleven days before *Bullets*.

There was utter disbelief when I said I had not known how much he had participated in the book and had been assured the project was off. And I could tell they found it hard to credit that he was not getting a percentage of the royalties for his co-operation. Then the killer punch. Surely I must have known from his diary that he was promoting the biography with the author in a nationwide tour of bookshop signings? There it was in the *Bookseller*.

I could not believe it. I knew nothing about it. This was utterly humiliating. I asked for a meeting the following day when I would produce evidence that I was telling the truth. I brought them my file of letters and memos to Scudamore and Spike, and Michael Joseph accepted I was telling the truth. Now it was time to deal with Spike.

I phoned to say I was coming to his house.

'Norm. Are you all right? What's wrong?'

'Too late for all that, Spike. I'm on my way.'

He sat in silence as I told him what had happened at the meeting with Michael Joseph.

'I don't know anything about a biography,' he said. In a situation like this lies meant nothing to him.

'That won't work this time. You've got yourself into this mess and you'll have to get yourself out of it.' I showed him the *Bookseller*. 'The chips are down, Spike. My professional integrity is on the line, so you take second place. I've told Jennie Davies to write to you here and when you get her letter you might appreciate the seriousness of the situation. She will be asking you to write to the *Bookseller* stating categorically that the only promotion you will be undertaking will be for *Bullets*.'

He looked utterly dejected, but I had to finish what I had come to tell him. 'As I signed the book contract on behalf of the company I've made an appointment with a solicitor to take out an injunction to stop the publication of the biography. This is to clear my name and nothing to do with the company. I've found out that large chunks of your work are quoted without permission from us.'

His head shrunk into his shoulders.

'And before I forget, you need to write a letter of apology to Jennie Davies. She's in trouble with her sales force because she briefed them on your book and made a big thing of it.'

I knew that would sting. But there was a final flick of rebellion and an attempt to get off the hook.

'I'll write the letter but I must tell her it was all your fault. I may have been lax in telling you at the outset, but I must point out to Jennie that you are my business manager as well as agent. You control my life and you should have known all about the book.'

'Hold it right there,' I said. 'If you're going down that road I'll arrange for a meeting with Jennie and the managing director. I'll take my file and we can get to the truth together.' I did not tell him I had already shown them the file.

'What bloody file?'

'My file on all the memos from me to you and letters to the author.'

He sat down and the injured Spike Milligan emerged. 'Please don't do this to me. I'm a writer. I'll do your bidding and write the letter you want.'

'And send me a copy – for my file.' I could not resist that and it went home. This time there were no jibes about being unchristian. Sorrowfully he said, 'How did I get into this position by just being kind and helping someone with my biography?'

'Too late for that, Spike.'

As he accompanied me to the door he asked, 'Are we still friends?'

That was usually the time for laughter and forgiveness, but not now.

'Not this time, daddy.'

My solicitor eventually succeeded in delaying the book's publication, and when I saw it I was astonished at how much he had talked to Scudamore. After it was all over I told him I thought he had betrayed me. He was horrified. Then I reminded him that a year before the *Bookseller* advertisement I had warned him on four occasions that trouble was coming.

'Well, you weren't strong enough then, were you?' he said.

After he finished *Bullets* he became manic, and in addition to starting volume six he immediately accepted all the work I asked him to do. He was a man possessed. He even said yes to an invitation to appear in the Bob Hope Birthday Gala, a special concert at the Lyric to celebrate the American star's eighty-second birthday at the end of May. But as usual there was a condition: he would not attend rehearsals. I was apprehensive at this but I need not have worried. The night went well and as a bonus, Spike shared a dressing room with the champion boxer Marvin Hagler, who became his new best friend. I had not seen him on such a high for a couple of years.

But the morning after the gala there was a completely different Spike on the phone.

'Cancel my day. My life is unbearable and I can't go on.'

What followed was Spike in one of his controlled rages. It had me in stitches and I wrote it down as soon as he had finished ranting.

'Jane's pet cat died yesterday. I had to bury the cat so I'm depressed. I mean, how much space would I need? So I went back into the house and got the live cat to measure him. He ran off and then I wondered how deep do I dig to bury the cat? Then I'm digging and the next door neighbour said, "Planting bulbs, Spike?"'

'"No. I'm burying the cat," I said.'

'"Honestly, Spike. Always ready with a joke."'

'And I said, "I'm burying the fucking cat."'

'So I had to come in and ring you to get away from it all.'

Before he put down the phone he said, 'Somebody should do for me what I did for Ronnie – save me from killing myself.'

And people ask me why I stayed with him. I never did find out if he went back and buried the cat.

But the following day he was back to normal. He telephoned at what for him was the early hour of eleven in the morning.

'I'm your parcel. Where do you want to deliver me today?'

He was due to record the quiz show *Give Us a Clue* for Thames Television so it was an easy-peasy sort of day.

A week later I was suddenly taken to hospital with a pulmonary embolism, which turned into a deep vein thrombosis. The flowers started to arrive from just about everyone I knew. Spike sent me two bouquets, one for me and another 'to your leg.' Jack Clarke knew Spike well but not his unexpected side, so was taken aback when Spike phoned him at home. Without preamble he said, 'If anything happens to her I'll be devastated,' and put down the phone. He did not stop to ask how Jack was coping or whether I was feeling better.

I had fallen ill in Yorkshire and so I recuperated at our house there, sitting in the conservatory, looking at the restful garden and listening to the soothing burble of the river. That made it a little less painful to give up smoking as well. I was away from the office for about three weeks but back in London in time for the September publication party at Kettners for *Where Have All the Bullets Gone?* Spike had agreed to Michael Joseph's plan for publicity, interviews, television appearances and book signings and they all went off without calamity, before he left for Australia to do a documentary for the BBC, *Spike Milligan's Australia*.

While he was there I had to ring him with the bad news that Eric had suffered a slight stroke. He loved Eric like a brother and I knew it would have a devastating effect on him, but if I had not told him and worse happened to Eric he would never have forgiven me. Spike had only four days' work left on the documentary before he returned to England, and if it had been much longer he would have dropped everything to be with Eric. On the return flight he suffered severe breathing difficulties. I believe this was brought on by his concern for Eric. As soon as he arrived home he rang to find out how Eric was and I was able to say that he was making a wonderful recovery. Spike said dejectedly, 'We are all starting to die,' and hung up. Fortunately, Eric pulled through completely and soon returned to work.

During the manic session earlier in the year Spike had agreed to do a pantomime at Richmond, and not long after he returned he was due to go into rehearsals. He was delighted when he was asked to appear in Kenny Everett's *Christmas Show*: he liked him and thought he was extremely talented. I was also in a good mood because Jack was about to take me on a wonderful holiday to Little Dix Bay on the Virgin Gorda. When we returned in January 1986 I found Spike very tired from the demands of the pantomime. During the last two weeks of the run I waited for him to say, 'Get me out of it,' but he did not. When he came to see me in my office his skin looked grey and he shuffled about slowly, whereas normally he bounced about the place and came in and out like a tornado.

'What's bugging you? Or is the black dog barking to get out?'

He said softly, 'No. It's just my life.'

After the panto he was due to go on holiday with Shelagh and I thought that would put him to rights, but then he cancelled it. A few days later he came to see me at Number Nine and sat in the armchair all day without saying a word. Early in the afternoon he went up to Room Fourteen and rested on the bed. Before I left for the evening I went up and sat with him.

'Are you pretending to be a jelly?' I asked after a while. I thought that might prompt a conversation.

Wearily he said, 'I need to go to my Alma Mater.'

He said he was in a constant state of panic, could not sleep and was walking round the house at two and three in the morning. By the end of the week he was in his Alma Mater, the Priory at Roehampton. It was a very quiet Milligan who came out of the Priory after a period of deep narcosis, the chemically induced sleep he occasionally resorted to. The entry in my diary for this time reads, 'Spike is so quiet. It's not normal. "Yes" to everything.'

When he came out of a depression he liked to have gigs lined up to help him return to 'normal' as soon as possible. But I wondered whether this time would turn out differently, because he had not been so lacklustre since the early Seventies. Yet he resumed work immediately and picked up where he had left off on volume six of his memoirs, to be called *Goodbye Soldier*. He reckoned he would finish it in a couple of weeks. I wondered what made Spike almost chain himself to his typewriter when he was depressed. It was either Dr Sydney Gottlieb or Professor Anthony Clare, who wrote *Depression and How to Survive It* with Spike in the early Nineties, who said that Spike was the exception to the rule, because when most authors wrote in a state of depression they realized later that they had written rubbish. Not so with Spike. At times like these he produced some of his best work.

Sure enough Spike finished volume six in two weeks and it was published later that year and became a bestseller. I reflected on how long it had taken to get him started on the last one, while this had materialized without so much as a nudge from me. As well as making all the usual guest appearances on television he had also finished another adult poetry book, *The Mirror Running*.

Spike came to see me some time after I had returned from a holiday and sensed something was wrong.

'How's your life?'

'Yes,' I said.

'Come on. It's got to be better than "Y-e-e-s-s". You can say "I own a bloke called Spike Milligan."'

When this did not get any reaction he insisted we have a talk.

'Please tell me your problems and I'll take them away from you.'

He often said that to me. When I said it was too painful to discuss he took my two office phones off the hook and said, 'You always help me. Please, please let me help you. We are part of each other's lives.'

I told him Jack and I had parted and I did not want to make it up. It was better to have a clean break because it was all too painful. 'Let's go for a walk in Kensington Gardens and look at the Elfin Oak.'

We left and, as we made our way there, he said he had never known two people so right for one another. Could he take Jack out for dinner and talk to him, because he too must be suffering? Or perhaps the three of us could have dinner. He was desperate that I should not do something I would regret. We had tea at the Orangerie in Holland Park and seemed to talk for ever. He was such a good friend.

When Jack and I subsequently settled our differences Spike sent us a simple card: 'I just want to say I'm glad you have got it together. Love, Spike.'

It always was that way. Whenever I was unhappy in my personal life he wanted to know what bothered me and never let me down. However, in business the other Spike more than made up for it.

After Richmond Spike decided not to do any more pantomimes because they were too much for him. He was near the end of his next novel, about an Irish labourer who thought he was the King of Ireland. Originally it was called *The King*, but this title was changed to *The Looney*. He called Harry Secombe to tell him about *The Looney* because he had the sense of humour to appreciate it. They spent almost an hour on the phone and Spike said it was wonderful. They laughed until he really did cry, and told each other the story of an overcoat, a ritual they had been following for years.

Apparently, in the early Fifties when they were broke and sharing digs in Shepherd's Bush with Michael Bentine, Spike was the only one in the flat with an overcoat. One day Harry borrowed it. I wondered how diminutive, rotund Harry must have looked in that coat if it was a reasonable fit for tall, chip-thin Spike. Nonetheless, it became the coat they shared – until one day Harry said he had lost it. Spike told me the story. 'About ten years ago we were having dinner at my house and I said to Harry, "Remember that fucking overcoat?" Instantly Harry

blurted out, "I sold it!" He had carried the guilt all those years.'
Like Pete, Spike had started to yearn for the old days when they
were all together.

The end of the year approached but Spike was now on a high.
On 11 December Eric was to attend an investiture to receive the
OBE he had been awarded. I believe he got more pleasure from
it than Eric. He told everyone who would listen that nobody
deserved it more because nobody had made as many people
laugh in the U.K. But his mood changed quickly and a few days
before Christmas I got a festive late night phone call. There were
no preliminaries. 'I thought I was going to lose my children in
1959 so I wrote *Silly Verse for Kids*.' He hung up.

As usual I was optimistic about the New Year and hopeful
that in 1987 things would get easier. Everybody told me that
Spike would mellow with age. But on 10 January I knew I
would not see the evidence of it during the next twelve months
because he phoned to say he had decided to move back into the
office.

Oh God no, I pleaded, silently. I had become accustomed to
a certain degree of tranquillity at Number Nine.

'Why the hell the women in my life can't get on I don't know,'
he ranted. 'I suppose women are just like that, but whatever, I
don't want any part of it.'

When he calmed down I learnt that the trouble stemmed from
a small family argument. I hoped the trouble would die down,
but two days later he rang to say Shelagh had been admitted to
a clinic.

'I am here now on my own keeping the family together.'

I felt like saying God help us all, but realized it would hardly
be diplomatic. My first thought was for Nanny, that dear old
lady. She had looked after Jane for over twenty years, nursed
Paddy through her cancer and cared for Spike after she died. It
was a nasty situation. Nanny was the same age as my mother
and I always thought of her in that way. I rang her to give some

comfort. She was too upset to say much more than, 'Shelagh resents my presence in the house. I can't take any more lies and deceit, but where am I to go?' She promised she would ring when she came to terms with the situation. When she did call again I could tell she was desperately unhappy.

Spike seemed to ignore Shelagh's stay in the clinic. He said simply, 'As I am now sailing alone I'd better work to buy the tucker.' He was strong and determined when I expected him to be down. But that changed all too soon. I had booked Spike to appear on the Thursday night on *Aspel and Company* and, as always, agreed to the condition that he would not appear on the rival BBC programme, *Wogan*. But that Tuesday Spike said, 'Get your diary out. I'm on Terry Wogan's show on Friday.'

'Where's that come from?'

'Neil Shand [who now worked on *Wogan*] telephoned me at home and said he wanted me to do the show.'

I told him he could not do it because I had already committed him to the Aspel show.

'I'll ring the *Wogan* office, tell them that Neil shouldn't have telephoned you at home and explain.'

I thought there might be a minor outburst with the usual line that I was stopping his livelihood, but I did not expect the mega tantrum I got. He insisted on doing both and I was not going to stand in his way. I explained that I had given my word to the *Aspel and Company* producer so would have to ring her and say that he was doing this against my advice; I had no intention of having my professional integrity put in doubt. Then he went wild. 'You are fucking up my career.'

I was feeling tetchy and said, 'You do a pretty good job of that yourself. I'm going.'

As soon as I had phoned the *Aspel* office and explained why he could not do it I left Number Nine. At home the next morning I received a letter from him insisting that I could have avoided the mix-up.

'The *Aspel* show think I pulled out in a fit of pique. This has harmed my professional standing about being awkward.'

Never let it be said, I thought. The letter went on, 'You should have covered up for me. I have an accountant who lets me down, my wife lets me down and you make a mess of the Aspel/Wogan shows for which I carry the can. It's all too much for me. I'm mentally ill. I should be in hospital but I can't afford it. My BUPA funds have run out so all in all I'm the innocent loser.'

That was Spike at his very best. He had worked himself into a daddy of a tantrum, cancelled both shows and then had to find someone to blame. It did not work because I ignored the letter. The next day he phoned and out came the emotional blackmail.

'If you desert me then there's no hope. You know more than anybody it's not me. It's the illness.'

I wondered why the same ploy worked on me every time. They say the Irish always stick together, and I was able to put the *Wogan* show on again later in the month. For three months he went in and out of depression, no tantrums but just walking about, drugged to the hilt. No sparkle, no repartee. He was fighting against going under. Then came the calm, when he was locked in his office, fires on no matter what the time of day and the blinds drawn.

One morning when I arrived at the office quite early it was just like old times. There was a note pinned to the door of Room Fourteen: 'FROM NOW ON IF GOD COMES THROUGH THE DOOR I WANT TO SEE HIS BIRTH CERTIFICATE.' What is all that about, I wondered, and questioned him when he surfaced.

'Don't get involved.'

I never did discover what had upset him. But soon afterwards I received a bombshell of a late night call.

'Norm. Can you talk?'

It was unusual for him to ask.

'Shelagh thinks I should retire Nanny.'

'What do you think?'

He did not answer that directly but explained it had got to the stage where it was his wife or Nanny. He was in tears. How the hell had he let himself get in this position?

In the end he retired Nanny and in an attempt to ease his conscience made sure she had an income. But as far as I was concerned there was not enough money in the world. He should not have allowed it to happen.

Chapter Twenty-two

After Nanny left Monkenhurst Spike reverted to type and, rather than start on the seventh volume of his war memoirs, he preferred to write poetry. Then out of the blue he came in one day to tell me that Patrick O'Neill wanted him to tour Australia in *The Sunshine Boys*. He was not in the mood to be dissuaded, so I simply said that if Patrick failed to pay him week in, week out I would immediately withdraw his services on behalf of Spike Milligan Productions. This time the contract would have a clause enforcing that.

Spike was furious. On the last tour, he said, I had got very nasty when payments came to a halt. He had wanted to let it ride, but he repeated my words of the previous year: 'You can give him your share if you want to but remember, my commission was in there, so you'll be giving away £6,000 of my money.' He had told me to take the sum owed from wherever he had got it and, even a year later, he was still bothered that I had refused to ease his conscience.

Spike was going through a very bad time with panic attacks

and insomnia. His GP told me he had never known his sleeping pattern to be so disturbed. He tried hypnotherapy again, with little effect, and as a last resort started to take five or six sleeping pills and drink two bottles of wine before going to bed. He decided to go to Australia by boat in the hope that he would find it relaxing. But then came the panic attacks and these brought on the worry that he might be even worse if confined to a cabin at sea. So the trip was cancelled at the eleventh hour and he told me he was finished. He never wanted to write or perform again.

A few days later I rang to tell him I was going to Yorkshire for a couple of days for a funeral. I knew his spirits were improving when he said, 'I'll be glad when I have one. I haven't been invited to a funeral recently.' Maybe the spark was about to ignite once more. I needed him to argue with me, as he always did when he was in the mood for work. And it arrived again within a couple of weeks when I was asked if he would be prepared to sing his old hit, *The Ying-Tong Song*, for a commercial. 'It's good money,' I said. But he could not do it, he could not remember the words because it was so long ago and Pete did it so much better. Pete, I said, was dead so I couldn't ask him.

'Don't bother, I'll find somebody to do it. It's only twenty-eight seconds so I'll get someone to impersonate you.'

There was an immediate reaction.

'Hey! Wait a minute. Nobody can do it as well as I can.'

The phone went down. Half an hour later he rang again.

'Norm. I've been practising. Tell them I'll do it.'

Those were the times that made me smile and it is those times I miss. Because I do Jack Clarke concludes there must be something odd about me.

When we were paid for the commercial Spike said, 'God! I never thought I'd get that amount of money all in one go when I sat on the tube and wrote it from Tottenham Court Road to Shepherd's Bush.' Work was his salvation. He had promised to appear in an episode of *Till Death Us Do Part* for Johnny Speight and he would never let him down. He thought he was the greatest observational writer in the country and understood that comedy offered a blazing insight into the truth, something few writers seemed to know.

After Tanis left for the final time in the mid-Eighties we had several secretaries. It no doubt seemed glamorous to be involved with Spike Milligan and work in the same office as Eric Sykes, not to mention Harry Secombe's agent, Jimmy Grafton. But it was understandable if they found it difficult to cope with Spike's mood swings and barrack room language. They came and they went, including one who went almost as soon as she arrived.

I settled her in over a cup of coffee and explained that at times Spike could be somewhat difficult but basically was all right. Well, she had had difficult bosses before. At ten o'clock Spike called her upstairs to take dictation. At ten to one she came back down, looking pale and drawn.

'Does he always work like that? He never stopped, not once.'

'He gets spells and works at that pace, then he'll sleep for a couple of days, so it evens itself out,' I said.

She said, 'I need a break so I'll take my lunch now.'

And she never came back. The worst thing from my point of view was that she took her shorthand notebook with her so the dictation had to be done again. To avert the Third World War I offered to do it myself.

'No. She's fucked off with it and I'm not prepared to do it again.'

I asked him what the dictation had been.

'Don't get involved,' he barked. 'That's an end to it.'

Then one day in spring he announced he had decided to sell his beloved Monkenhurst and move to the south coast. I could not believe it. He loved that house. He said he was worried his earning power would diminish and that he would not be able to afford to live there. This did not make sense. I reminded him that the house was paid for and asked if he had thought about the cost of renting a place and storing furniture until he found somewhere else to live, and then there were legal charges, removal expenses, alterations and decorations. This pessimism about his financial future was so unlike Spike. Whenever anyone had tackled him about having a pension he would use one of Johnny Speight's expressions. 'My talent is my pension.'

That evening Eric rang me, which was very unusual because unlike Spike he never bothered me at home. He had just finished speaking to Spike, who had told him about the sale and his intention to move to the south coast because Shelagh wanted to be near her mother. Eric said to him, 'But you can't do that. You're a North London man.'

We both wondered how Spike would cope without all the things he loved about the city, his friends, the theatre, concerts, jazz and late night dinners with whoever. He went ahead and sold Monkenhurst and moved temporarily into an oast house in Ticehurst, Kent in July 1987. He invested some of the proceeds from the sale of Monkenhurst in the stock market. But then on Black Monday shares crashed and, like everyone else, his investment suffered. He was advised to leave his investment where it was because the market was volatile and likely to recover, but Spike insisted that his money should be withdrawn and placed in an interest-bearing account. Twelve months later of course shares recovered and if Spike had left his money where it was he would not have made a loss.

Spike moved into his new house near Rye the following year. On the day of the move Jack Hobbs phoned.

'All I want to know is did you swap sideboards with him?'

'Yes.'

He laughed. 'I had a ten pound bet with Spike that you would. I actually said that you would say, "For God's sake take it."'

He was right. I had had the sideboard since the early Seventies, when Spike burst into the office one day saying, 'I've seen a marvellous mahogany sideboard for sale in a shop. It's far too large for the average house but it's ideal for your office.' I bought it for twenty pounds and, remembering what Ray Galton had once said, kept the receipt.

The sideboard was much admired over the years. Sean Connery occasionally dropped in to visit his pal, Eric, and when he once came into my office his eyes dwelt on the sideboard. He examined it in detail and pronounced it a fine piece of work. 'He would know,' said Spike. 'Once a carpenter, always a carpenter.'

When Spike had at last found the house in Rye, he dropped into the office. I asked what he wanted. There was no particular reason, he just wanted to see me. I could sense he was up to something. He had a cup of tea and chatted about this and that. Then out it came.

'That sideboard,' he said, looking at me for a response he did not get. He waited and grunted. 'It would be just right for my new house.'

'Sod off.'

'Don't be like that, Norma. My sideboard, you know, the magnificent oak one, a gem if ever there was one, doesn't fit in somehow. Now this mahogany one would be just right and the oak one is worth much more.'

'I said, "Sod off."'

He looked hurt. 'I was the one who bought you that Persian carpet hanging on the wall over there and persuaded you to have it instead of the John Bratby painting you wanted.'

'I thought it was a Christmas present.'

'If you loved me you'd do a swap.'

I had had that one before, more than once, and did not give in. I knew that before long he would be telling friends, 'I'm good to Norma but she won't swap sideboards with me.' Sure enough, he did. When that did not work I got the full treatment. He came many times and sat in my office and begged for it. He said he would not leave until he got what he wanted. He was relentless – and he was also in the way.

'Norm. You know I'm good to you and yet you won't help me.'

'I'm busy.'

Silence for no more than a minute or two.

'It's only a sideboard. And my oak one is very rare – worth a fortune, you know. It would look exactly right in here, much better than this mahogany one.'

After a week of this I could take no more.

'For God's sake do a swap and let me get on with my work.'

'I knew you loved me,' he said.

I could have hit him. So the sideboards were exchanged and although the oak one has never seemed quite right or happy in the office, Anthony sits on it and continues to smile. Jack won his ten pounds, but Spike never paid up. Once he got the sideboard he lost interest.

When Spike left for Rye things were never quite the same at Number Nine. On the plus side, Janet Spearman came into my life. She had worked as company manager for an impresario and toured at different times with the likes of Michael Redgrave and Douglas Fairbanks Jnr. Great, I thought, she is used to temperament. She was going to help out for a few months and fifteen years later she is still with me and has become for me what I was to Spike. Thank God she runs my life.

Spike came to London quite a lot to start with but soon tired of the two and a half hour car journey from Rye. At first he insisted the move would not interfere with his workload but I knew it would. After a time he said, 'No more voiceovers. I'm not coming to London just to work half an hour in a studio because the whole job takes me five and a half hours.'

For the first few years after the move he phoned me twenty and sometimes thirty times a day. Dorothy Parker's line, which

Spike and I had laughed at over the years, came to mind all too frequently: 'What hell is this?' I encouraged him to write to cut down on the phone calls, and in 1991, five years after the last, he published volume seven of his memoirs, *Peace Work*.

Now there was a new problem. For more than twenty years all his correspondence had come to the office but now, as he wrote letters from Rye without telling me, that was where the replies went. Often he did not bother to open them. Instead he waited a couple of weeks, put them all in a large envelope and sent them to me. It drove me mad and caused havoc. All Spike's subscription renewals for his magazines also went to Rye. Sometimes he would bin them so when they did not arrive he was furious. I remember a pathetic voice on the phone when he had not received his favourite, *Gunner Magazine*. 'My subscription expired, like I did. How I wish I could renew myself.'

When he knew I had tired of cancelling just about every bit of work I had lined up for him there was what I nicknamed one of his 'to make it right calls'. 'Norm. I'd like to do something nice for all of us,' he would say. This time he asked if I would arrange a box at the Albert Hall for one of the Proms on 26 July, lay on chilled white wine and reserve the best table at the Belvedere in Holland Park for dinner. It would be a happy night with all his family and I was invited along with Jack.

Laura and Silé were then married (both would marry twice) and went on to provide Spike with five grandchildren. Laura had moved to Australia where her children, Georgia and Jay, were born, which gave Spike great delight as he loved Australians and their way of life. Silé had three wonderful boys, Hastie, Brodie and Callum, who often went to stay in Rye. 'I've got the three trainee murderers coming this weekend,' Spike would say, delighted. 'If you want the definition of a combustion engine it's four-year-old Callum.' One of his proudest moments was when Hastie started to play rugby and loved it as much as he did.

Jane was the only one to follow in the footsteps of her parents.

She was adamant she would do it on her own and that is what she has done. She wanted to learn all aspects of show business and started on sound, and was so good that she did the sound for *Phantom of the Opera* in the West End. She is also a great dancer and has inherited Paddy's ability as a singer.

That night, before the car arrived to bring Spike and Shelagh from Rye, he telephoned.

'Have you got your diary? Well, write this in it, just as I say it. "What can go wrong? What will fuck up tonight?"'

'You're a real Cassandra.'

'I want everything to be right and nothing seems to go that way for me these days.'

It did not on this occasion. In fact it was a disaster. Jack and I left before the evening came to a close because I could not bear to see Spike so dejected. During the next two days I tried to phone him but he had unplugged his phone. It was a bad sign. I wondered whether his planned holiday would be off but in fact it was still on. He rang me the day before he left.

'Will you be here when I get back?'

'What the hell is wrong with you?'

What followed was so incredible I wrote it down in my diary.

'My angel of light. I hope you are looking after yourself with the commission you get from Spike Milligan Productions.'

Good God. What did he want me to do that I did not want to do?

'You'd better get it off your chest and say what you want me to do,' I said.

'Everything is boring. I'm fed up with being in bed.'

'Go on, you can tell me. You know I love you, Spike.'

'I know. It's a great feeling. Like going to a garage and filling up with free petrol for the rest of your life.'

This was amazing. All I could do was wait for the atomic bomb to go off. But it never did.

*

The years that followed were much quieter. Although there was still a Bayswater Harem it had diminished. He maintained the bedroom at Number Nine but when he came to London he often stayed with me. I made one condition – no birds in my flat. He said he was getting past it but I knew he was not because occasionally he would say, 'Don't forget. You and I had dinner tonight.'

Every now and again he got up to his old tricks, such as standing guarantor for a children's television programme called *The Ratties* without telling me. His daughter Laura, a very talented artist, had the original idea so he gave a bank guarantee to help finance the production. Of course, the bank called in the guarantee. He asked me to sort it out when that happened. I told him I knew nothing about it. 'You were on holiday and you weren't here to help me,' he said. How many times had I heard that line before?

I discovered that there were three or four other guarantors but the bank had somehow forgotten to mention them and asked Spike for the full amount, so luckily I was able to get him out of a nasty situation.

He still had his usual yearly dose of operations, one on his back and another on his eye. He was not still hankering after Lady Hamilton, I thought. And he did in fact do another pantomime in 1989, this time at Tunbridge Wells, but not, I thought, putting a lot of heart in it. Nevertheless it went well and the kids loved him. I think Spike got more enjoyment out of doing pantomimes than anything else. He loved children's laughter and would always have a crowd of them in his dressing room after the show. But the performances had been too much for him. He was exhausted. After the run I went to stay with him for a few days in Rye. I think I was company for Shelagh. It became clear to me that she was having a far from easy time with him and I got the impression that she was becoming rather a prisoner in the house because he rarely wanted to go out. When I stayed, at least, we always went out for dinner.

On one of these visits, just after New Year 1990, when I was playing bookends, as Paddy used to call it, chatting to him on his bed, Spike told me that this would be the year his mother would die. The previous night he had had a strange feeling that she was calling for him and had got out of bed and written this poem:

How many meals
did you cook for me mum
No computer can tell me.
You started feeding me
the day I was born
I can't remember
when you stopped
But I miss it
no food as ever tasted the same

Jan 1990 .0200am

Mum died 3 July 1990

Spike's premonition proved to be correct. In June Desmond rang from Australia to say Grandma was ill. He flew to Australia to be with her and stayed for three weeks, but came home when doctors said she would live for another six to twelve months. But they were wrong and he was devastated that he was not with her when she died. She was almost ninety-seven years old.

The day she died Spike phoned me. 'I want to tell you – I'd tell only you – I rang my mother's house just to be near her. I didn't know what else to do. She didn't answer.' After her death Desmond and Spike kept on the house at Woy Woy and Spike stayed in it when he worked in Australia. This reminded me how, after his father's death, he continued to address his Christmas cards to his mother, Captain Leo and Mrs. Milligan. He seemed to find it impossible to accept that certain things were in the past.

He became extremely depressed. He did not lie on top of the bed, he would not get out of it. When he phoned me he was sometimes so drugged I could not tell what he was saying, and at others he could speak coherently only in a very quiet voice. One day he said, 'I look at Jane. It makes me so sad – that she's not six any more. And my mother has died. The dynamo has gone from my life. I'll have to work twice as hard for her.' I never knew whether he was referring to his mother or to Jane.

Some time after this he rang to ask whether he could stay at my flat. Normally, this coincided with a job in London or one of those occasions when he wanted to take one of the Harem to dinner and did not want to make the late trip home. When he arrived I was taken aback by his appearance. He seemed to have shrunk. He was wearing his old black donkey jacket and black trousers, which was not unusual, but he was unshaven and looked as though he had not washed for a week. I remembered the days when he lived at Number Nine and we watched *The Magic Roundabout*, he in his office and me in mine. As soon as it finished he would shout down the stairs, 'Going into the bath.' That happened every evening. He was always fastidious about personal hygiene and the Devon Laundry picked up his clothes on a Tuesday and returned them a week later. Although never a sharp dresser he would always wear a clean 'Save the Whale' T-shirt, or one with a slogan about the rain-forests. This was a different Spike Milligan.

I asked him where he wanted to go for dinner, but he said he would rather have a few glasses of wine with me and then go to bed. I waited and waited and then out it came. He wanted a separation from Shelagh. He could no longer cope with her; he was not that strong any more and at the end of his tether. Where could he go? What would he do? he asked. He supplied the answers. She could have the house in Rye and he would find a flat in North London to be near Silé and his grandchildren. He could not live with Silé because the house had only three bedrooms. Could he stay with me for a few days? Of course he could. Then he said sadly, 'What a friend we have in Jesus, but I have a better one in you.' Within days Shelagh promised to change and they were reconciled.

Spike's depression worsened, however, and he was admitted to the Godden Green Clinic in October 1990. I visited him and thought he looked a little better, probably because he felt more secure. He said he had asked for electro-convulsive therapy. I pleaded with him not to have it. 'All it does is fry your brain. You can't possibly know what effect it will have.' I was wasting my time because he craved it. I visited him after three sessions of ECT. He had aged ten years. God knows, he was always slim but he had lost weight. I sat with him for a while. After a few minutes of silence he said, 'Suicide is a good prospect. There's no way I can come to terms with being old. I hate it. And I hate being a grandfather.' That was completely untrue. He loved his grandchildren and was enchanted when they stayed with him, and thrilled to hear their boisterous laughter when they were playing in the pool.

It seemed to me as though someone had drained him of all emotion. His condition remained the same throughout November. He had more ECT sessions, twelve in all, I believe. I could not bear to see him. On my second visit he sat silently and then after an hour or so he said, 'My faithful friend.' As I left he added, 'It's terrible to be your own murderer.'

In 1992 he was thrilled to be awarded an honorary CBE. Spike proved yet again he was the ultimate survivor and eventually climbed out of the depression. I cannot say we were back on track but we settled into a quiet rhythm. He telephoned me one day and said, 'I'll rewrite the Bible.' Yes, Spike, I thought, of course you will. But what I did not know was that he had already started. He read the first page to me and I knew then that he was on to a winner. It was pure Spike, taking the language of the good book and completely sending it up. The first chapter described 'the creation according to the trade unions':

In the beginning God created the heaven and the earth.
2. And darkness was upon the face of the deep; this was due to a malfunction at the Lots Road Power Station.
3. And God said, Let there be light; and there was light, but Eastern Electricity Board said He would have to wait until Thursday to be connected.
4. And God saw the light and it was good; He saw the quarterly bill and that was not good.

I encouraged Spike to complete it and *The Bible According to Spike Milligan* was published in 1993. It became a bestseller, with nearly 70,000 hardbacks sold. This was the beginning of his *According to . . .* series. Before he had completed the Bible he told me he would get a great deal of fun out of rewriting *Lady Chatterley's Lover*. He claimed that a woman close to Aldous Huxley, who did not like D.H. Lawrence, had derided the novel as 'a nothing book about a man's John Thomas and a woman's Lady Jane.' He told me that Lawrence had written another version of the novel called *John Thomas and Lady Jane*, which I did not believe, but it turned out to be true. His enthusiasm was aroused by this title and it became the next title to be revised by him. Then he wrote his version of *Rebecca*, but Daphne Du Maurier's estate did not like the idea and refused permission. I have kept the book and will try to ensure that it is published when *Rebecca* is out of copyright. Spike was not all that upset at the time because he was already fired up to rewrite *Wuthering Heights*, which came out the same year. Then he rewrote *Black Beauty, Frankenstein, Robin Hood, The Hound of the Baskervilles* and lastly, and very appropriately, *Treasure Island*.

A significant turning-point came in a telephone call in August 1993. 'Norm. I was out of breath after swimming twenty-five lengths today.' I laughed and said I could not do two lengths, but he insisted there was something wrong because until recently he had been able to swim sixty without a problem. He made an appointment to see a cardiologist in London and on the way from Rye telephoned me from the car. 'Get Janet to buy some Danish and I'll come and have tea after seeing the Doc.'

He never arrived. Instead he phoned again as he was on his way from Harley Street to London Bridge Hospital. The doctor wanted to do some tests. I said I would take the Danish to the hospital and we could have tea there. That is what we did and I caught a taxi back to Orme Court when they called him for the tests.

When I reached Number Nine about half an hour later a pale, anxious Eric was waiting in my office. Spike, he said, had had a heart attack while the tests were being carried out and was now undergoing a triple bypass. Of course nothing could be straightforward where Spike was concerned. Twelve hours after the operation a valve failed and he had to have another operation and a second anaesthetic.

The double dose on a seventy-five-year-old had a debilitating effect and after the operation his decline was marked. He complained that his powers of concentration had waned after so much anaesthetic. I thought it would help if he could write again and finish a poetry book he had started six years earlier. I could scarcely recognize the scrawl of the first poem he sent to me. His handwriting had always been so strong and bold, except when he was depressed. I realized then quite how much the operations had taken out of him.

He was at home recovering from the bypass operation when there came another devastating blow. Alan Clare died on 29 November 1993, and Spike was not well enough to attend the funeral. As I was leaving the office for the service Janet called out that Jack Hobbs's girlfriend, Judy, was on the phone.

'Not now. I'll be late for Alan's funeral.'

She said that Judy was crying. I took the phone call in the hall.

'Norma. Jack's died.' He had not been ill but had fallen in his son's flat. He had gone to hospital and complications occurred. He had died an hour or so earlier.

I could not believe it and at times I still cannot – both my great friends and allies dying within a week of each other. I sat in the taxi on the way to say goodbye to Alan, numbed by the double tragedy. I had a single long-stemmed red rose for Alan and wrote on the card, 'Love you. From your "Stella by Starlight" girl.' This was my favourite tune and every time I walked into the Trattoo Alan used to stop what he was playing and change effortlessly into a few bars of 'Stella'. I looked at the card and remembered the ragging that went on between him and Jack, also an accomplished pianist. If Alan was having a break or away doing a gig, as he sometimes did with Stéphane Grappelli, Jack took his place. When that happened I would insist that he did not play 'Stella' because there was no way he could play it as well as Alan, but one evening I made an exception.

'Play "Stella", Jack.'

He would not. Spike said he would, though, and did.

'That was terrible, Spike,' I told him.

'Learn to play the bloody thing yourself,' he said.

Of course Spike had an ally in Jack and for the rest of the evening they refused to play anything I requested. The incident came back to me as I looked at the card. My dear friends. I still miss them.

After the funeral I went back to the office to tell Spike about Jack. I was dreading it. All he said was 'I'm next' and put down the phone. Although I knew that was his way of coping, I hated his dismissive attitude, and he knew it. The next morning, although he had lost 'my two old mates', he was bright and jolly, as if nothing had happened.

'Good morning, sunshine girl. Do you love me?'

'Yes.'

'How much?'

'Twenty-seven years.'

He roared with laughter. 'You are supposed to say "Very much". You're like a British shop steward – twenty-seven years, four months, two weeks and four hours.'

He was denying the deaths of his two friends. I knew that a few days, perhaps even a few weeks, would have to pass before he mentioned either of them again. He did a while afterwards when he told me he had been playing his favourite tapes of Alan. Then there was another call. 'Norm. Will you get someone else to help you on my biography? You'll miss Jack. I know I do. I can't take his place but would you like me to help?'

This was rather heavy for Spike. To lift the mood I reminded him of something F. Scott Fitzgerald once said: 'There will never be a satisfactory biography of a writer. He's too many people if he's any good.' I told him I had no intention of writing his biography. It would be in the style of what Jack had called it, *Ups and Downs with Spike Milligan*.

'God help us,' he said.

He used the same expression when I asked him to write a letter to BBC Archives giving me his authority to examine any files relating to him.

'What for? They know we've been together for years.'

I explained that not every researcher at the BBC knew who I was and this is what he wrote:

> This letter is to acknowledge the authority of my manager,
> Norma Farnes, who is writing a book on me, God help us,

to have access to my life. She has the authority to speak on my behalf and on my business affairs, religion and civic. If there is anything else you want get her to give it to you.

Sincerely,

THE LATE SPIKE MILLIGAN.

Chapter Twenty-three

At the end of 1994 Spike caused a fuss at the British Comedy Awards, where he was given a Lifetime Achievement Award. Prince Charles had sent a tribute but as it was read out Spike said, 'Grovelling little bastard!' He meant it as a joke, but there was a furore. The following day he sent a telegram to Prince Charles saying, 'I suppose now a knighthood is out of the question.' His equerry assured us that they thought it was the funniest thing they had ever seen.

The next year Malcolm Morris, producer of *This is Your Life*, rang to say they would like to do Spike again. He had done one once before in 1973 when nothing had gone right. I will never forget it. Malcolm and I had worked together since Tyne Tees Television began in the late Fifties and in 1973, not long after he moved to *This is Your Life*, he rang to ask if there was anywhere I could guarantee that Spike would turn up on time as arranged.

'His Army reunion,' I said, 'apart from the times he's in Australia he never misses one.'

Completely unaware of what had been planned, Spike drove

to the reunion in Bexhill in his Mini. Malcolm decided he would have one of his researchers keep an eye on him. The researcher certainly would not have made a detective. When Spike left home that morning he noticed a car waiting outside his house and, when he checked his mirror, he saw it following. He decided to take a back road and once again the car followed, so he drove to a police station and said he was being tailed by a suspicious character. The police collared the driver and locked him up. Spike got back into the Mini and drove off like the clappers so as not to be late for the reunion. The researcher tried to get a message to Malcolm, asking him to confirm to the police that he was a researcher doing a job. Malcolm was loath to let the police know he was about to do a *This is Your Life* but he was in a pickle. He simply had to know where Spike was in case he had decided to stop off somewhere. So he let the police into the secret and obligingly they put out an alert over two counties.

I was supposed to travel to Bexhill in a car provided by Thames Television but Peter Sellers, who was of course to appear in the programme, insisted I travel with him in his car. He had decided to turn up in a German storm trooper's helmet and long black leather coat. At the time he was filming *Soft Beds and Hard Battles* and had had his head shaved for the part, and was desperate that nobody should see him bald. That was a logic typical of Milligan. What was the point when millions would soon see him on screen? Before he dozed off in the back of the car he asked me to wake him up ten minutes before we arrived at the reunion. When we did I got the gallant Sellers treatment. He summoned one of the researchers and ordered a bottle of champagne and smoked salmon sandwiches. For Pete that was done at the double. But he did not want them for himself, they were for me. I thought, that's just like Spike. When Malcolm walked in and saw me with a glass of champagne in one hand and a sandwich in the other he was furious because he thought I had ordered them. He calmed down when I told him it had been Pete's idea.

After the show, which was hilarious, I wanted to give the party a miss and get back to London as soon as possible. Pete knew this and said, 'Don't worry. We'll go back together. They won't refuse me an early car.' I did not know it at the time but he wanted to get back to Liza Minnelli.

The second *This is Your Life* was no more straightforward than the first. As Malcolm put it, Spike 'still moved on a different planet in a different time scale from us normal humans.' Spike was appearing for the BBC at Pebble Mill in Manchester on 23 January and he and I were returning the next day on the 11.30 a.m. train to Euston station. Malcolm's people alerted the station's management, and as they were all Milligan fans, they agreed to place on the main station arrivals board a notice saying, 'Spike Milligan. This is Your Life.' They said that they would only know which platform would be used five minutes before the train's arrival. I rang Malcolm on my mobile from the train's loo to say we were on our way and all was well. He was told that we would come in on platform five so he positioned his cameras, lights and sound there in readiness for our arrival. Then it was announced we would be arriving on platform two, so the crew ran over with the equipment and Michael Aspel stood by with the red book. In typical Milligan fashion the train then pulled up at platform five so, with only seconds to spare, they rushed back and Michael was ready to meet him. Malcolm recalled the moment of truth:

'Stand by,' I said into my railway phone to the computer centre that controlled the station notice board. There were Spike and Norma strolling along without a care in the world. The notice board flashed, 'Spike Milligan. This is Your Life.' Spike was in a world of his own and didn't notice it. Norma pointed it out to him and, as he looked up, Michael stepped in for the surprise. 'You've already done me and now everyone thinks I'm dead,' said Spike. As Michael ushered him to a waiting car he added, 'Anyway, there's certainly nobody alive to appear on it.' In fact the show ran almost double the normal running time.

For me it was worth all the tension of the previous forty-eight hours to see the expression on Spike's face when Toni Pontani came on to the stage. He was astonished that she was there. It was the highlight of the night for him. After the show she said, 'Let's run away together.'

He looked at her so sadly. 'Darling Toni, we're too old.'

After *This is Your Life* he continued to appear as a guest on television but he preferred to tour the country to do his poetry readings. It was a simple show; he read a few poems, chatted to the audience and after the interval read excerpts from his war memoirs. Then came a question and answer session. It was a huge success and he received many letters from audiences saying that they felt he had been in their own sitting room.

There was more sadness for Spike the following year when Ronnie Scott died. Spike's age was telling on him but still he kept on writing. Despite the fact that he had fought with the BBC for most of his life they decided to do a tribute to him for his eightieth birthday in 1998. I decided to keep it a surprise for him until a week before recording, but he was unimpressed when I told him. 'Oh, yeah?' he said. The BBC had wanted Clive Anderson to present the line-up, but I insisted it should be Terry Wogan, not because I do not like Clive Anderson, but I knew Terry would be more appropriate. Unfortunately I caught a virus and was in bed for the recording, so missed seeing Denis Norden, Johnny Speight, Eric and Spike together again. At this time I was collating material for *The Goons: The Story* which contained interviews with Harry and Spike, the first time they had talked about the show for years.

I had also wanted Spike to write an eighth volume of war memoirs, which would chart his progression into civvy street and cover the birth of *The Goon Show*. But he was dead against it; I realize now because the prospect of collating all the material and doing the research such a book would require was too exhausting for him. Instead he came up with the idea for an illustrated autobiography, using family photographs. He spent a while sorting out the images and looked forward to writing what he would call *The Family Album*, but when he sat down to do it the spark had gone and he found it a hard slog. That was terrible for him because writing had always been such a natural gift; it had always come off the top of his head, from a seemingly endless mine of hilarious and sometimes preposterous prose. But not any more. When the book was eventually published in 1999 he did the usual signing sessions. He enjoyed them but the travelling eventually got to him.

In 1998 it was Prince Charles's fiftieth birthday. He decided it was time for a bit of fun and wondered what he could buy him. He settled for a set of false teeth and a wig. Shades of the old Spike. Charles thought it was hysterical. That year he asked me to arrange some dates for more readings. I was apprehensive because he had become quite frail, but he was very keen so I spaced the dates to give him a few weeks between gigs. It was such a gamble that I decided to produce and back them, but I was wrong to worry. A tired old Spike would arrive at the theatre but a different person walked on to the stage.

I booked him for a sell-out night at the Gaiety Theatre in Dublin on 14 June 1998. Jack and I went a day or so earlier and were at the hotel when Spike arrived with Shelagh. He promptly had a row with her, lost his poems, did not know what he could possibly read, and said it would be better if I cancelled the show. As usual I had two extra copies of what he was going to read, but he was not to be placated. I nodded to Shelagh and Jack to leave the suite.

'Spike,' I said, 'you can't let the Irish down. You haven't appeared in Dublin for years. It's a sell-out and they've been queuing for hours for any returns.'

This struck a chord and I took him downstairs to the car that was waiting to take us to the Gaiety. In the dressing room he went through the extra copy I had brought with me, drank a glass or two of the Orvieto I had cooling in the fridge, and without any announcement walked straight on to the stage. That was the way he always did it. No 'Ladies and Gentleman, Spike Milligan' for him. The curtains were already drawn and before the audience realized he was centre stage, arms aloft, embracing them all.

'I've come home,' he cried.

The packed house erupted and he had a standing ovation before he started. After all the drama at the hotel I thought, you evil old sod. He was brilliant that night and the audience brought him back again and again. We had dinner afterwards and he knew he had been good, but Spike was modest about his performances and by that time he was far more interested in what wine he would drink.

I decided to put Spike on at the London Palladium with a similar show. I cannot say the same show because Spike extemporized to such an extent that I was never quite sure what was coming next. My father had always gone to the Palladium when he was in town and he would have been thrilled to see my name on the poster outside, 'Norma Farnes presents Spike Milligan'.

We did several more shows in the provinces and the tour put him in such good spirits that he went a few times to Paris to meet 'my only true love, Toni Pontani.' He started to come to the office now and again for a whole day, never giving a thought to the fact that he might be disruptive. For instance, I was having a meeting about my proposed book on Spike and he decided to sit in on the discussion to see what it was all about. He announced that he would write the foreword, and in typical

Milligan style said, 'Take it down, here and now.' The foreword to this book is what he dictated that day. Yes, I thought, the old spark may have diminished but it is still there.

Stirling Rodger, a friend of mine, was helping at Number Nine, and as an actor he had heard all about Spike's tantrums and eccentricities. Without any warning Spike turned up at the office while I was out with Eric, who was doing a recording. Stirling had nipped out for a sandwich but accidentally locked himself out, so was waiting at the steps of Number Nine until Eric and I returned. His heart sank when he saw Spike get out of a car.

'Sorry, Spike, I've locked myself out.'

'Don't worry, Stirl. I'll get us in.'

He took off his velvet cap, covered his fist with it, smashed one of the door's panes of glass and opened the door.

Stirling was aghast.

'It's okay, Stirl. I've done it loads of times. Norma will get it fixed when she comes back.' With that he walked into my office. When I returned he was sitting in the armchair, reading the *Evening Standard* and drinking a cup of tea, by kind permission of Stirling. He thought Spike's performance had been extraordinary and found my acceptance of it positively surreal. It is something he will always remember.

Everyone has occasions like that and mine came when Eric and I received an invitation to see the Hollywood singer and dancer Donald O'Connor at the Connaught Rooms. That impressed me, but I had not been aware that as resident writer Eric had written for Donald when he starred at the Palladium. Because of that old relationship Donald arranged one of the best tables for us. I did not know it but my big moment was about to occur during the interval. I could not believe my eyes when Anthony Hopkins walked across to our table.

'Hello, Eric,' he said.

'Hello, Tony,' said Eric.

This was not happening. Eric had never told me he knew my hero.

Eric said, 'Tony. This is Norma Farnes, my manager.'

He took my hand, bent over and kissed me on the cheek. After all this time! Chaste it might have been, but it was a kiss. Of course, after meeting big stars for most of my adult life I behaved like a complete idiot, went coy and whispered, 'Hello.' Jack was by my side and laughed himself silly. I could have killed him.

Who, among all my friends, would believe that Anthony Hopkins had kissed me? Spike would. I phoned him the next morning.

'Guess who I was with last night?'

'Who?'

'Anthony Hopkins.'

Without taking a breath he said, 'What did he say about my mother lighting all those candles for him?'

'I never told him.'

'What do you mean, you never told him? My mother saved his life, kept Price's candles going for years, and he doesn't know about it!'

'I went ga-ga and couldn't speak.'

'That was a treat I missed.'

'Yes. You would have enjoyed seeing him.'

'No. Not the Welsh lad. The Yorkshire bird – lost for words.'

Spike decided he wanted to do more poetry readings so I arranged the first at Hull. It was dreadful. After a few minutes in front of the audience he forgot what stage he had reached in the show. In the old days when he forgot he made it up as he went along, but this time he was disoriented and misjudged his timing. That threw me; his timing had always been brilliant. There were numerous complaints and rightly so. I arranged to refund the cost of their tickets.

We were committed to a reading at Chichester, although I had grave doubts as to whether we should cancel. But he wanted to do it. The same thing happened again. He misjudged his timing and signalled for the interval only twenty-five minutes after the start instead of an hour. We talked during the interval and he made amends by walking on and saying he would finish the first half before starting on the second. Very sadly, I decided it was not fair to him or audiences to put on any more shows.

One of his favourite expressions, used whenever someone was out of favour, was, 'He has all the charisma of an out-of-order telephone box.' It was the phrase I used when I told him he had lost his way at the last poetry reading, expecting it to lift his spirits a little. I was upset when all he said was 'I know, Norm, I know.'

He asked me several times to organize some more for him but I never did. This was further proof that his short-term memory was worsening, because in the old days he would have badgered me incessantly until I had done what he asked, but it saddened me that he started to forget his own requests.

As the grip on his memory loosened he relived the old days once more, recounting in minute detail what happened in the Army and his romantic time on Capri with Toni. The old Spike came alive in flashes. For instance, he had an argument with his brother, Desmond, by no means the first. Throughout the time I knew Spike Desmond was either 'my God-sent brother' or 'that stupid brother of mine'. Out of all the many disagreements they had one is etched in my memory. During one visit to Australia he took – stole I suppose is the correct word – family photographs belonging to Desmond and his mother, when she was still alive. He was an absolute sod for that sort of thing. Years earlier in London he and his Australian actor friend, Bill Kerr, went round old buildings, such as disused churches or offices, nurgling, as they called it. It was a polite term for stealing because they came away with old brass handles, lights, wrought ironware, anything that took their fancy. Throughout his life Spike assumed it was his right to take whatever he wanted. Whenever I called him a thief he was indignant.

On this occasion he went to his mother's house and rifled through the family album, taking whatever he wanted. Then he went to his brother's house and did the same. It was not the first time and over the years he had depleted both family albums, but now he had gone too far for Desmond, who was particularly upset that he had stolen from their mother. He asked Spike to return the photographs. Without a qualm, Spike denied taking them. Desmond went to a solicitor, who repeated the demand. Spike again denied he had them and in turn he hired a solicitor to demand an apology from Desmond for calling him a thief. Then, miracle of miracles, he accidentally found the photographs they wanted and returned them. This row lasted two years.

The next time Desmond visited his mother she said Terry had sent all the pictures back to her. Then she added, 'I don't need them any more, Desmond. Terry might as well have them.' And back they were sent to Spike. Desmond and I can laugh about it now, but was he furious at the time. Apart from these tiffs Spike loved Desmond. It was the sort of love-hate relationship he had with his mother and, unfortunately, with me. We were either the most wonderful people in the world or were ruining his life. That was Spike.

Although he now found it difficult to perform on stage he recorded his war memoirs for Audio Books in London and stayed with me. He thought he would like to go on a demonstration in Trafalgar Square in aid of Respect for Animals. I said I thought he had done his share for the planet and should leave the demonstration to those who were younger.

'I know you're right,' he said, 'but I'm overcharged emotionally. I get upset easily when I see cruelty and I can't stand injustice, so I'll have to go. I can't leave it to others.'

I tried to lift his mood with reminiscences about nights at the Trattoo with Alan Clare at the piano. It did not work.

'Alan is dead. There's no one.'

Spike called in July 1998 from Rye to say that he had written some more comic poetry, *A Mad Medley of Milligan*, and wanted to come and see me. When he arrived at the office I was shocked to see how much he had changed. He had lost even more weight and that once dynamic, athletic man shuffled rather than walked.

'What's this shuffle along to Buffalo in aid of?'

I wished I had not said it because he explained that his legs had weakened so much that sometimes he fell. It was said in a matter of fact way, which was so unlike him. Previously, whatever his ailment, imagined or otherwise, he sought a first opinion, a second and a third until he was satisfied he knew exactly the nature of his complaint. Now there was total acceptance. My God, I thought, a benign Milligan. I mentioned that Eric and I had decided to visit Johnny Speight. Spike knew Johnny was dying of cancer, and although the only person other than Paddy that he had visited when they were seriously ill was Peter Sellers, I thought he might make an exception for such a close friend. Spike looked at me sadly.

'Don't ask me to go. I can't do it.'

Johnny had only a few days to live, but apart from his appearance you would not have known it. His mind and his wit were as sharp as ever. After he died Spike asked if he could go to the funeral with me.

'I'm going to pay my respects to a wonderful man who had a giant talent.'

Why, I wondered, could he not have visited Johnny and said that to him? It would have meant so much to Johnny.

As we left the church after the funeral service the sun was shining and Spike took hold of my hand.

'Come on. Where's the laughter? Johnny gave it to thousands of people.'

I told him this was not the occasion for that.

'But oh yes, it is. He's out of his pain. Stan Getz played "Stars Fell on Alabama" to help him up there. And Eric, his friend for fifty years, said wonderful things about him. And then we left church to Johnny's all-time favourite, Frank Sinatra singing "The Shadow of Your Smile". What the hell's wrong with you, Norm? If you've got to go it doesn't get better than that.'

I knew he was right and to Sinatra's unforgettable voice was added our laughter, a reminder of something that Johnny had spent a lifetime making people do.

Some weeks later Spike came to London to attend a concert at the Barbican to celebrate Ronnie Scott's Jazz Club's fortieth anniversary. It was obvious that his health was failing and afterwards I had several calls from friends who were disturbed by his frail appearance. I decided to spend a few days with him at Rye. When I arrived Shelagh said he was in bed. He rarely left it, now, even during the day. It was a testing time for her because she had become a full-time nurse to him. She said she looked forward to my visits because he always made an effort to get up, dress and go out to dinner.

We had our usual bookends afternoons, lying on the bed, chatting and laughing. He told me I owed him thirty pounds. He had asked me to buy a case of a particular wine and subsequently found it cheaper elsewhere.

'You owe me thirty-two years. I can give you the thirty pounds but you can't give me the thirty-two years.'

'I know, I know. I'm having two medals made for you, one in nine-carat gold to wear round your neck with pride and the other in lead, so when I get too much for you, you can jump off Beachy Head. Shoot me in the back of the head when you're passing. I'll be the one lying down waiting for it.'

The next day we went to a tea shop in Rye where he wanted me to meet someone he described as 'a very courageous waitress'. The first time he went there he saw she had Down's Syndrome and was bald, which upset him because she had such a bright spirit. He asked the owners to find out whether it would be in order for him to buy her a wig in a modern hair style. The girl was overjoyed with the gift and I thought, here he is, in the last lap still trying to make life better for somebody.

When I left the next day I promised to visit the following week.

'Norm,' he said, 'remember, life is one long hell. I know you won't but don't let the bastards grind you down.'

I gazed at him and knew I had to accept that age and illness had taken their toll. That reminded me of a Christmas card Liz Cowley sent to me one year. The front of the card was black, relieved by a cluster of gold stars. She wrote inside, 'I know your star is up there somewhere. Try the door with "FUCK OFF."' I looked at the star on the bed. It was losing its twinkle.

Only a few days later he sent me a batch of serious poems with a note that he was doing my bidding and would send me more to complete the book. As promised, I went to see him the following week, but this time at the Conquest Hospital in Hastings where he had been taken as an emergency patient. I think that was the time when everything began to pack in for Spike. He was admitted when he developed septicaemia after some injections but was soon rushed to the Cromwell Road Hospital in London. His condition was deemed to be so serious that Shelagh phoned Laura in Australia and advised her to fly to England immediately. He was critically ill and a Roman Catholic priest was called to give him the last rites as his family gathered round him. I was at the foot of the bed and somehow I knew he was not going to die. It was such a strange feeling. I could not say goodbye to him, although he was in a coma, because I was convinced that before long he would wake up and start complaining about the conditions in the hospital or the food, the noise or there being too many people in the room. The grumpy Milligan would surface again. I waited with the family until four in the morning.

The following day Silé phoned to say that a miracle had occurred. He had survived the night and was conscious and talking.

'Is he complaining?'

'Not yet. That'll happen in about five minutes.'

But Spike's survival was not a recovery. After returning home he was in and out of hospital with kidney failure. Soon he was on dialysis three times a week at Brighton, the car trip there and back taking between three to four hours, depending on traffic. It was too much for him so treatment was arranged at a renal unit at his fondly remembered Bexhill, where he had spent his early years in the Army, so he had come full circle. Although the travelling time was cut to an hour or so it still sapped what little strength he had, and his appetite, always small, diminished until he existed on two Weetabix a day.

But Spike still had sufficient strength to make one last effort to make the world a better place. The manager of his personal bank at Rye telephoned me to say one of his cheques for £100 had been returned, because it had been sent to the wrong address. On the cheque he had written, 'Buy a teddy bear. Love Spike for Svenza Schmidt.' It came back with the envelope he had addressed to the *Daily Mail* in Fleet Street, London ('don't know the number'). Of course, the *Daily Mail* had long since left Fleet Street so the envelope did the rounds and eventually arrived at Spike's bank. I told the bank to send the cheque to me so I could sort it out. A story had appeared in the *Mail* in June 2000 about a little girl refugee not having a teddy bear. That touched Spike and his own brand of logic told him that by sending a cheque to the newspaper, whoosh!, the girl would get her teddy bear. Due to the kindness of Liz Rollanson of the *Mail* little Svenza Schmidt was traced to Berlin and she got her teddy bear. It was the last such typically humane gesture that Spike would make to an unknown.

Six months later the Prince of Wales came good, and Spike's

name appeared in the New Year's Honours, with an honorary KBE. The Prince of Wales made a special request to bestow the knighthood, because as a foreign subject it would normally be given by a representative of the Foreign Office. We went to St James's Palace with Shelagh, Jane, Silé and the three trainee murderers. Spike could barely walk now, but stood when Prince Charles came into the room. He told Spike to sit down and chatted to him with such kindness and sensitivity. I was bowled over by his charm. He said to me, 'I know who you are.' After the ceremony we went to the Ritz for tea. As we walked in the pianist started playing 'Rainy Day'. We thought this extraordinary, but then he came up to Spike and said how pleased he was to meet him. Alan Clare had spread the word about Spike's favourite tune.

Soon afterwards I had to tell him that Harry Secombe was seriously ill. He wanted to visit him at his house in Surrey. It had to be the day after dialysis when he usually rested but had a little more energy than usual. He made a gigantic effort and the two of them spent several hours together. I think both men knew they would not meet again. Afterwards Spike was troubled about what would happen to Myra when Harry died, because she and Harry had one of those rare show business marriages in which neither had eyes for anyone else. Fortunately, when the sad time came, her loving children and grandchildren surrounded her.

Spike was too ill to attend the memorial service at Westminster Abbey on 26 October 2001. His simple message was read out. 'Harry was the sweetness of Wales.' Eric and I attended the service and when the congregation stood for 'Bread of Heaven' we sang it at the top of our voices. Eric said, 'This is for you, Spike. You got your wish.' Afterwards several people asked why we sang it with such gusto and we told them about Spike's hope that Harry would die before he did so he could not sing 'Bread of Heaven' at his funeral.

A few days later Spike was admitted to hospital and when I arrived a junior doctor was trying to persuade him to walk with the aid of a walking stick. Spike was not having any of it.

'Come on, Spike. It'll help you to get round and then you can go home.'

Spike turned quickly and said to the doctor, 'Do you know what freedom is?' He did not wait for a reply. 'It's telling you to fuck off!'

I laughed. 'You're getting better, Spike.'

The doctor stared at us and thank goodness he laughed too.

Spike was able to go home but the next few months were as much as he could bear. Dialysis three times a week was more than his frail body could take but he knew if he did not keep going to Bexhill he would die. He held on and on my next visit to Rye, just after Christmas, I could see he was fighting for his life.

The old Milligan emerged some time later when a visitor asked what was his favourite piece of music. 'Right now, the fucking "Funeral March."' I would like to have been there for that. When I visited again in January Shelagh said he was no longer reading or watching television. On his bed was a biography of Rommel.

I lay on top of the blankets.

'This is not exactly like bookends, but not far off. Would you like me to read the Rommel book for you?'

'Yes please, Norm.' His voice was as faint as a bird's tremulous fading song.

Shelagh looked in and I could see tears in her eyes when she said, 'That's a nice sight.'

I knew instinctively that there would be no more bookends. After I had read for a few minutes he slept, a rosary in his hand, his breathing fluttering and uneven. I got off the bed and looked at him as he fought for his life. And I remembered our worst moment of all.

The image returned as if I were looking at a photograph of

the scene. It was 1972 and he had been ill for two weeks. He had not emerged once from his office and did not want anyone to see him. This was one of those depressions when his face was distorted with great dark pouches beneath his eyes. He rang soon after I arrived home from the office and said he wanted to see me, so I drove back to Number Nine. He had unlocked his door so I walked in. I can still feel the heat that hit me, as if a furnace door had just been opened. The atmosphere was suffocating, with the windows closed and the blinds drawn. A small table lamp barely lit the room. Spike announced that he had come to the conclusion that there was no point in living, because if he did, inevitably he would sink into depression once again and he could not face that any more. He went, as if in slow motion, to a grey filing cabinet and took out a brown leather case. Out of it he pulled a revolver.

'It's loaded,' he said, and begged me to shoot him. Suicide was out of the question. I was the only person that would do this for him. It would be easy. He would turn his back and it would take no more than a second.

The heat was unbearable and in that unreal atmosphere I thought for one split second that I would do it. He was crying silently, the tears running down his cheeks, pleading with me to pull the trigger. But then I knew I could not do it.

'What about your mother? It would kill her. And how about Paddy and the children?'

None of that mattered to him at that moment. He felt nothing but a large black emptiness that drained him of any other emotion. I saw an empty bottle of Tuinol on the table, and realized how much the drug had deadened him. I started talking, and talked and talked until very late. At last he took four sleeping pills – one was the normal dose – and I watched over him until he slept and I knew that it was safe to go home. I did not take the revolver with me but put it back in its case and into the filing cabinet, sure that the danger had passed.

Thirty years later, as I looked at his tired face and heard his fitful breathing, I knew it was time for him to die.

'Don't fight any more, Spike. For once in your life give in and go.'

It was a hard thing for me to say but I meant it and prayed his end would be peaceful. Soon afterwards he made the brave decision to end the dialysis. He knew what he was doing. There was time for his children to see him before he died, which he did at last on 26 February 2002. Romany flew from her home near Vancouver to be at the funeral and Sean, Laura, Silé and Jane made her welcome as one of the family, unlike James.

I gave a great deal of thought to the memorial service, which I arranged at St Martin-in-the-Fields on 24 June 2002. My top billing was Eric. But I had a problem. Eric had had a minor stroke in May and after his rehabilitation the doctors told him to rest. How sad I would be saying farewell to Spike without Eric beside me.

I had to be practical. I knew it would be an ordeal for Eric, even if he had not had the stroke, so we talked at length and I tried to persuade him to stay at home. After all, only seven weeks had elapsed since his stroke and he had not so much as left the house. I could only think of one other person that Spike would have approved of, Michael Parkinson. I telephoned him and explained the situation. Eric was adamant that he would attend, but just in case, could I call on Parky if at the last moment Eric decided he was not up to it? He did not hesitate to say yes.

Three days before the service Eric rang and said he had better start thinking of what he was going to say at the memorial service. Again, I tried to talk him out of it and told him that Parky was more than happy to be his stand-in. Sheer guts and grim determination got Eric to the service.

The demand for seats was enormous and the church could have been filled many times over. Many people prominent in show business clamoured to pay tribute to Spike at the service but I decided to select those he had liked and admired most. My first choice was Joanna Lumley. He had often sent her telegrams asking, 'Will you marry me?' She was very fond of one of Spike's poems, 'Boxer my Boxer', and I asked her to read it, which she did, beautifully. Next on my list was Peter O'Toole, because Spike had admired his 'free Irish spirit'. He chose to read a Shakespeare sonnet because Spike once told him he liked them as they were short. Then came Eddie Izzard. Spike thought he was the best of the new generation of comedians and he read my favourite of Spike's poems, 'Have A Nice Day'. Stephen Fry read a passage from John the Baptist, and then ever so touchingly his daughter Jane sang 'Alice in Wonderland', the words of which had been written by Spike, and the music by Alan Clare. I asked Barbara Dickson, who had also sung at his funeral, if she would sing his favourite, 'Rainy Day'. She did not know the number but rehearsed it for the day. Her wonderful true voice singing his favourite song was too much for me. I had hoped I would not cry but it summoned the memories of the hundreds of times I had heard Spike play it over the years.

Last of all came the man Spike called 'a bit of gold in show business'. Eric paid a wonderful tribute to him. He told anecdotes of their early years together and all the laughter they had shared, and included a surprise tribute to me, which moved me greatly. He ended by telling the story of how he and Spike used to eat at an Italian restaurant in Shepherd's Bush. Next door to the restaurant was a funeral parlour and one day Spike lay on the pavement outside the undertakers and shouted 'Shop.' Eric said, 'Do you know it's taken fifty years for someone to answer the door?'

Eric thought I should say something too but I did not want to. I had something else in mind. I had called Myra Secombe to ask if she had a recording of Harry singing 'Guide me, O thou great Redeemer'. She was aware of Spike's joke and was delighted to let me have it. David, Harry's son, agreed to explain the story before it was played. As Harry's wonderful voice rang out with 'bread of heaven' I said to Eric, 'It's taken me nearly thirty-six years to get one over on Spike. He would have loved every minute of it and he'd say, "Those two bloody stubborn northerners are having the last laugh".' That was what he always called us.

The church was filled with sunflowers, his favourite. As we left after the service the sun was shining and the church bells were ringing. I said to Spike, 'At Johnny's funeral you said it didn't get any better than that. Well, the same goes for you.'

Spike, I miss you, you old sod.

Index

P.S.

Ideas,
interviews
& features ...

Q & A

Why did you write the book?
Because one day Spike said, 'You are the only one who really knows me. Others will write biographies but you know me better than anyone.' It wasn't until after he died that I actually started to work on it.

How would you describe your relationship with Spike?
In the literal sense it was a love-hate relationship. Sometimes he loved me while I hated him and vice versa.

Other assistants came and went before you arrived at Number Nine. Why did you stay for nearly 36 years?
Because it was a daily challenge and very stimulating.

Did you ever wish you had been a performer?
No, never. I don't have the temperament and I couldn't endure the anxiety. At my first introduction to television in the Fifties I was fascinated by the production side of the business. I had no desire to be in front of the camera.

What was your reaction when on separate occasions Spike told you that two of his girlfriends were expecting his child?
I thought he was an idiot to believe they were on the pill. I couldn't comprehend his naivety. I felt he should have taken precautions and told him so.

What interests do you have outside the business?
I go to the theatre as often as possible, enjoy

dining out and in Yorkshire, in the winter, I love to entertain at home beside big log fires. I read biographies, arrange flowers and walk on the beaches nearby.

Have you always had a retreat in the country?
No, I'd always fancied the Cotswolds but Jack has his roots in North Yorkshire and has lived there for most of his life. That's where I go most weekends and I've grown to love the moors as much as he does. He's walked and ridden them for most of his life. My mother loved the peace of the garden and she ended her days there. Perhaps I will.

Do you ever take your business problems home with you?
No, never. The first thing I do when I get home is run my bath and light the candles that surround it, then I have a half-hour's soak and a glass of champagne. If there is a problem my dictum is that it can wait until tomorrow. It never interferes with my sleep. As my mother always said, 'It's only a job.' That's how I survived.

What was Spike's worst trait?
His disloyalty. But he was such a complicated character: he could be one hundred percent disloyal one day and one hundred percent loyal the next. In my personal life he never let me down but in business he let me down and betrayed me almost every day.

Are there plans for any more Milligan books?
Yes. I'm working on another compilation of extracts from his works to follow *The* ▶

LIFE
at a glance

Author photo © Monica Curtain

BORN

1934, Thornaby-on-Tees.

EDUCATED

Robert Atkinson
Secondary School,
Thornaby.

CAREER

Shorthand typist, ICI
Stockton. PA to Jack
Clarke, journalist.
Information Officer at the
Independent Television
Companies Association.

FAMILY

Norma was once married
but divorced after four
years. She decided many
years ago that she did not
want any children. She has
lived with Jack Clarke for
twenty-six years.

Q & A *(continued)*

◄ *Essential Spike Milligan.* My partner,
Jack Clarke, came up with the title, *The
Compulsive Milligan,* and it will be published
later this year. The royalties from this, and
other ventures I have in the pipeline, go into
a trust for the benefit of Spike's children. In
1995 he asked me to promise that I would
look after them and that is what I intend to do.

Will you take on any more clients?
No. I look after Eric Sykes, a really quite
incredible man, as creative and as busy as
ever, and of course Eddie Braben, who was
the scriptwriting genius behind Morecambe
and Wise.

When will you retire?
As long as my boys want to work I'll be here
to look after them.

**What's the secret of being a good manager
and agent?**
Much of it is common sense, being a good
organizer, sorting the good work from the
bad and knowing where to pitch the fee for
your client. It's got to be equitable to both
sides but you've got to be firm, particularly
with some impresarios and the new breed of
negotiators in television and in advertising
agencies. Some know what they are doing,
but others seem to me to be fresh out of
university with a media studies degree,
little experience, a bad telephone manner
and not the slightest idea of what my
clients are worth. I tell them to go back
to their bosses and come up with a
realistic offer.

Is the new breed of impresario difficult to deal with?
Some are and they try it on. But they tire before I do.

Who's your favourite?
Bill Kenwright. Top of the tree for me. Very professional. Tough when he has to be. But he knows what he's doing. He'll take a chance with new talent but is loyal to those who've done well for him. Above all he's a man with great emotional warmth, sensitive to others and caring.

So what was your ambition when you finally realized your career was going to be as a manager and agent?
To be one of the best in the business and to do my all for my clients.

What is your lasting memory of Spike?
He was my best friend. ■

Top Ten
Favourite Reads

Great Expectations, Charles Dickens

Tender is the Night, F. Scott Fitzgerald

Goddess: The Secret Lives of Marilyn Monroe, Anthony Summers

Lewis Carroll: Complete Works

The Prophet, Kahlil Gibran

Farewell to Arms, Ernest Hemingway

Violet to Vita, edited by Mitchell A. Leaska and John Phillips

Pygmalion, George Bernard Shaw

The Importance of Being Earnest, Oscar Wilde

The Sayings of Dorothy Parker

Life Drawing

WHAT is your idea of perfect happiness?
Sitting on the terrace of my home in
Yorkshire with Jack on a warm spring
evening with blackbirds singing and the
ever-present burble of the river as it flows
past the garden.

What is your ambition?
To have peace of mind.

**What are you planning to do with the rest of
your life?**
To keep going.

What objects do you always carry with you?
A shoehorn. But I can't tell you why. ∎

A Critical Eye

WITH *Spike: An Intimate Memoir* Norma Farnes fascinated most of her reviewers and intrigued them all with her insight into what more than one described as 'this tortured comic genius'.

In the **Financial Times** Alex Gaines wrote: 'Farnes was blessed with an unflappability which seems to have acted like a cold towel on Milligan's head – most of the time. Unfussily written, it is an intimate memoir, with none of the sentiment or point scoring that often mars a widow's tale. He was lucky to have such a woman at, or by – but not always on – his side.'

For the **Observer** Sean O'Hagan described the book as 'part showbiz memoir, part personal exorcism': 'It is one of those books you wish you had never started but, almost shamefully, cannot stop reading, so nakedly revealing is it of the tortured individual that lurked behind the public façade.'

In the opinion of Peter Lewis in the **Daily Mail**: 'Without her to save him from himself and coax him into fulfilling his bookings, [Spike's] career would have foundered early on ... His self-absorption came out again when Farnes was seriously ill. Spike rang her husband – not to ask how she was or to commiserate, but to say "If anything happens to her I shall be devastated."'

In the **Sunday Times** Humphrey Carpenter wrote: 'The book is always readable and written with infectious verve ... it is much to Farnes's credit that she does not try to whitewash Milligan ... she doesn't restrain herself from exposing his almost ▶

◄ full-time infidelity to his second wife, Paddy.'

The **East Anglian Daily Times** concluded: '[Farnes] provides readers with a multi-faceted portrait of a man who had more personality traits than an entire hospital of schizophrenics', whilst in Norma's home-town newspaper, Teesside's **Evening Gazette**, Barbara Argument, after quoting the memorable scene when Norma cuddled up to Spike on his death bed, 'like book ends', summed up Norma's role in the life of one of the UK's greatest comics: 'She was his bloody stubborn northerner agent who guided his career and soothed his tortured mind, the trouble shooter behind this comic genius, always fighting his corner.' ∎

About the book

If You Loved This,
You Might like ...

Read on

The Essential Spike Milligan
Compiled by Alex Games. Foreword by Eddie
Izzard. Fourth Estate

'A joyous and wondrous thing ... Alex Games
has done a fine job ... A sound and neatly
timed volume and perfect for filling a
Milligan-shaped gap in anyone's life.'
Literary Review

Puckoon
Spike Milligan, Penguin

Adolf Hitler: My Part in His Downfall
Spike Milligan, Penguin

Mussolini: His Part in My Downfall
Spike Milligan, Penguin

Monty: His Part in My Victory
Spike Milligan, Penguin

Where Have all the Bullets Gone
Spike Milligan, Penguin

**Surviving Spike Milligan: Mad Memories of
Life with the Arch Goon**
John Antrobus, Robson Books

**Tragically I Was an Only Twin: The Comedy
of Peter Cook**
Peter Cook, William Cook (Editor), Arrow

Remembering Peter Sellers
Graham Stark, Robson Books

Comedy Heroes
Eric Sykes, Virgin Books ∎

BOOKSHOP

Now you can buy any of these great titles from
HarperCollins at **10%** off recommended retail
price. *FREE* postage and packaging in the UK.

The Essential Spike Milligan
Compiled by Alex Games 0 00 715511 5   £8.99
....

Morecambe and Wise
Graham McCann 1 85702 911 9   £7.99
....

Dad's Army
Graham McCann 1 84115 309 5   £7.99
....

Sunshine on Putty
Ben Thompson 0 00 718132 9   £8.99
....

Billy
Pamela Stephenson 0 00 711092 8   £7.99
....

Total cost
....

10% discount
....

Final total
....

To purchase by Visa/Mastercard/Switch
*simply call **08707 871724** or fax on **08707 871725***

To pay by cheque, send a copy of this form with a cheque
made payable to 'HarperCollins Publishers' to: Mail Order
Dept. (Ref: B0B4), HarperCollins Publishers, Westerhill
Road, Bishopbriggs, G64 2QT, making sure to include your
full name, postal address and phone number.

From time to time HarperCollins may wish to use your
personal data to send you details of other HarperCollins
publications and offers. If you wish to receive information
on other HarperCollins publications and offers please tick
this box ☐

Do not send cash or currency. Prices correct at time of press. Prices and
availability are subject to change without notice. Delivery overseas
and to Ireland incurs a £2 per book postage and packing charge.